Food & Wine
of France

Food & Wine of France

Bordeaux to the Pays Basque
a gastronomic guide

MICHAEL AND SYBIL BROWN

NEW YORK

Published in USA 1983
by Exeter Books
Distributed by Bookthrift
Exeter is a trademark of Simon & Schuster
Bookthrift is a registered trademark of Simon & Schuster
New York, New York

ISBN 0-671-05968-8

Reprinted 1984

Printed in Czechoslovakia

*To
the late Gerald Nutt*

Acknowledgments

Our grateful thanks are due to the following who kindly assisted us in our researches: Monsieur and Madame Artisié, 'Nicoy', Pujols, Lot-et-Garonne; Madame Barde, Auberge à la Ferme, Bossu, Monflanquin, Lot-et-Garonne; Monsieur Brana, Caves du Brana, St-Jean-Pied-de-Port, Pyrénées-Atlantiques; Monsieur Chigé, Cru Lamouroux, Chapelle de Rousse, Pau, Pyrénées-Atlantiques; Madame Gayraud and Madame Lasbenne, Genouillacou, Pujols, Lot-et-Garonne; Monsieur and Madame Grassa and Monsieur and Madame Dubuc, Château du Tariquet, Eauze, Gers; Peter and Bridget Holt, 'Les Plantiers', Degagnac, Lot; Monsieur Dominique Idiart, Sauveterre-de-Béarn, Pyrénées-Atlantiques; Mr George Mortimore, The Old Chelsea Wine Stores, London; Monsieur A. Mur, Les Vignerons Réunis des Côtes de Buzet, Buzet-sur-Baïse, Lot-et-Garonne; Monsieur Ramos and his daughter Madame Mercadier, Villeneuve-sur-Lot, Lot-et-Garonne; Monsieur Denis de Robillard, Château de Peyros, Corbères, Lembeye, Pyrénées-Atlantiques; Monsieur Louis Vales, Aguessac, Aveyron; Monsieur Emile Viguier, Les Buis, Entraygues, Aveyron; *Food from France*, London; and finally Jenny Dereham, who organized the index.

Jacket photography: (front) Bill Richmond (back) J.-P. Ferrero.

The Author and Publishers wish to thank the following for permission to reproduce their colour photographs: Anthony Blake, 11; Ray Delvert, 1, 2, 3, 5, 6, 7; Jean-Paul Ferrero, 4, 8, 9, 10, 12.

Contents

List of colour photographs

between pages 120 and 121

List of maps

Foreword

There have long been processions of the British to and through south-western France. First, in the twelfth century, came the soldiery, whose marauding, we trust, was offset in the God's-eye-view by the lines of pious pilgrims *en route* to Santiago de Compostela. After we had lost military possession of Aquitaine, shippers and merchants continued to frequent Bordeaux on the civil business of wine, and still continue. In the nineteenth century the Fashionables, and even the Royals, adopted Biarritz as their haunt. Then, with the discovery of the Périgord caves, came the palaeographers. Most recently there has been a trickle of British settlers, like our authors the Browns, who have found the south-western climate, scenery and culture so agreeable as to wish to make their homes there, and have commendably restored ruined farmsteads and dilapidated cottages to this end.

There are tourists too, of course, but most hurry through the area in a rush to the more favourable exchange-rate of the *peseta*. So the South-West remains perhaps the least-known to our countrymen of all the beautiful regions of France. Certainly it is the least beset by coach tours and package-holidaymakers.

This book is primarily a gastronomic guide, but it touches also on the scenery, the buildings and the inhabitants of a region where almost every prospect pleases and man (and woman) is very far from vile. They are, indeed, sturdily independent people, perhaps a bit suspicious of strangers, even of strangers from other parts of their country. But they are readily won to friendship with those who appreciate their values; and when they know you and accept you they are helpful, hospitable and loyal.

There are numerous extensive volumes devoted solely to the wines of Bordeaux, which is the largest area in the world for the production of fine wine; and here the authors, on account of the scale of their book, have necessarily been somewhat summary. But I am pleased that, together with their listing of the great classified *crus* that few of us can any longer buy, they combine descriptions of the lesser-known *communes* and make sound selections from the *crus* bourgeois that are specially worthy of attention. Likewise, in the subsequent sections of the book, they introduce us to a fascinating range of minor *appellations contrôlées*, *vins de qualité supérieure*, *vins de pays* and even *vins de table*, at which we can no longer afford to turn up our noses. It would be foolish to do so anyhow, however rich we may be, for these south-western growths go so well with the local *cuisine*, and are in fact, in many cases, not only locally interesting but also positively good.

The food of the South-West is different from the classic *cuisine française* based on butter and cream – the *cuisine*, say, of the Lyonnais. You will notice a slightly sweet taste that comes from the use of goose fat and, with saladings, from the walnut oil. It is not a delicate *cuisine*, but it is hearty rather than heavy: fare for a people who are hardy workers but with refined palates. Yet you cannot call it a *cuisine bourgeoise*, when it includes *foie gras*, truffles, caviar, lampreys and salmon.

The detailed recipes may in places seem a bit daunting to the amateur. This is not instant cookery, nor cookery for the working hostess who dashes away from her office at 6 p.m. to serve a dinner party at 8.30. It is cooking for those who love the art and are willing to devote time and attention to it. Still, there are many dishes for which you not merely can do much of the preparatory work a day ahead, but for which indeed you *must* so do. And there are suggestions for simplifying the rich, slow, patient cookery of this area, and for the substitution of materials available in Britain for the local *spécialités de la région*. Yet for those who simply must have delicate food there is the famous *cuisine minceur* of Michel Guérard at Eugénie-les-Bains; but this is an expensive taste.

The authors have much ground to cover, yet have found space for numerous attractive vignettes of the local life. I venture to mention also the prehistoric caves of the Périgord, and their astonishing paintings, for which they have not found space; with the caution however that the interested tourist should inform himself in advance about current facilities for visiting Lascaux, the greatest of these, where years ago I had the fortune to be conducted by one of the then-young men who had discovered this treasure of historic and aesthetic interest.

But apart from that you are in good hands with these experienced guides, the Browns. Read their book, explore their country, follow their advice about wine and food, and try their recipes. If you do so, you will find a rich reward in every aspect they reveal of the life and landscape of this lovely France of the South-West.

H.W. YOXALL
Former Chairman, the International Wine and Food Society
Grand Officier, La Confrérie des Chevaliers du Tastevin

Preface

TELL A FRENCHMAN that you are going to the South-West for a holiday and he will invariably reply '*on mange bien dans le sud-ouest*', mentally ticking off the region's gastronomic delights as he does so: *foie gras, confit d'oie*, truffles, *prunes d'Agen*. Yet, despite its reputation for good food, the South-West has been sadly neglected, not only by English writers on French cuisine but by the French themselves. So, when my wife and I first visited the region, nine years ago, and tried to find a book that would tell us what specialities to look for, we were disappointed to discover how little had been written on the subject. True, there was plenty of literature on Périgord (Dordogne), both in English and French, but for some areas, like Armagnac (Gers), there was nothing except a locally produced guide on sale in some of the larger towns. The only solution was to start collecting our own material: this book is the result.

One of the problems when writing about the South-West is to decide exactly where it begins and ends. Some books take in an enormous area stretching northwards from the Pyrénées as far as La Rochelle and Poitiers, but we felt it would be impossible for us to cover such a huge territory adequately. Instead, we have confined ourselves to the Pays Basque and Béarn (Pyrénées-Atlantiques) and the lands included in the ancient duchies of Guyenne and Gascony. Guyenne, at its greatest extent, stretched eastwards from Bordeaux to the Massif Central and included the modern *départements* of Gironde, Dordogne, Lot-et-Garonne, Lot, Aveyron and a part of Tarn-et-Garonne. Gascony lay to the south of Guyenne and covered the Landes, Gers, Hautes-Pyrénées and part of Haute Garonne.

We chose this part of the South-West for a number of reasons: first all of it lies within a reasonable distance of our house near Villeneuve-sur-Lot, Lot-et-Garonne; second, we knew that more and more English people were taking their holidays in the Dordogne or settling there and we felt that the area we had chosen was the one that they would most likely wish to explore, just as we ourselves had done; third, the whole region has strong historical links with England: during the Middle Ages much of it actually belonged to the English crown and there are many reminders of the English connection to this day, including towns like Libourne on the river Dordogne, that were founded by Englishmen. Later, the Pays Basque and Béarn became one of Europe's earliest tourist playgrounds, and towns like Pau and Biarritz were

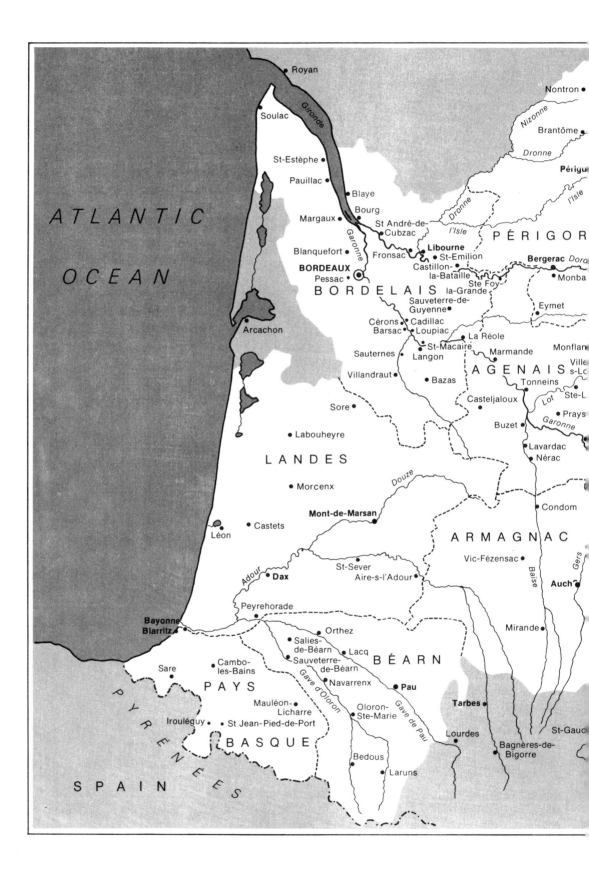

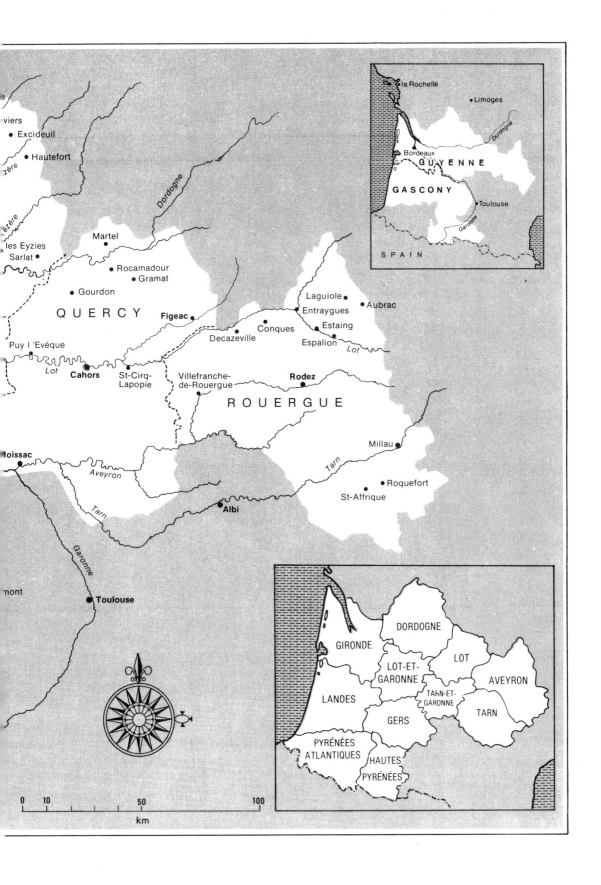

viers

• Excideuil

• Hautefort

zère

les Eyzies
Sarlat •

• Martel

• Rocamadour
  • Gramat

• Gourdon

QUERCY

Figeac •

Dordogne

Puy l 'Evéque

Lot

Cahors • St-Cirq-
              Lapopie

Laguiole
Entraygues • Aubrac
       Estaing
Conques
Decazeville   Espalion Lot

Villefranche-
de-Rouergue   **Rodez** •

R O U E R G U E

Millau •

Tarn

• Roquefort
St-Affrique •

Moissac •

Aveyron

Tarn

Garonne

• **Albi**

mont

• **Toulouse**

0   10   50   100

km

la Rochelle • Limoges

Dordogne

Bordeaux

GUYENNE

GASCONY

• Toulouse

Garonne

S P A I N

GIRONDE

DORDOGNE

LOT-ET-
GARONNE   LOT

AVEYRON

LANDES   TARN-ET-
         GARONNE

GERS   TARN

PYRÉNÉES
ATLANTIQUES

HAUTES
PYRÉNÉES

favourite resorts for Edwardian holidaymakers.

In describing the region we have stuck to the old names such as Périgord instead of Dordogne, and Armagnac rather than Gers. This is because the local dishes still carry the old names; for example, you would never talk about *omelette dordognoise* for *omelette périgourdine*, any more than you would call Yorkshire pudding Humberside pudding! Moreover, just as the people who live in the part of Humberside that used to be called the East Riding still think of themselves as Yorkshiremen, so the people of the Gers still think of themselves as Gascons, as do those of the Landes. The modern *département* names date only from the time of the First Republic and although administratively they are firmly entrenched they have quite failed to eradicate the old names from the consciousness of most of the local inhabitants. It has to be admitted, however, that the departmental boundaries do not always coincide exactly with those of the old regions (these fluctuated anyway during the Middle Ages according to the fortunes of war), but this is a gastronomic guide, not an academic work of history or geography, and so we need not be too concerned on that score.

Most of the book is based on personal research. Wherever possible we have visited a vineyard to sample the wine or an individual producer to find out how his specialities are made. The only exception is the Bordelais. The sheer size of the Bordeaux wine industry would have made a personal investigation the work of a lifetime. Fortunately, Bordeaux wines are well documented already and we are confident that the information in this section is accurate.

Unlike most writers on wine, we have not dwelt over-long on the top end of the market. Eulogies of luxury wines like Château Latour or comparisons with great prewar vintages are not much use to the majority of tourists. Most people, however interested they may be in wine, are looking for good value rather than the exotic. With this in mind, we have tried to mention as many of the middle-range wines as possible – not the plonks, because these can be found anywhere, but good-quality local wines that are relatively inexpensive because they are less well known than those from more famous areas such as the Médoc or St-Émilion. In particular, we have included the addresses of a number of reliable co-operatives where you can buy very good wines in 11-, 25- or 32-litre plastic containers (*cubitainers*) with a tap. These are a good idea if you are staying in a villa or farmhouse for a week or two. You can, of course, taste the wine first to make sure you like it.

We have not given the names of any hotels or restaurants. You can never guarantee that an establishment will not change hands with a consequent change in standards, whether for better or worse, and so this kind of information needs constant updating. Instead, we would recommend one of the excellent established guides, either the Michelin or Kléber.

Our research has taken us to many interesting places that we would never otherwise have seen and we have met many charming and delightful people.

In the process we have often found that the information that we had found in books was out of date or just plain inaccurate. This was especially true of some of the more obscure areas. We hope that this guide will prove reliable and will serve to introduce the reader not only to some new gastronomic experiences but also to some little-known but beautiful parts of this fascinating region.

Bonne cuisine et bons vins, c'est le paradis sur terre.

HENRI IV OF FRANCE

Introduction

IN 1969 a safety organization called Sécurité Routière mounted a massive publicity campaign to dissuade French motorists from driving on top of a large lunch. A striking advertisement showed a self-satisfied diner about to tuck into a good spread. The caption read: 'In one hour this gentleman will be driving at 140 kilometres an hour.' The inference was clear: too much food impairs one's driving skills and can be dangerous.

Just when the publicity was at its height and evoking an anxious response from French restaurateurs, a motorist went on trial somewhere in the South-West for dangerous driving. The police alleged that he had been meandering in a dazed fashion all over the road. The motorist protested that he was feeling dizzy because he had not had enough lunch, and his case was dismissed with the stern warning: 'In future, don't drive on too few dishes.'

The prolonged, substantial midday meals that are still traditional in the South-West are a reflection of the pace of life in this rural and in some ways rather backward region where *le sandwich* and *le snackbar* have so far made little headway. Here mixed farming still holds sway and there are numerous smallholdings with a few fields devoted to crops, orchards, pasture land for cattle and sometimes a little vineyard as well. The *métayage* or share-cropping system, by which the farm labourer works the land in return for a share of the harvest and sometimes tools and accommodation as well, still goes on, even today. The French government is encouraging the consolidation of small farms and the concentration on single cash crops, but progress is slow. Yet it is precisely because the region has remained behind the times that the tradition of good food and good cooking has survived.

The South-West has always been one of the poorest and most undeveloped regions of France. Right up to the last quarter of the nineteenth century the peasants in the remoter regions were still leading a life that was close to the Stone Age. In 1836 an army officer who was making a survey of the area round Navarrenx and Oloron, in Béarn, copied out the previous report written in 1698, noting that nothing much had apparently changed in 150 years. In parts of the Pyrénées ploughs only started to replace the old hand tools (shovels, spades, hoes and wooden mallets for breaking up clods of earth) in the 1880s. In the Landes it was not until the beginning of the twentieth century that wooden ploughs began to give way to metal and that the introduction of artificial fertilizers brought increased yields and for the first time raised the peasants above subsistence level.

The French agricultural revolution took place at different times in different parts of the country. Daniel Faucher, a French social historian, has divided the process into four stages: during the eighteenth century the practice of allowing land to lie fallow, sometimes for two or three years at a time, was abolished. It was followed by improvements in crops, the growing of fodder for animals and the planting of new root crops, especially potatoes. The third stage saw the introduction of chemical fertilizers, which not only increased crop yields but meant that areas like the Ségala, on the edge of the Massif Central, where previously only indifferent crops of rye (*seigle*) had been grown, were able to produce good harvests of wheat. Finally, came the machines, which not only increased the efficiency of farming but allowed fewer hands to achieve better results and freed the unemployed workers to migrate to the towns. The true picture, however, was not as clear-cut as Daniel Faucher's scheme would suggest. There were overlaps between the various stages and progress varied from one part of France to the next. In the South-West, because of poor communications, the pace of change was painfully slow. No one stage can be counted as more important than the others, but the arrival of chemical fertilizers on the scene was certainly a vital development. In the Quercy and the Agenais today, the Parisians who own second homes are building *pigeonniers* – simple stone towers with tiled or slate-covered pointed roofs which are commonly found on the older farms in this part of the South-West. The pigeons that lived in the roof of the *pigeonnier* were kept, not as a supplementary food supply, but for the sake of their droppings. In areas where there were few cattle, the guano from the birds' droppings was a valuable source of nitrates. So strong was the pigeon fertilizer that it could not be spread on the ground until rain was starting to fall, otherwise the stalks and surface roots would have been burnt by the concentrated nitrates. Until the revolution, the *pigeonnier* and its valuable guano belonged exclusively to the local lord of the manor who thus controlled the sale of this precious fertilizer. Today pigeon droppings are no longer used but a certain cachet still belongs to possessing a *pigeonnier*, even though it is more likely to contain a smart, tiled bathroom than pigeons.

If the farming life and methods were primitive, the farmhouses themselves were equally simple. At the turn of the century they were a basic four-walled construction, sometimes with a chimney, and with 'rooms' made by planked partitions. There were few doors or windows, because both were taxed until 1917 and also because they added to the expense of construction. Houses were built to keep out the hot summer sun as well as the draughts and cold of winter, so the openings faced away from the worst of the weather. In this part of France the prevailing wind is from the south-west and, as in Britain, it often brings cloudy weather accompanied by strong winds and heavy rain, so the windows and doors in old farmhouses generally face east and south. As building techniques and material became more sophisticated and the country people saw the improvements being introduced into the bourgeois houses in the towns, the farmhouses became more comfortable and roomy as well, with cellars below and even a second storey above the ground floor. Tiles took the place of thatch on the roofs, and for the really wealthy, slates were imported into the region from the north.

The fireplace was the centre of the farmhouse and was built on such a large scale that old people could sit comfortably in the chimney corner away from draughts, keeping an eye on the fire and stirring the cooking pot. Even when wood-burning stoves were introduced, the open fire was still used for cooking much of the time. Ovens were a luxury in the country districts until butane and propane gases revolutionized both the cooking and the kitchen utensils. But old customs and traditions die hard and as late as 1972, when we were looking for a house in the Quercy, we saw jam being made on an open fire in one of the farmhouses we visited. The farmer's wife tended both jam and fire, stirring the one and feeding the other with twigs and small pieces of wood. We asked why she cooked her jam on the fire when she had a large gas cooker in the corner of the kitchen. She shrugged and then laughed: that was how her mother had always done it, she explained, and besides jam needed very little heat and she could control it with two or three twigs at a time. We tasted a spoonful before we left; it was melon jam, smooth and sweet with all the ripeness of autumn days.

Lacking an oven, and with strictily limited fuel supplies, the farmer's wife learned to provide a variety of appetizing food cooked with a minimum of fuel.* The basic utensil was the cauldron, a large cooking pot with a handle and three small legs: it could be hung from the *crémaillère* (the series of hooks over the open fire) or set securely on the hot fire itself, or even stood in the hearth near the fire to keep warm and continue cooking slowly. Inside the cauldron such composite dishes as the *garbure*, the *pot-au-feu* and the *poule-au-pot* would be cooked. Puddings could be boiled in cloths in the water and, like the suet dumpling, these could be sweet or savoury. Many desserts and sweetmeats were made by boiling cereals with water until they formed a thick mass which was spread on a board and allowed to cool and thicken; the slab of porridge was then cut into shapes and fried in lard or goose fat and sprinkled with sugar or cheese. One such accommodating mixture is the *cruchade*, made with semolina and flavoured with orange flower-water and sugar and honey if it is served as a tea-time snack, or sprinkled with grated cheese if eaten with aperitifs. Even a shortcrust pastry, enriched with a beaten egg or two can be rolled out and cut into squares and then deep-fried in neutral fat or oil, in the same way that pancakes can be either sweet or savoury.

Cakes, tarts and sweet puddings that we would automatically cook in the

* Before the revolution the landlord often had a feudal right prohibiting collection of fuel on his land by his tenants.

oven were made either in a covered frying pan or a heavy copper or iron dish with a close-fitting lid on which glowing embers were piled, so that when the vessel was put on the fire there was *feu dessous, feu dessus*. Many desserts were made simply in the open frying pan, including the *clafoutis* (black cherries in a custard batter from the Limousin) and the *flaugnarde* (the same mixture, but with prunes instead of cherries, from the Périgord and the Agenais), which were fried slowly on one side, turned carefully and fried again.

Much of modern bedsitter cooking has a great deal in common with the methods traditionally used in the South-West; but with a couple of gas rings, a grill and an electric crockpot or slow-cooker, today's flat-dweller has at his command a range of energy sources that until a few years ago was just not available to the French farmer's wife. Now, however, most houses in the South-West have electricity, and the advent of bottled gas means that even the remotest farms have a refrigerator and a modern cooker with an oven.

An unexpected addition to the French cook's *batterie de cuisine* was the eiderdown. At times like the *vendange*, when all hands, including grannies and great-aunts, were in the vineyard, the eiderdown came into its own. The thick, feather-filled duvet, relegated to the top of the *armoire* (wardrobe) during the hot summer months, was brought down and wrapped round the tureens and *faitouts* to keep meals hot and allow the *ragoûts* and *estouffades* to continue their long, slow cooking, leaving the women free to take their scissors and start snipping off the bunches of grapes. Besides keeping the food hot, the ciderdown also maintained the yeast paste (so essential to bread-making) at a constant temperature and served as a cocoon for the bread dough, which was put into a warm bed and covered with the eiderdown so that the yeast would work and the dough rise.

Every household kneaded its own dough which was either baked in an oven belonging to a neighbouring family or taken in a handcart, wrapped in its eiderdown, to the communal oven, which might be several kilometres away in the next village In the Rouergue there are still people today who remember how families and neighbours co-operated in making the bread: one minding the yeast paste and feeding it between one baking and the next; another providing the wood to heat the rough stone communal oven; a third releasing her children from work for the day to keep the oven supplied with wood or to assist the baker, if the village could afford the services of a professional to bake for them. Each loaf was marked with the family's cross or sign, or could be distinguished by its shape. Some loaves weighed 8 kilos or more and were almost the size of a cartwheel, one or two of them sustaining a family for two weeks until the next baking.

The cooking of the South-West is firmly rooted in the land. The quality of the produce is usually high. Indeed in specially favoured areas like the Périgord it even includes such luxury items as truffles; what is more, because most of the region is mixed farming country, there is a great variety of foodstuffs, changing constantly, of course, according to the season of the year. But no matter how good the ingredients they still have to be turned into an appetizing dish, and all through the South-West there is a long tradition of good, plain, economical country cooking.

The two basic ingredients of this cuisine are goose and pork fat. Goose fat has the advantage that, if kept cool, it does not go so stale or rancid as other fats do, but it is now expensive and less commonly used, whereas pork fat (or lard as we call it) is relatively cheap and easily obtained. At one time the use of butter in cooking was restricted to the Pyrénées, where the lush pastures supported herds of cows, but this is no longer the case and, despite its high price, butter is now used throughout the region. The olive tree does not grow in the South-West, so olive oil has traditionally played little part in the local cooking, but here again the use of sunflower and maize oils is becoming widespread. Nevertheless, goose and pork fats give the region's cooking its authentic flavour. Goose fat is used wherever lightness is essential; for example, pastry is brushed lightly with melted goose fat as layer after layer is rolled to produce the *pâte feuilletée* (flaky pastry) for the large shallow tarts called *tourtières* – one of the region's special delights for those who possess a sweet tooth. Pork fat, on the other hand, comes into its own when rich, succulent sauces and gravies are needed, and the rind from a piece of pork is an essential ingredient in nearly all stocks and stews.

Of course, the goose and the pig contribute more than just their fats to the gastronomy of the South-West and both turn up in many guises in the local *charcuterie* shops; their respective roles are covered in more detail in the sections on the Périgord and Béarn. Anyone who would like to go into the art of *charcuterie* in some depth should read Jane Grigson's invaluable *Charcuterie and French Pork Cookery*.

In the Middle Ages one of the chief sources of bulk in the peasant's diet was millet, but after the discovery of the New World it was gradually superceded by maize. Nevertheless the name survives in *milhas*, also known as *le millassos* or *le millas*, a thick porridge-like mixture once made from millet and now from maize. You can try it with semolina, ground rice or, if you live near an Italian delicatessen, polenta. Boil 500 ml (1 pint) of water in a thick saucepan with the grated rind of a lemon and add little by little as much semolina as you need to make a thick porridge dough. Mix in a beaten egg when the mixture is off the boil, stirring well to eliminate the lumps, pour into a flat buttered cake tin and leave to cool. The *millas* will become quite solid; cut into pieces and fry gently until brown and crisp; serve hot, sprinkled with sugar and lemon juice. The *millas* is just one of a number of similar recipes found in the South-West. *Cruchades* are savoury biscuits made in the same way as *millas*, omitting the lemon peel, but dipped in beaten egg and dredged in flour before being fried and served hot with grated cheese on top. *Cruchades* are delicious as a cocktail snack and like many dishes of the South-West turn up under a variety of names: *la rimote*, or *la pous* in

Périgord and *brove* in Béarn.

As one would expect, herbs and spices play an important part in the regional cuisine. Cinnamon, saffron, cloves and ginger are all used and, very important, the herbs of *St Jean*. These are gathered on St John's Day (at least they are supposed to be), which falls on 24 June, and consist of thyme, bay leaves, savory, sweet marjoram, oregano, coriander, parsley, chervil and tarragon. One herb that does not find much favour in the South-West, however, is mint. Our custom of serving mint sauce with lamb is regarded as barbaric by the French and in a book on the gastronomy of the French regions we found this cautionary and shameful tale: the author, who was on holiday in the Quercy, was invited to dine with some French friends who had brought a charming old farmhouse just north of Cahors. The main course was to be two joints of lamb, a rare treat, for the succulent lamb of the causses du Quercy is famous throughout France. The lamb had been entrusted to the tender mercy of a foreign *au pair*; eventually, after much banging about in the kitchen, interspersed with long silences, the joints were presented at table: they had been boiled until they were grey and were swimming in a sea of mint sauce. As one guest later commented in stricken tones: '*On a fusillé pour moins à la Libération!*'.

The Romans called the South-West Aquitania, 'land of waters', a description that accurately underlines the importance of the river system that links the southern and eastern limits of the region with Bordeaux in the north. By far the most important waterway is the stately Garonne which, rising in the Pyrénées, on the Spanish side of the frontier, flows in a great curving arc, first eastwards to Toulouse and afterwards north-westwards, until eventually it joins the Dordogne at Bec d'Ambès, just north of Bordeaux, to create the majestic estuary of the Gironde. En route the Garonne is swollen by numerous tributaries; some like the Baïse and the Gers, quite small; others, like the Tarn, important rivers in their own right.

One of the major tributaries, the Lot, has its source high up in the mountains of the Massif Central, as does the Dordogne. The Lot flows south-west for some way before swinging westwards to join the Garonne at Aiguillon, linking in the process the Rouergue, the Quercy and the Agenais, which together with the Périgord and the Bordelais made up the ancient duchy of Guyenne.

In the south-west of the region the chief river is the Adour. Like the Garonne it starts high up in the central Pyrénées, south of Bagnères-de-Bigorre, but after flowing north for some way turns west towards the Atlantic which it meets near Bayonne. The Adour's main tributaries are the Gave d'Oloron, the Gave de Pau and the Nivelle.

Right up to the end of the nineteenth century these rivers, all of which flow towards the Atlantic, were the chief means of communication between different parts of the region, in the days before the railway tracks had been laid and when the roads were so bad that in winter it was possible for a man on horseback to sink into a pothole, never to be seen again.

The best farming land in the South-West is nearly all to be found where the rivers, having left the confines of the mountains, flow through pleasant alluvial valleys and meander slowly across the flat lowland plains. Not all parts of the region have been equally endowed by nature, however. Much of the Pays Basque, in the foothills of the Pyrénées, is barren heathland, the sandy soil of the Landes can only sustain plantations of pines, while in the Périgord, the Quercy and the Rouergue there are great stretches where the limestone soil is so arid that only sheep can thrive there: these are the *causses*.

The Basin of Aquitaine, as the South-West is called by geologists, was for millions of years covered by sea, whose waters lapped the western shores of what is now the Massif Central. This mountain range, which belongs to the oldest European system, emerged from the waters that covered the earth over 250 million years ago. Gradually erosion ground down the rocks until the surface of the Massif was reduced to an almost flat plateau. Round about 200 million years ago a massive fault resulted in a major subsidence and the sea entered the 'Gulf of Causses'. The western profile of the Massif was now roughly crescent-shaped with blunt horns formed by what is now the plateau of the Limousin in the north and by the Cévennes mountains in the south. In the shallow bay so formed the erosion caused by the movement of the tides resulted in layers of sand and clay that formed a hard impermeable sea bed. Here deposits of fish bones and seashells slowly built up to form a bed of limestone 1,000 metres deep. Very gradually the level of the land rose and the limestone shelf, the future *causses*, emerged from the sea.

Then 50 million years or so ago the earth's crust was subjected to the most enormous internal stresses and in the course of the ensuing convulsions new mountains, the Alps and the Pyrénées, appeared. The hard crystalline rock of the older mountain range took the strain but great fissures appeared in the softer limestone of the *causses* and there were massive landslips. Escaping waters found their way through the cracks in the limestone and biting downwards until they reached the original hard bedrock of the former sea produced deep canyons like those of the upper reaches of the Lot or the Gorges of the Tarn.

The trouble with the *causses* is that they suffer from a chronic shortage of water. The limestone soil, although potentially very fertile, is so porous that any moisture sinks rapidly through it until a layer of hard rock is reached. Here underground lakes and rivers are formed whose waters re-emerge above ground only where some fault in the strata permits; sometimes this is many miles away.

In the highlands of the Massif the problem is quite the opposite. Here the ancient rock is so hard that it is impervious to water, which either runs swiftly away down the steeper slopes or accumulates in the lower-lying areas so that the thin topsoil becomes waterlogged and turns sour. The climate here is cold and damp with long hard winters, so it is hardly surprising that with such conditions the population is small.

The birth of the Pyrénées was accompanied by the production of great quantities of debris that poured down the flanks of the new mountains to be deposited in a series of undulating ridges that make up the foothills we see today. The most remarkable example of this process is the plateau of Lannemezan, just east of Tarbes, where the debris reached the flat plain and spread out in the shape of a great fan intersected by a network of small rivers and streams. All this land is very infertile and consists mostly of barren heathland called 'touyas'. Recently, however a large area to the north and west of Pau has been reclaimed and successfully planted with maize.

North of Lannemezan, in Armagnac (Gers), the soil consists mainly of clay with a high lime content. It is very difficult to work and in the past the combined strength of a pair of oxen was needed to drag the plough through the heavy earth. Now the oxen have nearly all disappeared to be replaced by tractors; perhaps the fuel crisis will bring about their return.

On its western borders, Armagnac runs into the forests of the Landes, which covers most of the coastal region from the Gironde down to Bayonne. The soil here is sandy with an underlying layer of hard red sandstone, which makes for poor drainage. Before the planting of the forest, which started in the first quarter of the nineteenth century, the Landes was notorious as one of the most inhospitable places in the whole of France, inhabited only by a few shepherds and their flocks: even today the population remains small. The reclamation of this wasteland is described in more detail in the chapter on the Landes.

Although so much of the South-West consists of poor farming land there are still very large tracts, especially in the lowlands and the river valleys, where conditions are ideal. Not only is the soil rich but the climate is mild with plenty of rain; nevertheless it can be very hot in the summer with a period of drought in July, August and September. The region falls under the influence of two conflicting weather systems, one originating in the Atlantic and the other in the Mediterranean. The Atlantic system is the dominant one and is responsible for the high annual rainfall. The wettest part (over 1,200mm annually) is the western end of the Pyrénées, where the great swollen rainclouds that roll in from the ocean are brought up short by the mountains of the Pays Basque and Béarn, but the area of high rainfall extends a long way northwards into the Landes. As you go further north and east away from the coast and the mountains, the rainfall is less and the land begins to acquire the parched look associated with the Mediterranean climate. The line of demarcation between the two systems of weather extends very roughly from Albi on the Tarn south to Toulouse, after which it follows the course of the river Ariège upstream as far as the Pyrénées, where it becomes wetter again. East of this line the influence of the drier Mediterranean becomes much more marked, especially if you take the traditional route to the Mediterranean coast through the gap between the Cévennes to the north-east and the Pyrénées to the south. In the Rouergue, on the edge of the Massif Central, on the other hand, the weather is much colder and wetter.

When the light easterly winds are blowing over the region and the skies are a limpid blue the weather is fine, but the westerlies bring more changeable weather with heavy rain alternating with clear periods as a succession of depressions sweep in from the Atlantic. The weather is often very stormy and in the summer there are sometimes spectacular electrical storms.

But extremes of heat and cold are rare in the South-West. The average annual temperatures range between 4°–20°C (40°–68°F) in the north of the region and 7°–20°C (45°–68°F) in the south. Snow is seldom seen, except in the mountains, and in the central lowlands there are usually only a few days of frost, although in 1977 a late snap at Easter nipped the blossom in the bud and ruined the soft fruit harvest for that year. Frost is quite common in the Bordelais (Gironde) in the winter months but at that time the vines are dormant and no harm is done. Although Bordeaux lies at sea level and close to the ocean, it can be very cold there in the winter, especially when the *bise*, a bitter northerly wind, is blowing. The effect of the *bise* is felt as far south as Auch, the capital of Armagnac. Bordeaux also suffers from frequent mists and fogs, caused by the difference in temperatures between the waters of the Gironde and the land, but similar conditions are to be found all over the South-West in the autumn and winter months.

Spring comes late in April but when it does there is a brief, glorious flowering which is particularly spectacular in the orchard country of the Agenais (Lot-et-Garonne). The three months of April, May and June are unusually wet for France but are followed by several months of fine weather which often lasts until late in October, allowing very late grape harvests in the Sauternes area of the Bordelais (Gironde) and in the Bergeracois in Périgord (Dordogne). The summer months are so dry in the Armagnac region that the clay soil is baked hard, great cracks appear and the surface turns to dust. Ensuing heavy rainfall in the mountains to the south sometimes results in serious flooding which washes away the topsoil. The floods of 1977 were the worst experienced in the region for half a century; Armagnac was the worst-hit area and at Auch two people were drowned and two bridges swept away. The previous year, by contrast, had seen a severe drought, but this was not confined to the South-West and conditions in the north of France were even worse.

Despite these occasional extremes of weather, the South-West enjoys a moderate climate and on the whole life there is very pleasant with mild winters, hot summers and long golden autumns. Béarn and the Pays Basque have been popular retirement areas for more than 150 years, ever since Wellington's troops were quartered in Pau following the defeat of Napoleon's armies in Spain. More recently, and especially since the Second

World War, more and more foreigners, with the Dutch and English predominating, have been settling in Périgord (Dordogne) and the Quercy (Lot), attracted by the climate and the slow pace of life.

For a hundred years or more the population of the region has been declining as more and more young men and women have moved away looking for work and a better standard of life. The steady influx of retired people has aggravated this problem by pushing up the average age and imposing an additional burden on the working population that has remained. The situation has been alleviated to some extent by the arrival of poor immigrant workers from Italy, Spain, Portugal and, after the loss of the French colonies, from Algeria and Vietnam; even so the decline continues in most parts of the region and the department of the Gers has the lowest density of population in the whole of France.

The depopulation of parts of the South-West is the result of centuries of neglect that has left much of the region largely undeveloped. The reasons for this neglect are both geographical and historical. Cut off from Paris and the north by the Massif Central, the South-West evolved its own distinctive culture during the early Middle Ages, and throughout the subsequent centuries nurtured a fierce opposition to the central government.

In the thirteenth century the heretical sect called Cathars became firmly established in the kingdom of Toulouse which lay east of the Garonne and stretched as far north as the Quercy and the Rouergue. Pope Innocent III preached a crusade against the heretics and an army led by Simon de Montfort, father of the leader of the Baron's Revolt in England in the thirteenth century, marched from the north to suppress the Cathars with great ferocity. The struggle lasted for 20 years and resulted in the territories of the Count of Toulouse passing to the French kings. Although the crusade was for the most part confined to an area east of the one described in this book, the Agenais, the Quercy and the Rouergue all suffered at Simon de Montfort's hands and the ruthlessness of the crusading armies left a legacy of bitterness that bedevilled future relations between the government in Paris and the people of the South-West.

There was however a more serious obstacle to the efforts of the French kings to extend their sway over the rest of the region. When Eleanor of Aquitaine married Henry Plantagenet, the future king of England, in 1152, she brought him as her dowry an enormous stretch of territory in the west of France, including Gascony and with Bordeaux as its port of entry. On Henry's accession all this passed into the control of the English kings. The English presence in Gascony was a running sore that the French kings could not leave alone and led inevitably to the outbreak of the Hundred Years' War. The French territories adjacent to Gascony, such as Armagnac and the Quercy, suffered terribly during the ensuing conflict and the numerous thirteenth and fourteenth century castles, fortified churches and specially built walled towns called *bastides* testify to this day to the uncertainty of life at that period. Eventually the English were defeated at the battle of Castillon in 1453 and driven out of France.

But the troubles of the South-West were by no means ended. In the sixteenth century the region became a Protestant stronghold and the wars of religion were largely fought there, to end only when Henri of Navarre became King of France in 1589.

No doubt because of this history of unrest and disaffection, the kings of France never looked kindly on the South-West. It has remained until quite recently one of the most backward areas of France and only since the Second World War has the creation of Sud-Ouest Aviation and the building of the Concorde brought prosperity to Toulouse and the surrounding country. Unfortunately the recession has hit the aircraft industry and unemployment is rising again. Apart from Sud-Ouest Aviation, the only other major industries in the region are coal-mining at Decazeville in the Rouergue, where unemployment is also on the increase, and the natural gas plant at Lacq, near Pau. But this is not much in such a big region and the South-West remains largely agricultural in character. It is true that the EEC has brought prosperity to some of the more favoured farming areas, like the Agenais, but elsewhere in Armagnac, the Rouergue or parts of the Pays Basque, for example, time seems to have stood still and to visit one of the small sleepy villages in these parts is like stepping back in time to before the First World War.

However difficult communications between the South-West and northern France may have been, the region was open to many other influences that have played an important part in the development of its gastronomy. The Romans made the major contribution: it was they who first introduced the vine to south-west France and it was during their 400 year benevolent rule that Bordeaux came into prominence and that the wine trade started, although in those days the wine was for the most part exported up the Garonne to Toulouse and thence to Narbonne. France also owes its great chestnut forests to the Romans who brought the nut with them from Italy. When times were very hard chestnuts became the staple diet of peasants who lived in the poorer parts of the region, such as the forests of Périgord or the Rouergue.

It may well be that the Romans were also responsible for the custom of *gavage* that is so widespread in the South-West, for it is known that they force-fed their geese with figs and this fruit is common in the region.

The Dark Ages have left so few records that there is nothing to show whether the numerous invaders who harried the South-West for the next 600 years or so made any mark on the region's food or not. What is certain is that they did no good to the wine trade.

Not until the Crusaders started to return from the Middle East were there any important changes. They brought home with them not only improved skills in warfare and building castles but a heightened awareness of good food learned from the Arabs, and more specifically the sweet dessert grape called the 'Chasselas' and fruit trees, particularly the plum, which flourished in the Agenais and from which is derived one of the South-West's most famous delicacies, the succulent prune, so different from the withered black objects of our childhood memories.

English rule in Gascony, while it seems to have had little effect on the region's food, played a vital role in the development of the wine trade. Indeed the level of exports of wine to England in the fourteenth century has never been surpassed and Bordeaux under English rule was one of the wealthiest cities in France, a prosperity that reached far into the hinterland. Although the connection was interrupted after the battle of Castillon, it was never completely broken and to this day England remains one of Bordeaux's biggest customers for fine wines. What is more, Britons living and working in Bordeaux have played a significant part of building up the wine trade and there are still many British firms like Bass Charrington with substantial financial interests there.

The discovery of the New World resulted in some important innovations in the South-West's diet. In many areas maize replaced millet as the staple food of the peasants and was also fed to poultry. Today maize is no longer an important food for humans but it is still used to fatten the geese and ducks that are reared for the sake of their enlarged livers (*foie gras*), and to feed the plump yellow chickens of the Landes. Maize is also refined and sold as cooking oil. Chocolate, pumpkins, peppers and tomatoes all made their first appearance in the sixteenth century: chocolate, which originated in Mexico found its way to Bayonne by way of Spain, while peppers and tomatoes came to play an important part in Basque cooking in dishes like *poulet basquaise* and *pipérade*. The tomato grows well in the region and has become the principal cash crop of the Marmandais, based on the town of Marmande in the Agenais.

At the end of the sixteenth century the South-West was the main battleground for the rival Protestant and Catholic factions in a bitter civil war, but with the accession of Henri IV to the throne, stability gradually returned and it was during the next 150 years that the chefs and *traiteurs* (catering middlemen) of Périgord created the sophisticated cuisine for the local aristocracy which is the culminating glory of the gastronomy of the South-West. The revolution threw these artists out of work and many of them opened *charcuterie* shops; in this way their skills were disseminated to a much larger clientele.

During the sixteenth and seventeenth centuries it was the Dutch who provided the most important outside influence on the region. They had acquired a taste for the sweet muscat wines of Greece, but these were denied to them because the Ottoman Turks controlled the eastern Mediterranean.

So the Dutch encouraged the *vignerons* of the Entre-deux-Mers, in the Bordeaux region, and the Bergeracois in Périgord to plant varieties of vine that would give them the kind of wine they preferred. These are still predominantly white-wine-producing areas to this day and in the Bergeracois the emphasis is still on sweet rather than dry.

The Dutch built up a considerable trade with northern Europe in fortified wines. They bought very cheap wines and added sugar, spices and spirit to disguise the poor quality and to stop the wine deteriorating, for in those days, before there were corks and bottles, the wine went sour within the year. The need for spirit* led the Dutch to promote the distillation of wine in the South-West, especially in the Armagnac area. The resulting *eau-de-vie* became known as 'brandywijn', which in Dutch means 'burnt wine' and refers to the early method of distillation in a pot over a wood fire. The tough Dutch sailors started to drink brandywijn and thus helped to stimulate the refinement of the original coarse spirit into the smooth brandies we know as armagnac and cognac.

The Dutch also made a very important contribution in the Médoc at the end of the seventeenth century, for it was their engineers who organized the draining of the marshes and thus paved the way for the planting of some of the Médoc's most famous vineyards.

The end of the eighteenth century saw the beginning of the agricultural revolution already referred to, but this would not have been possible without the improvement in communications that began under Napoleon at the start of the nineteenth century. Until then the rivers were the main highways, the roads being so bad that it took four days to reach Bordeaux from Paris, travelling by stagecoach. Many parts of the region, such as Armagnac and the Causses de Quercy were so far removed from Bordeaux that they operated as enclosed economies with the small local market towns reduced to an interchange of goods with each other. In the case of Armagnac the transport problem was so bad that the producers were compelled to convert their wine to *eau-de-vie* rather than see it turn sour. Even so the distance of the Armagnac vineyards from Bordeaux meant that their brandy remained comparatively unknown compared with that of the better placed Charente, which of course produces cognac.

The building of good roads by Napoleon was a start, but it was not until the coming of the railways that the region really began to open up to the outside world, although this did not happen in some of the remoter parts, such as the Rouergue, until the 1870s. Once the tracks were laid, however, the enclosed economies no longer worked and the peasants, seeing the prospect of an easier life, voted with their rail tickets and left to seek work in Paris or the industrial north-east.

But one of the biggest changes in the economy of the South-West was the

---

* It was also used as an anaesthetic.

result of the introduction of a tiny insect from America, the phylloxera. This parasitic louse, less than a millimetre long, burrows into the roots of the vine where it multiplies at the rate of twelve generations a year. Gradually the roots shrivel and the vine withers and dies. The phylloxera was first discovered in the Bordelais, just across the river from the city of Bordeaux, in 1866 and during the next decade it spread throughout the South-West leaving a trail of disaster. By the mid-1880s the wine harvest in the Bordeaux region was a quarter of what it had been in the record year of 1875. All kinds of remedies were tried: spraying with chemicals, fumigation; in desperation, some *vignerons* even resorted to flooding their vineyards – all to no avail.

Eventually the only solution was the replanting of the vineyards with vines imported from America on to which were grafted the original native stock. On their own the American vines produced a very inferior wine but they had the great advantage that they were immune to the phylloxera. When the native Bordeaux varieties were grafted on to them the result was a phylloxera-resistant vine capable of producing a good quality wine. Replanting began in 1877 and in two years the Bordelais was nearly back to pre-phylloxera levels of production, although these are never likely to be reached again for a variety of economic reasons. Nevertheless, the stocking of the vineyards proceeded very slowly. What is more young vines do not immediately produce good wine, so although production increased quickly it was not until 1893 that fine quality Bordeaux wines were widely available once more, whilst the first exceptional post-phylloxera vintage was not until 1899.

But although the vineyards of the Bordelais were saved, those in some other parts of the South-West, such as the Périgord, the Quercy and the Rouergue, lacking the financial resources needed for restocking and replanting, never fully recovered and the ones found there today cover a much smaller area than before. The phylloxera brought ruin to many small producers in the South-West, but there were long-term benefits as well. Many of the vineyards had been tiny, producing very indifferent wine and these were no great loss. Another long-term result was the passing of the *appellation contrôlée* legislation. This had to be introduced to prevent the *vignerons* replanting their vineyards with vines that were more prolific but gave inferior wine and selling it under the original name as if it were the same as that produced from the pre-phylloxera vines. This legislation is discussed in more detail on pages 35–40.

It was during the nineteenth century that the Parisian habit of eating in restaurants began to spread throughout France as improved roads and the railways made the population more mobile. This brought the classic French cuisine to the South-West and that is what you will find on offer today in most restaurants in the region. The local specialities often take some time to prepare, so don't expect to be able to walk into any restaurant and find a famous local dish; instead it is best to speak to the *patron* in advance and you will find him only too delighted to co-operate. Having said that, you can usually rely on finding *foie gras*, *confit d'oie* and *pâté truffé* on the menus of all but very small establishments.

The twentieth century has seen the steady decline in population of the South-West, reversed in some parts by an influx of immigrant Italian workers and refugees from the Spanish Civil War and the overseas French colonies, Vietnam and Algeria. These newcomers seem to have made only a minimal contribution to the cuisine, apart from the occasional appearance of macaroni with casserole dishes and the addition of the famous North African dish, *cous-cous*, to restaurant menus. Otherwise the most important changes are taking place in the larger towns where housewives are increasingly patronising supermarkets and hypermarkets and buying convenience foods for quick cooking. This trend is likely to accelerate as the younger women increasingly come to expect greater leisure and independence than their mothers enjoyed, but in the country areas – and the South-West is mostly country of course – the old traditions still flourish.

Quantities and measurements

THE QUANTITIES for the recipes given in this book are in metric first, with approximate imperial measurements in brackets. These are not really equivalents: juggling with decimal points and exact conversions is pointless for most of the recipes. The robust country cooking does not depend on exact proportions and you will find that a few grammes or even ounces more or less of a particular item will not, on the whole, change the balance of a recipe out of all recognition. The methods described and the quantities suggested may encourage some cooks to develop their own *spécialités de la maison*, with a little more of this item or a little less of that. Nor are the oven measurements exact in Gas Marks, Centigrade or Fahrenheit; each cook will know the temperature of her oven for the type of dish being prepared, and what one may describe as Mark 4 could depend on whether one is using town gas, natural gas or bottled gas. Slow cooking may be preferred for a chicken casserole instead of a quick braising.

Those cooks who worry about exact quantities can follow either the metric or the imperial, but should not mix the two sets. Fluid ounces are given for liquid measures for the benefit of cooks in the USA and Canada. The size of a glass of wine or armagnac depends on the generosity of the cook.

Liquids

Metric	Imperial	Fluid ounces (approx)	
		British	American
1 litre	1.76 pints	35	28
0.5 l (50 cl)	0.88 pints	18	$14\frac{1}{2}$
0.25 l (25 cl or 250ml)	0.44 pints	9	7
1.14 l	2 pints	40	32
0.57 l (57 cl or 570 ml)	1 pint	20	16
0.28 l (28 cl or 280 ml)	$\frac{1}{2}$ pint	10	8
0.14 l (14 cl or 140 ml)	$\frac{1}{4}$ pint	5	4

Weight

Metric	Imperial	Imperial	Metric
1 kg	2.20 lb	2 lb	0.91 kg (907 g)
0.5 kg (500 g)	1.1 lb (1 lb 2 oz)	1 lb	0.45 kg (454 g)
0.25 kg (250 g)	9 oz	$\frac{1}{2}$ lb (8 oz)	0.211 kg (227 g)
0.01 kg (100 g)	3.5 oz	$\frac{1}{4}$ lb (4 oz)	0.113 kg (113 g)
50 g	1.8 oz	2 oz	56.7 g
25 g	0.88 oz	1 oz	28.4 g

Cup measures

A British Standard measuring cup approximately equals 10 fluid ounces; an American Standard measuring cup approximately equals 8 fluid ounces.

British Cup Measures	American Equivalents
2 fl oz	$\frac{1}{4}$ cup
$2\frac{1}{2}$ fl oz	$\frac{1}{3}$ cup
4 fl oz	$\frac{1}{2}$ cup
$5\frac{1}{2}$ fl oz	$\frac{2}{3}$ cup
8 fl oz	1 cup ($\frac{1}{2}$ US pt)
10 fl oz ($\frac{1}{2}$ imp pt)	$1\frac{1}{4}$ cup
16 fl oz	2 cups (1 US pt)
20 fl oz (1 imp pt)	$2\frac{1}{2}$ cups

Oven temperatures

	Gas Regulo Mark	Degrees Fahrenheit (F)	Centigrade (C)
Cool	$0 - \frac{1}{2}$	225–250	105–120
Very slow	$\frac{1}{2} - 1$	250–275	120–135
Slow	1 – 2	275–300	135–150
Slow to moderate	2 – 3	300–350	150–180
Moderate	4	375	190
Moderately hot	5	400	205
Hot	6 – 7	425–450	220–240
Very hot	8 –10	475–500	240–260

Measurement of alcohol

The alcoholic strength of wines and spirits is expressed in degrees of alcohol by volume throughout.

About the Wine

IN BRITAIN south-west France is probably best known for its fine red wines, but in France the region is also famous for its sweet whites, some of which can lay claim to being amongst the best in the world. It is an unfortunate fact that sweet white wines have a bad name in Britain and the fashion is now for very dry whites like Muscadet from the Loire. This prejudice, for that is all it is, has been fed by some of the poor-quality sweet wines that used to be sold under the name of Barsac or Sauternes. Usually these wines did not even originate in France and they certainly bore little resemblance to the real thing, but unfortunately they were most people's only experience of sweet whites and they literally left a nasty taste. Yet it would be a sad mistake for anyone travelling through the South-West to ignore the fine dessert wines of Sauternes, Monbazillac or Jurançon, for to do so would be to miss some of the region's most delicious products. In our experience, friends who have been introduced for the first time to a classic dessert wine, such as a Barsac, have never regretted it. To be at their best these wines should be served chilled.

Wine is made throughout the region and generally the standard is very high. Alongside the famous wine-producing areas, like Bordeaux, Cahors and Bergerac, are many others where you will find very drinkable local wines. More detailed information on these *vins de pays*, as they are called, will be found on page 39.

To take full advantage of the wide range of wines to be found in the South-West and the information about them contained in this book it is essential to understand how the French classify their wines and the way they are described on the label.

The description of wine is subject in France to very strict legislation which controls the right to use place names like Bordeaux, Sauternes or Bergerac. These are the laws of Appellation d'Origine Contrôlée (AOC for short) which are administered by the Institut National des Appellations d'Origine (INAO) whose headquarters is in Paris. The object of the legislation is to guarantee that a wine genuinely comes from the place it says it does on the label and is not a blend of wines from somewhere else. Thus, if you were in the wine-making district of the Médoc, in the Bordeaux region, and wished to buy a good local wine you would look for the words Appellation Médoc Contrôlée on the label. This means that the wine has been made exclusively from grapes grown in the Médoc itself. To earn the right to use a specific place name the *vignerons* (wine-growers) must meet certain quite rigorous conditions laid down by the INAO. Summarized briefly these are:

1 *The area of production* Only vineyards that lie within a strictly defined geographical area are entitled to the name, provided they also comply with all the other regulations. The composition of the soil as well as the traditional boundaries are taken into consideration when the permitted area is marked out.

2 *Permitted vines* The wines must be made from certain varieties of vines that have by tradition been established in the area. This regulation is not immutable. The INAO will allow new and better varieties of vine to be introduced provided this does not in any way alter the essential character of the wine or degrade it. In Cahors, for example, the Tannat grape has been recently introduced with INAO approval in preference to the Jurançon Noir which was prone to mildew.

3 *Permitted alcoholic content* To be entitled to the appellation the wine must have a minimum alcoholic strength and this must be derived from the natural sugar content of the grape itself. The wine you actually buy will normally be a degree or so above this minimum level and in bad years the regulations allow chaptalization, that is the addition of sugar to raise the level of alcoholic strength, but this is only allowed if the permitted minimum has been reached.

4 *Permitted harvest* Over-production usually results in a poor-quality wine so strict regulations lay down the number of hectolitres of wine that may be made per hectare of vineyard. In a very good year vineyards often exceed this amount, but the excess wine may not be sold under the *appellation* name. This has led to excellent château wine being sold to the trade under separate labels which do not carry the AOC guarantee. These wines can be bargains.

5 *Viticulture* The INAO lays down specific regulations governing the care of the vine. These can vary from one area to another, for example in the Pyrénées the vines are trained high to avoid the winter frosts, whereas in the Médoc they are pruned low so that they are close to the stony soil and benefit from the reflected heat. The regulations are based on established practice but their object is to discourage the *vignerons* from adopting practices that produce bumper crops of indifferent quality.

6 *Viniculture* The actual wine-making process is also controlled with regulations governing such matters as the length of time the wine is left in contact with the skins and how long it is kept in cask before bottling. The whole purpose of the *Appellation d'Origine Contrôlée* legislation is to guarantee the authenticity of the wine and to preserve its local characteristics and its quality. Very sensibly the regulations are based on local traditions and customs: the areas are those where the named wines have

always been made, the grapes employed are the ones that have always been used locally and the methods of cultivation are those that have always been associated with those particular vineyards. Nevertheless the INAO is dedicated to eliminating bad old customs and encourages the *vignerons* to concentrate on raising the quality of their wine. This can bring outstanding results as is the case with the Côtes de Buzet wines of the Agenais (see page 90).

The need for some kind of legislation became apparent at the end of the nineteenth century after the phylloxera disaster. Once the answer to the disease had been found, many vineyards were replanted with new hybrid stock which was often quite different from the old pre-phylloxera stock. The result was too often large crops producing mediocre wine. Much of the wine sold at this period was in fact a blend of wines from many different areas, sometimes far removed from the place name on the label. The first legislation was concerned mainly with defining the geographical place of origin of a wine, with further laws following in 1908 and 1919 and 1927, but it was not until 1935 that the regulations in force today were finally codified and the INAO was set up to administer them.

Under the *Appellation d'Origine Contrôlée* system the more closely an area is defined the more authentic the wine should be. Take the wines of the Bordeaux region, for example, and you will find that most of the wine made there carries the simple message *Appellation Bordeaux Contrôlée* on its labels; this means that the wine has been made somewhere within the officially recognized Bordeaux wine area (see map on page 45) and will almost certainly be a blend of different wines from within that region. If it is red wine it must have been made from the following grapes, Cabernet Sauvignon, Cabernet Franc, Merlot, Malbec, Carmenere and Petit Verdot; if white, only Sémillon, Sauvignon, Muscadelle and Merlot Blanc may be used. The permitted minimums of alcohol are 10 degrees for the red and 10.5 degrees for the white. A Bordeaux Supérieur is not, as might be thought, a higher quality wine but one that has a higher alcoholic minimum. For the *Appellation Bordeaux Supérieur Contrôlée* red the permitted alcoholic minimum is 10.5 degrees and for the white 11.5 degrees, of which 10.5 must be derived from the natural grape sugar.

Within the Bordeaux region are a number of wine districts such as the Graves or St-Émilion which have their own recognized *appellations*, so that the label would read something like '*Appellation St-Émilion Contrôlée*', indicating that this is a blended wine from the St-Émilion district. If, however, the label reads, for example, '*Château Bellevue, Appellation St-Émilion Contrôlée*', then you know that the wine comes from a single estate in St-Émilion.

In the Médoc district of Bordeaux, the definitions become more complicated still. The district is subdivided into Haut-Médoc and Médoc, of which Haut-Médoc produces by far the better wine. The Haut-Médoc producers put '*Appellation Haut-Médoc Contrôlée*' on their labels but the Médoc uses only '*Appellation Médoc Contrôlée*'. Some communes in the Haut-Médoc make such fine wine that they are entitled to their own *appellations*, so you need to know their names. They will all be found in the section on the Bordelais, but the most famous of them are Pauillac, Margaux, St-Julien Beychevelle and St-Estèphe. Thus the label for one of the most famous of all the Haut-Médoc châteaux reads: '*Château Mouton-Rothschild, Appellation Pauillac Contrôlée*'.

To confuse the issue still further, in 1855 sixty-two of the best châteaux of the Médoc were included in a list that arranged them in five classes. The wines are called *crus* (growths) in the list and the *premiers crus* (first growths), that is to say the wines included in the first of the five classes, numbered only four, Château Lafite, Château Latour, Château Margaux and Château Haut-Brion, the last being the only château in the whole list that physically lies outside the Médoc (Haut-Brion is in fact in the Graves but in 1855 it was so highly regarded that it was felt it could not be left out). These four wines, together with Château Mouton-Rothschild, which was promoted to the rank of *premier cru* in 1973, are outstanding; but the others in the remaining four classes, while seldom reaching the same heights as the big five, are also very good. The 1855 classification has stood the test of time and is still used as a guide to the finest wines of the Médoc, even so it can be misleading. It looks like a petrified league table with the last château of the cinquième crus (fifth growths) permanently on the edge of relegation; in fact, leaving aside the premiers crus which are literally in a class of their own, any of the wines included in the original classification may be regarded as rather special and there is no reason to suppose that a third growth is of necessity any better than a fifth. Unless you wish to go into the whole matter very thoroughly it should be enough to know that the wine of a particular château is classified and this you can discover by looking at Appendix 1. It should also be pointed out that the class to which these wines belong rarely appears on the label, the more usual form of words used being *Grand Cru Classé*.

The white wines of Barsac and the Sauternes were also included in the classification of 1855, but those of St-Émilion and Graves were not classified until 1955 and 1959 respectively. The last two classifications do not as yet have the same prestige as the 1855 classification of the Médoc. Luckily it is only in the Bordeaux region of the South-West that the description of wine becomes so convoluted.

The words *Appellation Contrôlée* must by law appear on the label of an AOC wine this is your best guarantee when looking for a better quality wine, but since 1949 there has been a secondary classification of French wines; the '*Vins Délimités de Qualité Supérieure*' (Delimited Wines of Superior Quality) or VDQS for short. These are wines that did not fall within the AOC regulations of 1935 but which in 1949 were considered good enough to be covered by some system of control. The VDQS legislation is not as extensive as that imposed on AOC wines but the territory is defined in the same way and the *vignerons* have to conform to regulations governing the grape varieties that may be used and the strength of alcohol that is permitted. Some wines like that of Cahors have benefited from the regulations to such an extent that they have been promoted to full AOC status.

Until quite recently all the remaining wines on sale in France were classified as '*Vins de table*' but now that the AOC and even the VDQS ones have become so expensive the INAO has introduced a new classification designed to encourage the production of good quality local wines at reasonable prices somewhere between those paid for VDQS and table wines; these are the '*Vins de Pays.*' New regulations were introduced in 1973, the principal ones being:

1 The wines must be made from grapes from specified vines. These differ from one locality according to the nature of the soil.
2 They must have an alcohol content obtained naturally in the region of production. In the South-West the permitted minimum is 9.5 degrees.
3 *Vins de Pays* must be made and kept separately from other table wines.
4 The wines have to pass tasting checks carried out by an approved professional body.

These regulations ensure that *vins de pays* are blends of wines that come from well defined local areas. Those made in the South-West are listed below under the names of the *départments* where they are to be found:

GERS (Armagnac)
Côtes du Condomois (also made in the southern part of Lot-et-Garonne)
Côtes de Gascogne
Côtes de Montestruc
Côtes de Saint-Mont

LOT (Quercy)
Coteaux du Quercy (also made in the northern part of Tarn-et-Garonne)
Coteaux de Glanes

LOT-ET-GARONNE (Agenais and northern part of Armagnac)
Côtes du Condomois (also made in the Gers)
Agenais (also made in the northern part of Tarn-et-Garonne)
Côtes du Brulhois

TARN-ET-GARONNE (Bas Quercy)
Agenais (also made in Lot-et-Garonne)
Coteaux du Quercy (also made in Lot)
Saint-Sardos

AVEYRON (Rouergue)
Côtes du Tarn (also made in the Tarn)

If you are looking for a good *vin de pays*, the best place to go to is the local cooperative, although you may have to buy a minimum of ten litres in a plastic container called a *cubitainer*, or *cubie* for short.

Cheaper still than the *vins de pays* are the *vins de table*. These are blends of wines that may originate either exclusively from French wine-growing regions or from other EEC countries. If the wines are from France alone the label must say 'Produce of France'. The label must also give the alcoholic content. *Vins de table* often have brand names like 'Nicolas' or 'Castelvin'.

One of the best guarantees of any French wine are the words *Mis en Bouteille au Chateau*, because they mean that the wine has been bottled on the estate where it was made, and one assumes that the proprietor would not do this unless he was concerned about its quality. *Mis en Bouteille dans nos Caves* means nothing since the cellars in question could be anywhere. Another sign of a good quality wine is the name on the label of a leading shipper like Calvet or Sichel.

The label often gives additional information such as whether the wine is still or sparkling; sweet or dry; red, white or rosé. Here are some of the terms commonly met with:

Blanc de Blanc A white made solely from white grapes.

Champenoise A sparkling wine made by the same method as Champagne with a secondary fermentation taking place in the bottle.

Demi-sec Sweetish (literally half-dry).

Doux Sweet.

Liquoreux A rich sweet dessert wine such as a Sauternes or a Monbazillac. Usually with a high alcoholic strength.

Moelleux Literally marrowy. A mellow luscious wine. Usually applied to white wines similar to, but not as full and strong as, the *liquoreux* wines mentioned above. The term can also be applied to smooth, well-rounded red wines such as those of Pomerol.

Pétillant A slightly sparkling wine, the result of a minor secondary fermentation in the bottle.

Sauvignon Usually linked with another word, e.g. Blanc Sauvignon or Sauvignon Sec. Indicates a dry white wine from the Sauvignon grape.

Sec Dry.

GUYENNE

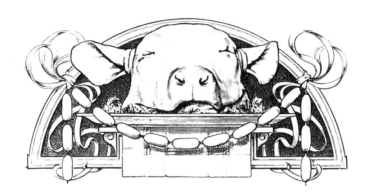

Bordelais

IT WAS A foggy morning in February when we arrived at Château Margaux. We had spent the night in a small hotel in the old part of Bordeaux and had decided on the spur of the moment to visit one of the famous châteaux of the Médoc. Driving northwards through the flat vineyard country was a weird experience; we could see little except occasional road signs, but the names on the signs read like a wine merchant's catalogue: Château La Lagune, Château Cantemerle, Château Boyd-Cantenac, Château Kirwan, Château Palmer, Château Giscours, all these and so many more within 30 kilometres of the heart of Bordeaux.

At Château Margaux all seemed deserted and the rows of black vine stumps looked quite dead; it was difficult to imagine the heavy black grapes that would be harvested there eight months later. Certainly it was not an ideal day for a visit, but even so we could not help being impressed by the elegant eighteenth-century front of the château as we drove into the courtyard with its fine pedimented portico supported on beautifully proportioned Ionic columns. Despite the damp gloomy weather we were treated with great courtesy and taken on a conducted tour. The highlight of the visit was undoubtedly seeing the *chai* where the barrels of new wine are stored. It is an enormous airy room whose roof is supported by a long line of slim white classical columns. The architectural design is purely functional but the visual effect produced by the contrasting shapes of the round fat brown barrels and the vertical lines of the Tuscan columns is quite remarkable.

In some respects this combination of commercial functionalism and elegance is the key to Bordeaux itself. 'Take Versailles and add Antwerp and you have Bordeaux,' wrote Victor Hugo. Sitting in a café in the Place de la Comédie, right in the heart of the city, one sees what Hugo meant. Opposite the café stands the Grand Théâtre, built by Bordeaux's famous architect Victor Louis between 1773 and 1780 on the instructions of the governor, the Duc de Richelieu. Looking at this harmonious classical building, with its magnificent colonnaded front, one tends to forget that only 400 metres away is the river, its banks lined with warehouses and cranes marking the port whose traffic created the city's wealth.

Bordeaux lies on the river Garonne, 98 kilometres from the sea at the first place that is narrow enough to afford an easy crossing, although it was not until 1821 that work was finished on the first bridge. The river is tidal up to and beyond the city and so it was natural that a great port should grow up here, especially in the days when the only reliable form of transport was by river and sea. Twenty-three kilometres to the north of the city, however, is Bec d'Ambès, the narrow spit of land that marks the confluence of the rivers Garonne and Dordogne. Below this point the estuary is known as the Gironde. The reason why the port of Bordeaux developed where it did, rather than on the Dordogne, was because the Garonne offers easier access to a large hinterland to the south-east, whereas east of Bergerac navigation on the Dordogne grows increasingly difficult. The long estuary and comparative shallowness of the Garonne, however, has meant that in recent years Bordeaux has lost a great deal of trade to the deep-water ports of northern Europe. Even so it is still the fourth largest in France as well as being the fourth biggest conurbation, with a population of 226,000 within the boundaries of the city proper.

The origins of Bordeaux are obscure. It is possible that there was a Bronze Age settlement on the site, but it is not until the arrival of the Romans in 56 BC that there are any hard facts. The Romans brought the vine to south-west France and by the end of the first century AD Burdigala, as the Romans called Bordeaux, was already surrounded by vineyards. Roman rule was benign and Burdigala flourished, becoming by the end of the second century AD the political and economic capital of Aquitania. The city grew in size and prosperity and as it did so there emerged an aristocratic élite, one of whom was the poet Ausonius. This famous scholar, who became a prefect of Gaul and a consul, retired to Burdigala where he seems to have spent his declining years without regret, enjoying the mild climate and relaxed way of life which then as now characterized Aquitania. It was during this time that Ausonius wrote a charming poem about his native city which tells us that Burdigala was already famous for its wine and its oysters.

This age of affluence was followed, after the fall of Rome in AD 410, by a series of invasions punctuated by periods of calm. Goths, Vascons, Arabs, Franks and Normans all sacked Bordeaux, but somehow the city and the surrounding vineyards survived.

It was during this period that Aquitaine became virtually an independent kingdom under the rule of its dukes. Eventually these overmighty subjects were brought to heel by the time-honoured expedient of arranging a royal marriage. In 1137 Eleanor of Aquitaine married the future Louis VII of France in Bordeaux cathedral. This piece of practical statesmanship was confounded by the incompatability of the marriage partners. Eleanor behaved less than discreetly, was divorced by the furious king and promptly married Henry Plantagenet, the heir to the English throne. Two years later in 1154 Henry became king and Eleanor's immense possessions in the south-west of France passed to the English crown, thus sowing the seeds of the long, bitter struggle known as the Hundred Years' War.

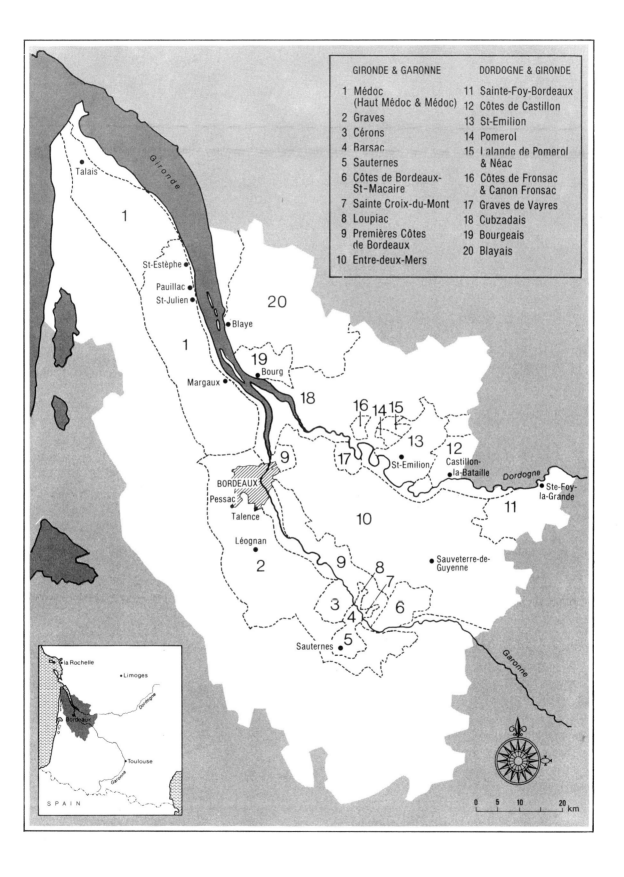

GIRONDE & GARONNE

1 Médoc
  (Haut Médoc & Médoc)
2 Graves
3 Cérons
4 Barsac
5 Sauternes
6 Côtes de Bordeaux-
  St-Macaire
7 Sainte Croix-du-Mont
8 Loupiac
9 Premières Côtes
  de Bordeaux
10 Entre-deux-Mers

DORDOGNE & GIRONDE

11 Sainte-Foy-Bordeaux
12 Côtes de Castillon
13 St-Emilion
14 Pomerol
15 Lalande de Pomerol
   & Néac
16 Côtes de Fronsac
   & Canon Fronsac
17 Graves de Vayres
18 Cubzadais
19 Bourgeais
20 Blayais

However ruinous the war may have been for France as a whole, Bordeaux did very well out of it. The English kings developed a taste for Gascon wine and so did their subjects. In 1308 Edward II alone ordered a thousand barrels (roughly 1,152,000 bottles) to celebrate his marriage to Isabelle of France. Bordeaux became a thriving port again and by the middle of the fourteenth century was exporting in the region of 180,000 hectolitres of wine a year to England – this at a time when our population numbered four million.

Every autumn a fleet of merchant ships left London for Bordeaux, the time of sailing being linked to the date of the new vintage in the Bordelais. Froissart describes the flotilla as containing as many as three hundred ships and its arrival in the port was one of the highlights of the year and was celebrated by great civic festivities. The ships remained in Bordeaux for about ten weeks (while the merchants bargained and the wine fermented and settled), and then sailed for London arriving there just before Christmas. A second voyage was made in the new year, returning to England at Easter.

The Gascon wine so beloved of the English was very different from the Bordeaux wine of today. It was made from a blend of red and white grapes and was light red in colour, from which it derived the name of claret (a corruption of the French word *clairet* which is used to describe light-bodied wines with a clear colour). In those days the wine was also what we now call a *vin de l'année*, in other words it had no long-lasting qualities and was best drunk young. So the first shipment, received before Christmas, was much sought after.

During the period of the Hundred Years' War, Bordeaux enjoyed a privileged position under the protection of the English kings, a situation that the Bordelais exploited quite unscrupulously to promote their own wines at the expense of those that were shipped through Bordeaux but came from higher up the Garonne, the Dordogne and the Lot, such as Cahors and Monbazillac. These Haut Pays wines as they were called, were not allowed within the city confines until the feast of St Martin (11 November) which gave the merchants of Bordeaux plenty of time to sell off their own wines first. It has to be remembered, however, that the Bordeaux wine-producing area was much smaller than it is today and that most of the wine came from the area that we now call Graves. Conversely the Haut Pays produced more wine than they do now and thus the Bordeaux traders were vulnerable to their competition.

The Hundred Years' War ended in 1453 when the English commander, Talbot, was defeated and killed at the battle of Castillon on the Dordogne, 49 kilometres from Bordeaux. The city fell to the French and for a short time lost all its privileges as a punishment for having supported the English cause, but such an important trading centre could not be subjected to penalties and restrictions for ever and Bordeaux soon regained its commercial freedom. Gradually, despite the disturbed state of Europe, the city regained its former trading position until by the eighteenth century it was once again a major exporter of wine. The magnificent architecture dating from this period is sufficient testimony to the city's prosperity at this period. Nevertheless, the long conflict between the French and English, culminating in the Napoleonic wars, did not help the Bordeaux wine trade, which had to look for markets further afield.

It was not until the second half of the nineteenth century, after the free trade treaty with Britain of 1860, that exports of Bordeaux wines climbed back to the level they had reached early in the fourteenth century, when the total for the whole of the Bordelais region was 900,000 hectolitres. By the 1870s annual harvests of two million hectolitres were quite common and in 1872 the export figure rose to an all-time record of 1.5 million hectolitres. Unfortunately this boom period was destined not to last. In the late 1870s disaster struck in the shape of the phylloxera louse, which attacked and destroyed the vines, not only in the Bordelais but throughout the South-West. The onslaught of this disease, combined with a bad outbreak of mildew, threatened to wipe out the wine industry in Bordeaux altogether, but the answer was found by grafting the vines on to American stock that was immune to the disease. The process began in 1887 and by 1889 the Bordelais were back in business. Many other wine-growing areas, such as the Rouergue and most of Périgord, never fully recovered, but in Bordeaux production levels gradually returned to pre-phylloxera levels. Exports on the other hand are still well below one million litres, although because of the high proportion of fine wines included in today's figures the value is very much greater.

The Bordeaux region now has approximately 140,000 hectares planted with vines producing between four and five million hectolitres a year, or about 6 per cent of all French production. But what is more important than the superficial area under vines is the very high proportion of quality wine made in the area. In this respect Bordeaux has no equal. Certainly Burgundy produces wines that rival those of Bordeaux in excellence, but there are far fewer of them. Over two-thirds of the region's wine are entitled to the *Appellation d'Origine Contrôllée* (AOC) label that guarantees its authenticity (see pages 35–40 for details of the AOC system). In 1970, for example, the production of AOC wines in France as a whole was 11.45 million hectolitres of which Bordeaux's contribution was 3.37 million hectolitres. Of this figure just over two million hectolitres was red.

Most Bordeaux vineyards producing AOC wines belong to single estates called châteaux, a description that can cause some confusion to the uninitiated. Here a château means nothing more than a building, or group of buildings, where wine is made from the proprietor's own vineyard. Some of them may indeed be beautiful buildings like Château Margaux or Château Beychevelle, both in the Médoc; others are little more than simple farm buildings with outhouses: it is the function that is important. Every château, whatever its size, must however have its *chai* where the wine is kept in barrels prior to bottling; the *maître de chai*, who is responsible for harvesting the grapes and making and storing the wine is the most important man of the château, the owner excepted, although often they are one and the same.'

Many châteaux are quite small but some are very large indeed, like Château Pontet-Canet, in the Médoc, which has 80 hectares planted with vines and produces 3,500 hectolitres of wine annually. This is in complete contrast with the situation in Burgundy where vineyards tend to be small and are often divided between several different owners. The famous Le Montrachet vineyard in the Côte de Beaune, for instance, covers only seven and a half hectares, makes 205 hectolitres a year and is shared between thirteen different owners.

There are over 3,000 wine-making châteaux in the Bordeaux region; clearly it would be impossible to cover them all in detail in a book like this, so instead we shall describe the different wine districts that make up the region, concentrating on the characteristics peculiar to each and mentioning any outstanding châteaux to be found there as we go along.

You will not be able to buy any wine at the famous estates, since most of their annual production is sold even before it is bottled, but you should be able to enjoy a tasting and make a purchase at most of the châteaux mentioned. However, if in doubt, you can check with the Maison du Vin, 1 cours du 30 juillet.

The estuary of the Gironde and the rivers Garonne and Dordogne form a kind of upside-down letter Y with the Gironde representing the shank and the two rivers the arms. Our description of the districts starts with the Médoc on the left (west) bank of the Gironde and works anti-clockwise down the Garonne, across the space between the arms (the Entre-deux-Mers) and back along the Dordogne to the right (east) bank of the Gironde. A glance at the map on page 45 should make this clear.

For greater ease of identification all the districts described have been numbered from 1 to 20. They are in order:

Gironde and Garonne
  1 Médoc
    (Haut-Médoc and Médoc)
  2 Graves
  3 Cérons
  4 Barsac
  5 Sauternes
  6 Côtes de Bordeaux-St-Macaire
  7 Ste-Croix-du-Mont
  8 Loupiac
  9 Premières Côtes de Bordeaux
  10 Entre-deux-Mers

Dordogne and Gironde
  11 Ste-Foy-Bordeaux
  12 Côtes de Castillon
  13 St-Emilion
  14 Pomerol
  15 Lalande-de-Pomerol and Néac
  16 Côtes de Fronsac and Canon Fronsac
  17 Graves de Vayres
  18 Cubzadais
  19 Bourgeais
  20 Blayais

1 The Médoc

The Médoc is the most famous district of Bordeaux. It produces a higher proportion of fine wine than anywhere else in the region and contains an extraordinary number of famous châteaux, making some of the greatest red wine in the world (white wine is rare in the Médoc). It consists of a narrow strip of land, 98 kilometres long, stretching northwards from Bordeaux to the mouth of the estuary. To the west lie the pine forests of the Landes and the coastal sand dunes, and to the east the waters of the Gironde. The Médoc is only 25 kilometres at its widest point, but the area where the best vineyards are to be found is an even narrower band no more than 4 kilometres from the banks of the Gironde, hence the saying in the Médoc that the best wine is made within sight of the river. Furthermore, the Médoc is subdivided into Haut-Médoc and Médoc, but apart from the odd château all the finest wine is made in the Haut-Médoc which starts at Blanquefort, just north of the city of Bordeaux, and extends as far as St-Seurin-de-Cadourne.

The landscape is an unpreposessing one, flat and sandy for the most part but undulating gently towards the river bank where gravel and stone hummocks mark the area where the vines flourish. At intervals small irrigation canals and streams (known here as *jalles*) wind their way from west to east to join the Gironde. Odd as it may seem, wine has not been made in the Médoc for very long. The name is supposed to be a corruption of the Latin '*in medio aquae*', meaning 'in the middle of the waters', and to refer to the appearance of the landscape before the Médoc was drained at the end of the seventeenth century (up until then it consisted of unhealthy marshes and scattered woodland where a scanty population of poverty-stricken peasants eaked out a living). So, for the most part, the vineyards of the Médoc are only 200 years old. Nevertheless, once the work of draining the land was finished it was quickly discovered that conditions were especially favourable for growing vines, particularly close to the river where ancient glaciers have left behind deposits of gravel and pebbles brought down from the Pyrénées. The stones hold the heat of the sun and reflect it back to the low-pruned grapes at night; they also force the roots of the vine to dig deep for moisture, and wherever this is the case the vine seems to flourish. These factors, together with Bordeaux's temperate climate, were soon to be an unbeatable combination and already by the middle of the nineteenth century the Médoc was famous for the quality of its wine. So famous, in fact, that, when in 1855 a special list of great wines of Bordeaux was drawn up for the Paris Exhibition of that year, all but one of the red wines, out of a total of sixty-two, were from the Médoc.

The wines, or *crus* (growths) as they are described in the list, are subdivided into five classes, from the *premiers crus* (first growths) to the *cinquièmes*. The list of *premiers crus* contains five names only:

	Commune
Château Lafite	Paulliac
Château Margaux	Margaux
Château Latour	Pauillac
Château Haut-Brion	Pessac
Château Mouton-Rothschild	Pauillac

Of these five, Château Haut-Brion is the only *cru* that comes from outside the Médoc. The commune of Pessac is in the Graves district, but in 1855 the reputation of Haut-Brion's wine was so great that it was felt it could not possibly be left out of any comprehensive list of fine Bordeaux wines. Château Mouton-Rothschild was not, on the other hand, originally included in the list of *premiers crus*, but was classed as a *deuxième*. This was widely regarded as a mistake at the time but it took until 1973 for Mouton-Rothschild to be elected to its rightful place amongst the *premiers crus*. It is, in fact, the only *cru* in the whole list to have been reclassified and, on the whole, most experts would agree that the original classification has stood the test of time and that the sixty-two châteaux originally selected still represent the best of the Médoc, although their respective positions in the five classes may be open to question. For example, many people today think that the last in the list, Château Cantemerle, has improved the quality of its wine so much that it should be a *deuxième cru*: but this is a field for the pundits; the layman can rest assured that any château in the list is likely to make an above-average wine. The complete 1855 classification is given in Appendix 2 on page 232 but all the individual châteaux are also listed in this section, under their respective communes.

There are, of course, many other excellent wines produced in the Haut-Mèdoc besides those included in the 1855 classification and these are also subdivided according to merit. One rung below the *cinquièmes crus* are wines nominated as *crus exceptionnels* and below them again are the *crus bourgeois*. The quality of some of these is so good that many experts believe that were the wines of the Médoc ever to be reclassified some *crus exceptionnels* and *bourgeois* would have to be included in the new list. To avoid confusion only a few of the best known of them will be mentioned here.

Nearly all the well-known châteaux of the Haut-Médoc are concentrated in eight communes: Pauillac, Margaux, St-Julien, St-Estèphe, Soussans, Arsac, Cantenac and Labarde, of which the first four are by far the most important. Let us look at them in more detail.

PAUILLAC

Pauillac lies towards the top of the Haut-Médoc, bounded to the north by St-Estèphe and to the south by St-Julien. It takes pride of place because of the fame of its finest vineyards. Altogether it has eighteen classified growths,

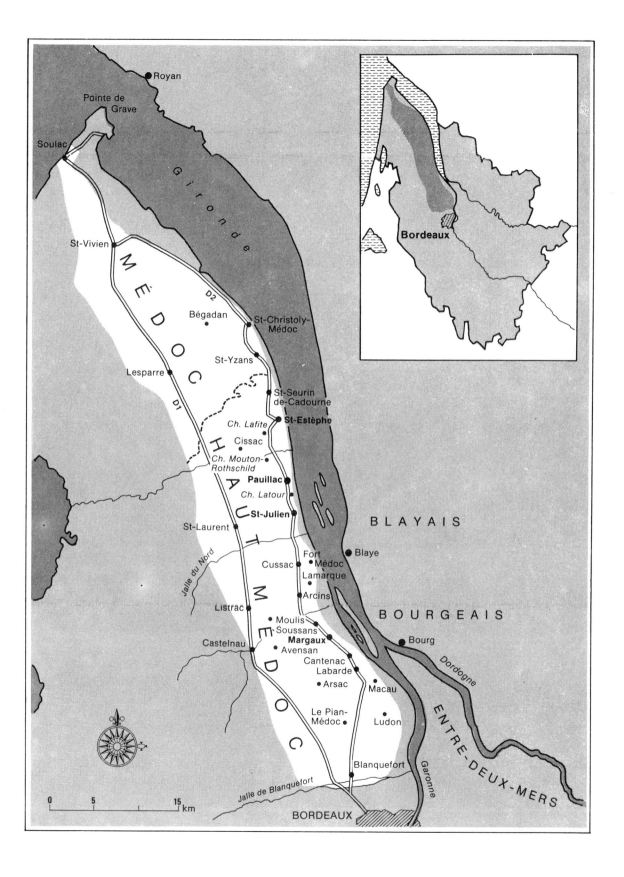

Royan

Pointe de
Grave

Soulac

Gironde

St-Vivien

D2

Bégadan

St-Christoly-
Médoc

St-Yzans

Lesparre

M É D O C

D1

St-Seurin
de-Cadourne

Ch. Lafite

St-Estèphe

Cissac

*Ch. Mouton-
Rothschild*

Pauillac

H A U T

Ch. Latour

St-Julien

St-Laurent

BLAYAIS

Jalle du Nord

Fort
Médoc

Blaye

Cussac

Lamarque

Arcins

Listrac

M É D O C

BOURGEAIS

Moulis
Soussans

Bourg

Castelnau

Margaux
Avensan

Cantenac
Labarde

Arsac

Macau

Dordogne

Le Pian-
Médoc

Ludon

ENTRE-DEUX-MERS

Blanquefort

Garonne

Jalle de Blanquefort

0   5   15
km

BORDEAUX

Bordeaux

three of them *premiers crus*, the highest number of any commune in the Médoc. The list is:

First growths (premiers crus)
Château Lafite-Rothschild
Château Latour
Château Mouton-Rothschild

Second growths (second crus)
Château Pichon-Longueville
Château Pichon-Longueville –
    Comtesse-de-Lalande

Fourth growths (quatrièmes crus)
Château Duhart-Milon

Fifth growths (cinquièmes crus)
Château Batailley
Château Haut Batailley
Château Clerc-Milon
Château Croizet-Bages
Château Grand-Puy-Ducasse
Château Grand-Puy-Lacoste
Château Haut-Bages-Libéral
Château Lynch-Bages
Château Lynch-Moussas
Château Mouton-Baron Philippe
    (formerly Mouton-d'Armailhacq)
Château Pédesclaux
Château Pontet-Canet

Château Lafite is widely held to be the finest of all the Haut-Médoc wines. It is a large estate of more than 80 hectares dating back to the Middle Ages, although the present classical building, with its long terrace planted with cedars, is eighteenth century. Lafite's annual production is in the region of 225,000 litres, of which 45,000 litres is sold as the château's second wine under the name of Carruades. The wine made at Château Lafite is not as hard as those of its great neighbours, Château Latour and Château Mouton-Rothschild. This is in part due to the difference of the soil, which is a little less stony here, and partly to the fact that Lafite uses more of the Merlot grape than the other first growths. The proportion of grapes employed is two-thirds Cabernet Sauvignon, one-sixth Merlot and one-sixth Cabernet Franc. This gives a supple, elegant wine with a beautiful perfumed aroma.

Chatèau Lafite is open to the public but visitors are not allowed into the *chai*. Nor will you be able to buy any wine, for with its world-wide reputation Lafite's annual production is all sold even before it is bottled.

Château Latour is a smaller estate of 59 hectares producing about 195,000 litres annually. Like Château Lafite, Latour makes a small quantity of a second wine called Les Forts de Latour. It sells for half the price of the senior wine and is well worth looking out for.

The estate was already famous in the sixteenth century and is mentioned by Montaigne in his *Essays*, although the vineyard itself was not planted until 1680. The tower – La Tour – was erected as recently as the end of the nineteenth century, but where it stands was once part of a fortified wall raised in the Middle Ages against pirates.

Château Latour's wine is robust and hard when it is first made. It takes a long time to mature but then becomes satisfyingly rich and mellow. The hardness of the wine matches that of the soil which is full of big polished stones, some as big as an egg. The story is told of a former owner of Latour, the Marquis de Ségur, who amazed the court when he appeared at Versailles wearing a glittering waistcoat. Seeing him, Louis XV was heard to remark, 'Here is the richest man in my kingdom; his land produces nectar and diamonds.' The 'diamonds' were in fact polished quartz from the vineyard of Latour.

The wine of Château Latour contains 80 per cent Cabernet Sauvignon grapes and 10 per cent each Cabernet Franc and Merlot. It is this very high proportion of Cabernet Sauvignon combined with the stoniness of the soil that largely accounts for the hardness and the longevity of this splendid wine.

Château Latour is not open to the public without special permission of the proprietors, but Baron Philippe de Rothschild, the owner of Château Mouton-Rothschild, welcomes visitors. If you are short of time this is probably the best of the châteaux to go and see. You enter first a superbly furnished room decorated with paintings and sculptures connected with wine. From here you are taken to the banqueting hall, which is hung with a magnificent series of tapestries representing the harvesting and making of wine. At the side of the hall double doors lead to the *chai* where the new wine is stored in well-ordered rows of barrels stretching far into the distance. If you telephone in advance you can also visit the museum created by the Baron for his late wife, Pauline. Here again the theme is wine and the *objets d'art* range from a gouache by Picasso to the most exquisitely engraved glasses, everything beautifully mounted and displayed. The Baron's love of art and his flair for publicity combined happily when in 1945 he had the brilliant idea of asking a different artist each year to design a wine label for the new vintage. The list contains the names of Cocteau, Braque, Dali, Chagall and Henry Moore. But this is not all, for in the cellars there is a 'library' of fine old wines, both those of Mouton itself and of other châteaux, including some from other districts of Bordeaux like St-Émilion and Pomerol.

The wine of Château Mouton-Rothschild, like that of Château Latour, takes a long time to reach perfection. This is because it has an even higher proportion of Cabernet Sauvignon grapes (approximately 90 per cent with 7 per cent Cabernet Franc and 3 per cent Merlot). What is more, the grape juice is left in contact with the skins and other residue of the pressing for a month, which is two weeks longer than is normal. It is mainly the tannin that is responsible for making a hard wine and giving it longevity; so by leaving the skin, where most of the tannin resides, in contact with the juice for such a long time the Baron ensures a slow-maturing, powerful wine.

Across the road from Château Mouton-Rothschild is another estate owned by Baron Philippe, Château Mouton-Baron Philippe (formerly known as Château Mouton-d'Armailhacq). It is classed as a fifth growth but under the baron's energetic management (the estate has belonged to him since 1933) its wine has improved considerably and is now certainly as good as most growths. More recently Baron Philippe has acquired another fifth-growth château in Pauillac, Château Clerc-Milon, whose wine is bound to improve as a result.

The other classified wines of Pauillac all make very good wine, of course, but there are a number that are unclassified that are well worth noting. These include Château La Couronne in the south of the commune, Château Fonbadet, just off the D2 north of the village of Daubos; Château Haut-Bages-Avérous, near the more famous Château Lynch-Bages; Château La Tour-Pibran, north-west of the town of Pauillac itself, and further north still, near the unsightly petrol refinery, Château La Fleur-Milon.

If you are thinking of buying some wine and like us cannot afford the fabulous prices charged by the better-known châteaux of the Médoc (you are likely to find them cheaper to buy in England anyway) you might do worse than to visit the local co-operative of Pauillac. Here you will find an excellent blended wine sold under the name of La Rose-Pauillac. Remember that in Pauillac the conditions are so favourable that a co-operative wine made here may well be better than a château-bottled wine from another area where the soil and climate are less good.

MARGAUX

Margaux is the southernmost of the four great communes of the Haut-Médoc. Its soil is thin and full of gravel rather than the larger stones found in Pauillac, but the drainage is good. The resulting wines are lighter and more supple than those of other communes. Château Margaux in particular, makes a wine of great finesse, having a delicately perfumed bouquet that makes it our first choice amongst the great wines of the Médoc.

Château Margaux is a large estate covering more than 70 hectares and making approximately 140,000 litre of wine. The grapes employed are 75 per cent Cabernet Sauvignon and 25 per cent Merlot. A small amount of white wine is also made here under the name of Pavillon-Blanc de Château Margaux. In 1976 Château Margaux changed hands after a period of financial difficulties which some experts believe may have affected the quality of recent vintages. The new owners are Félix Pontin, a major French grocery chain, who are expected to quickly restore Margaux's great reputation.

Altogether five neighbouring communes are entitled to add the prized name of Margaux to their labels: Margaux itself, Soussans, Arsac, Cantenac and Labarde. Between them they can boast twenty-one classified growths, eleven of them in Margaux, seven in Cantenac, two in Labarde and one in Arsac. Here they are:

First growth (premier cru)
Château Margaux (Margaux)

Second growths (deuxièmes crus)
Château Rausan-Ségla (Margaux)
Château Rauzan-Gassies (Margaux)
Château Lascombes (Margaux)
Château Durfort-Vivens (Margaux)
Château Brane-Cantenac (Cantenac)

Third growths (troisièmes crus)
Château Kirwan (Cantenac)
Château d'Issan (Cantenac)
Château Giscours (Labarde)
Château Malescot-Saint-Exupéry (Margaux)
Château Boyd-Cantenac (Margaux)
Château Cantenac-Brown (Cantenac)
Château Palmer (Cantenac)
Château Desmirail (Margaux)
Château Ferrière (Margaux)
Château Marquis d'Alesme-Becker (Margaux)

Fourth growths (quatrièmes crus)
Château Prieuré-Lichine (Cantenac)
Château Pouget (Cantenac)
Château Marquis-de-Terme (Margaux)

Fifth growths (cinquièmes crus)
Château Dauzac (Labarde)
Château Le Tertre (Arsac)

There are so many excellent châteaux in Margaux and the adjacent communes that it is hard to know which to single out. Mention must be made, however, of Château Palmer, in Cantenac, whose wine has improved so much in recent years that many experts consider it the equal of the *premiers crus.*

Of the unclassified châteaux one to look out for is the *cru exceptionnel,* Château d'Angludet, in Cantenac, whose excellent wine has a growing reputation. Other estates making good quality wine are Château Bel-Air-Marquis d'Aligre (Soussans), Château Labégorce Zédé (Soussans), Château Paveil-de-Luze (Soussans), and Château La Tour-de-Mons (Soussans). Chateau Villegeorge in the nearby commune of Avensan is a small estate making wine not entitled to the Margaux appellation but similar in style. It is classified as a *cru exceptionel.*

The most southerly part of the Médoc, near to Bordeaux, has a number of interesting chateaux which, however, only qualify for the appellation Haut-Médoc. The fifth-growth Château Cantemerle has already been mentioned; further south in the commune of Ludon-Médoc, Château La Lagune makes a good third growth.

At the other side of Margaux, going north, are several communes, Listrac, Avensan, Moulis, Arcins, Lamarque and Cussac, where although good wine is made, the names of the estates are not well known because none of them are in the list of 1855. Many of the wines made here are good value and worth looking out for; Château Villegeorge (Avensan) has already been mentioned above and Château Chasse-Spleen (Moulis) and Château Fourcas-Hostein in Listrac are also worth noting. Here is a select list of chateaux in these communes:

Château Chasse-Spleen (Moulis)* Cru Exceptionel
Château Citran (Avensan)
Château Courant (Arcins)
Château la Closerie-Grand-Poujeaux (Moulis)*
Château Dutruch-Grand-Poujeaux (Moulis)*
Château Fourcas-Hostein (Listrac)*
Château Fourcas-Dupre (Listrac)
Château de Lamarque (Lamarque)
Château Lanessan (Cussac)
Château Malescasse (Lamarque)
Château Maucaillou (Moulis)*
Château Poujeaux-Theil (Moulis) Cru Exceptionnel
Château la Tour du Haut-Moulin (Cussac)

ST JULIEN

North of Cussac you come to the third of the great communes of the Haut Médoc, St-Julien-Beychevelle, to give the name in full, commonly known as St-Julien. Here the soil is not as thin as that of Margaux or as stony as that of Pauillac. The transitional nature of the terrain is reflected in the wine which, while not as powerful as Pauillac, has more body but less finesse than a Margaux. This blend of characteristics results in a splendid wine that combines many of the best qualities of both its illustrious neighbours, while retaining its own individual style.

There are eleven châteaux in St-Julien whose wines were included in the 1855 classification, five of them second growths, the highest number of any commune of the Haut Médoc. They are:

Second growths (deuxieme crus)
Château Léoville-Las-Cases
Château Léoville-Poyferré
Château Léoville-Barton
Château Gruaud-Larose
Château Ducru-Beaucaillou

Third growths (troisièmes crus)
Château Lagrange
Château Langon-Barton

* The wines of Moulins and Listrac are entitled to their own appellation.

Fourth growths (quatrièmes crus)

Château St-Pierre*	Château Branaire-Ducru
Château Talbot	Château Beychevelle

Although the three Léoville estates probably produce the best wines of St-Julien, the most interesting is Beychevelle. The château, which was built in 1757 on the site of a mediaeval fortress, is very beautiful, and the elegance of the building is matched by that of the wine. The name is supposed to derive from *baissez les voiles*, meaning lower the sails, and there is a very nice picture of a one-masted vessel doing just that on the label. Apparently this was a tribute of respect offered to the Grand Admiral of France, the Duke of Épernon, by passing ships as they entered or left the Gironde.

The grapes used at Château Beychevelle are 68 per cent Cabernet Sauvignon, 28 per cent Merlot and 4 per cent Cabernet Franc. There are 48 hectares under vine and the annual production is about 180,000 litres.

Another interesting property is Château Talbot, named after Sir John Talbot, Earl of Shrewsbury, 'Old Talbot', who led the English army and was himself killed in the final battle of the Hundred Years' War, which took place in 1453 at Castillon-la-Bataille on the river Dordogne. It seems unlikely that Talbot had any connection with the château, but there is a tradition that it was his headquarters on the eve of the battle and that he hid some treasure there in the cellars that has never been recovered. Château Talbot makes a full-bodied wine admirably suited to its name. It is a big estate of 85 hectares producing about 360,000 litres annually. The grapes are 70 per cent Cabernet Sauvignon, 25 per cent Merlot, 3 per cent Cabernet Franc and 2 per cent Petit Verdot.

St-Julien has only a few unclassified estates, but one of them, the *cru bourgeois*, Château Gloria, makes superb wine, regarded by most experts as the equal of any of the classified growths of the commune. Its price is correspondingly high.

West of St-Julien is the commune of St-Laurent which boasts three classified growths, although the non-classified wines produced here are only entitled to the *appellation* Haut-Médoc. Château La Tour-Carnet is a fourth growth and Châteaux Belgrave and Camensac are both fifths. The best is Camensac, which after a long period of neglect was replanted in the 1960s and has since made a good full-bodied wine.

ST-ESTÈPHE

After St-Julien we cross Pauillac and come to the most northerly of the communes of the Haut Médoc, St-Estèphe. Here the soil contains a higher proportion of clay, is therefore heavier and drains more slowly. The resulting wines are more robust than those of the communes further south

---

* The Wines of Ch. St-Pierre-Borleurge and Ch. St-Pierre-Sevaistre, both in the original 1855 classification, have now been amalgamated.

and have a higher acid content. They certainly lack the finesse of the Margaux wines but they are full of flavour, have a powerful bouquet and are popular in England. St-Estèphe has five classified growths:

Second growths (deuxièmes crus)	*Fourth growth (quatrième cru)*
Château Cos d'Estournel	Château Lafon-Rochet
Château Montrose	
	Fifth growth (cinquième cru)
Third growth (trousième crus)	Château Cos-Labory
Château Calon-Ségur	

Château Cos d'Estournel is the most famous of the St-Estéphe estates. It stands just across the road from Château Lafite and as they share much the same soil it is not surprising that Cos d'Estournel's wine is very good indeed. The building is even more remarkable: it was built in the early ninteenth century in the Chinese gothic style fashionable at the time and looks more like a stage set for *Madame Butterfly* than a building devoted to the serious business of making wine. The sight of its ornate towers, looking like miniature pagodas, on the Médoc skyline is a weird one indeed. However fanciful in appearance, Château Cos d'Estournel makes very good wine using a grape mixture of 60 per cent Cabernet Sauvignon, and 40 per cent Merlot. The vineyards extend over forty-seven hectares and produce roughly 180,000 litres.

There are many excellent unclassified estates in St-Estéphe, although none of them are *crus exceptionnels*. Château de Pez and Château Mêyney both have very good reputations. Others to look out for are:

Château Beausejour*	Château Marbuzet
Château Beau-Site	Château Les Ormes-de-Pez
Château Le Boscq	Château Plantier Rose
Château Capbern	Château Pomys
Château Canteloup	Château La Tour-de-Marbuzet
Château Haut Marbuzet	Château Tronquoy-Lalande

As in Pauillac there is also a well-known co-operative which markets its wine under the name of Marquis de St-Estèphe.

MÉDOC

Beyond St-Estèphe is the Medoc, formerly called Bas-Médoc and now officially known as Médoc Maritime. There are no outstanding châteaux in the Médoc but one or two estates make good-quality, reliable wine that is not to be despised. The best is probably Château Loudenne, a beautiful estate on the river at St-Yzans that ranks as a *cru bourgeois* and is considered just as good as most *crus bourgeois* of the Haut-Médoc. Château Loudenne

---

* There is a Château of the same name in Listrac which also produces a decent wine.

also makes a well-known blended Médoc sold under the name of La Cour Pavillion.

Other estates worthy of mention are Château Laujac (Bégedan), Cru Patache d'Aux (Bégedan), Château Potensac (Ordonnac-et-Potensac) and Château La Tour-de-By (Bégedan). Most of the communes also have co-operatives whose wine is good and reasonably priced.

2 Graves

The vineyards of Graves are amongst the oldest of the region. They were planted outside the walls of Bordeaux during the Middle Ages and the growers went out to them each morning and returned to the protection of the city walls each night. As the suburbs grew, many of the vineyards were swallowed up by property developers and only one or two major estates, such as Château Haut-Brion, survive, islands of green in a sea of urban buildings.

The name 'Graves' derives from the gravel soil which near the city is similar in character to that found in the best vineyards of the Haut-Médoc, which the Graves adjoins just north of the city. The district comprises a narrow strip, not more than 15 kilometres wide, sandwiched between the Garonne to the east and the forest of the Landes to the west. It extends southwards for 65 kilometres along the left bank of the Garonne, the soil becoming heavier and less stony, with clay covered by a top layer of sand as one gets further away from Bordeaux. The southern part of the Graves is green and heavily wooded with isolated vineyards in occasional clearings. Some of the châteaux here are very beautiful, especially the moated Château de la Brède, which is famous not so much for wine, although there was once a vineyard here, but because it belonged to the writer Montesquieu and still contains his library. Further inland, near Langon, is the impressive château of Roquetaillade. It was built by a nephew of Pope Clement V at the beginning of the fourteenth century and still looks very formidable with its six towers and high keep. From the battlements there is a fine view of the Graves and Sauternais and in the distance, across the river Garonne, the Entre-deux-Mers.

The Graves is predominately a white wine-producing area. They are made from Sauvignon, Sémillon and Muscadelle grapes (as is usual throughout the region for white wines) and tend to be dry or medium dry in the north and sweet in the south. The dry whites have a permitted alcoholic minimum of 11 degrees and their appellation is Graves Blancs. The sweet white wines carry the appellation Graves-Supérieures if they have a minimum of 12 degrees of alcohol by natural fermentation. This does not mean that the sweet wines are better than the dry, of course, on the contrary the best white Graves are by common consent Château Haut-Brion Blanc and Château Lavile de la Mission Haut-Brion, which are both dry. In fact many people consider them to be the finest dry white wines produced in the

Bordelais. Both are recommended for drinking with the local oysters.

Apart from these two dry whites the best of the Graves wines, even though they represent a small proportion of the whole, are all reds. Château Haut-Brion in particular rivals the best châteaux of the Haut-Médoc in fame. In fact, when the red wines of the Médoc were classified in 1855, the reputation of Haut-Brion stood so high that it was felt it could not be left out of the list and was included amongst the first growths (see page 38). The vineyards of Château Haut-Brion are believed to have been planted by Jean de Pontac who bought the estate in 1553. A hundred years later it was already famous as we know from Pepys' diary. The entry for 10 April 1663 reads: 'here (the Royal Oak tavern in the City) drank a sort of French wine called Ho Bryan that had a good and most peculiar taste'. It is indeed a noble wine with a very full rounded flavour. The château is situated in the suburbs of Bordeaux and is therefore the easiest of the famous estates to visit for someone with little time to spare, but visits are by appointment only. The Maison du Vin (see Appendix 7) will give you addresses of individual châteaux. The vineyard covers 42 hectares and is planted with 55 per cent Cabernet Sauvignon, 25 per cent Cabernet Franc and 20 per cent Merlot, the same grape varieties used in the Médoc. The soil is very stony here (so conditions are similar to those of Pauillac), which partly explains the high quality of the wine. The annual production is 117,000 litres.

Across the road from Château Haut-Brion lies Château La-Mission-Haut-Brion, whose vineyard used to be part of the Haut-Brion estate. In 1682 La Mission was left to a religious order called Prêcheurs de la Mission (hence the name) founded by St Vincent de Paul. The friars lived there until the French revolution and their chapel is now a small museum including amongst other treasures a superb collection of Delft ware. The château is now owned by Monsieur Fernand Woltner whose father, Henri Woltner, was largely responsible for building the château's present high reputation. It is a small estate of only 18.5 hectares producing roughly 76,500 litres annually. The grape mixture is 60 per cent Cabernet Sauvignon, 10 per cent Cabernet Franc and 30 per cent Merlot.

The third of the famous red wine châteaux of the Graves is Château Pape Clément which like the other two is to be found in the commune of Pessac. Château Pape Clément is believed to be the oldest single vineyard in the whole of the Bordeaux region. It was originally part of the archipiscopal see of Bertrand de Gott who was elected Pope in 1305 and subsequently made it over to his successor Archbishop Arnaud de Canteloup. Soon after, the vineyard was renamed in the new Pope's honour. The fortunes of the estate fell to a low ebb after the last war but have revived since 1955. The soil here is not as stony as that of Haut-Brion and La Mission Haut-Brion and the wine is therefore lighter and more fragrant. The annual production is about 45,000 litres from 27 hectares.

The wines of the Graves were not classified until 1953, and after much

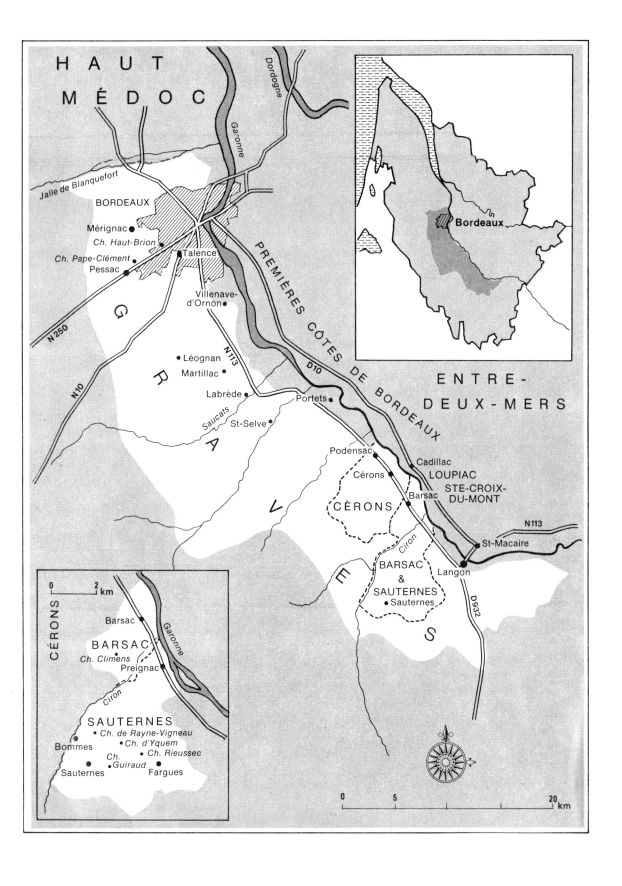

HAUT
MÉDOC

Dordogne

Garonne

Jalle de Blanquefort

BORDEAUX

Mérignac ●
Ch. Haut-Brion
Ch. Pape-Clément ●
Pessac ●

Talence ■

Villenave-
d'Ornon ●

N 250

N113

N10

G

R

A

V

E

S

Léognan ●
Martillac ●

Labrède ●

Saucats

St-Selve ●

Portets ●

Podensac ■

Cérons ●

CÉRONS

PREMIÈRES CÔTES DE BORDEAUX

D10

Cadillac ■

LOUPIAC

STE-CROIX-
DU-MONT

Barsac ●

BARSAC
&
SAUTERNES

Ciron

Sauternes ●

St-Macaire ●

N113

Langon ■

D 932

ENTRE-
DEUX-MERS

Bordeaux

CÉRONS

0   2 km

Barsac ■

Garonne

BARSAC

Ch. Climens ●
Preignac ●

Ciron

SAUTERNES

● *Ch. de Rayne-Vigneau*
● *Ch. d'Yquem*
Ch. ● *Ch. Rieussec*
Bommes ●
● *Guiraud*
Sauternes ● Fargues

0   5   20
                              km

dissatisfaction again in 1959. The revised list is given in Appendix 3 (page 224).

3 Cérons

Cérons, also known as Les Petits Graves or Seconds Graves, is an enclave within the larger Graves district. It lies, together with the adjoining districts of Barsac and Sauternes, on the left bank of the Garonne just down river from the town of Langon. All three are white wine districts, planted with Suavignon, Semillon and Muscadelle vines. The N113 which runs through Cérons is lined with stalls, some of them comically representing giant bottles or sham castles, offering tastings. The wine of Cérons is neither as dry as a Graves nor as sweet as a Barsac or Sauternes. Because of this in-between character of the wine it is relatively unknown outside France, but it is a fresh, attractive wine with a fruity bouquet and makes a very good aperitif, although it is strong (it has a minimum strength of 12.5 degrees, only half a degree less than a Sauternes). Recently, in response to changing tastes there has been a tendency to concentrate on making dry wines, but these cannot carry the *appellation* Cérons, which is reserved for sweet wines made by the traditional methods used also in Sauternes and Barsac (see below), and are marketed under the *appellation* Graves. The best estates are:

Château Archambeau (Illats)
Cru le Brouillaou (Podensac)
Château de Cérons (Cérons)
Château Grand Chemin (Cérons)
Château Lalanette-Ferbos (Cérons)
Château de Madère (Podensac)
Château Cru Madérot (Podensac)

4 Barsac
5 Sauternes

Barsac and Sauternes can justifiably claim to make the finest sweet wines in the world, rivalled only by the Trockenbeerenauslese of the Rhine and the Moselle or Hungary's Imperial Tokay.

Sauternes have unfortunately earned a bad name in Britain because of the indifferent sickly-sweet stuff from countries other than France, that has been passed off under this label in the past, before the laws were tightened up. A true Sauternes is something very different; it is a rich, luscious wine with the satisfying sweetness of a ripe plum or peach, although the incomparable flavour is quite different, of course. It is also powerful wine that sometimes achieves 17 degrees of alcohol (the permitted minimum after fermentation is 13 degrees) and it has a magnificent heady bouquet. Such a wine is to be savoured by sipping it slowly either on its own or at the end of a meal. It should be served chilled (but not frozen!).

The secret of Sauternes' and Barsac's excellence is found in the process of 'noble rot' (*pourriture noble*), induced by a mould called *Botrytis cinerea* that attacks the skin of the grape and causes it to shrivel, while at the same time concentrating the sugar content. The grapes are harvested late in the Sauternais and two or three pickings may be needed to make sure that they have all reached the desired state of rottenness. The process is described in more detail in the section on Périgord where the wine of Monbazillac is made in the same way (page 116).

The wines of Barsac and Sauternes are closely related. Today the Sauternes district comprises five communes, Sauternes itself, Barsac, Bommes, Preignac and Fargues. At one time Sauternes and Barsac sold their wines independently, but eventually it was decided that, because their individual production was small, it would be sensible to combine the five neighbouring communes under the name of Sauternes. Although Barsac was included, because of the high repute of its wine, it was permitted to use either Sauternes or Barsac on its labels.

The reputation of the wines of Sauternes goes back at least to the eighteenth century when the American President, Thomas Jefferson*, who was knowledgeable about wine, wrote: 'Sauternes. This is the best white wine of France and the best of it is made by Monsieur Lur-Saluces.' The descendant of Jefferson's Lur-Saluces still owns Château d'Yquem which is not only acknowledged to make the finest Sauternes, but ranks with the first growth châteaux of the Haut-Médoc and Château Haut-Brion in the Graves as one of the Bordeaux élite; some would say it is *the* supreme estate of the region.

Set on a small hill, giving a fine view of its surrounding vineyards, Château d'Yquem, with its corner turrets, is not a grand building but it has the comfortable charm of an old manor house. Parts of the building go back to the twelfth century, others date from the Renaissance period and the seventeenth century. Château d'Yquem is famed not only for the high quality of its wine, but for the immense skill and dedication that goes into the making of it. So rigorous are the château's standards that although the vineyard covers 90 hectares, the annual production averages only 108,000 litres.

It is said that the archdukes of Russia were so inordinately fond of d'Yquem that they would drink nothing else. In 1869, an especially fine year, the wine was bottled for the archduke in cut glass decanters engraved in gold with the name of the château and the year.

The wines of Sauternes and Barsac were the only ones, besides those of the Médoc, to be included in the 1855 classification. The list is given in Appendix 4 (page 225).

The wines are very long lasting. On New Year's Eve, 1978, we opened a

* In Jefferson's day Sauternes was a semi-sweet wine. The *pourriture noble* method of wine making had yet to be introduced to the Bordelais.

bottle of 1923 Château Suduiraut. Although it had turned the colour of amber, we were amazed to find when we opened it how rich the bouquet was, while the wine itself was mellow yet still full of subtlety. We agreed it was the finest wine of any kind that we had ever tasted. Sauternes, by the way, start a deep golden colour and gradually grow darker and richer in hue as time passes.

At one time, apart from a negligible amount of red wine, Barsac and Sauternes produced only sweet white wine but, sadly, the lack of demand for dessert wines has driven some of the *vignerons* to start making dry whites. Even Château d'Yquem now produces a small amount under the name Ygrec. It is made from half Sémillon and half Sauvignon grapes. Châteaux Filhot and Guiraud also offer dry whites, but the best are made by Château Doisy-Daëne from an unusual combination of grapes: 20 per cent Sémillon, 60 per cent Sauvignon and 20 per cent Riesling. It is bottled after six months and is best drunk young.

6 Cotes de Bordeaux—St-Macaire

At Langon you can cross the Garonne and enter the enchanting mediaeval walled town of St-Macaire through one of its three fortified gateways. St-Macaire is built on a limestone bluff and enjoys commanding views of the Sauternais vineyards. The wine district of Côtes de Bordeaux-St-Macaire extends eastwards in the direction of La Réole as far as the commune of Caudrot and northwards into the Entre-deux-Mers as far as St-Martial. There are ten communes altogether: St-Macaire, St-Martial, Le Pian-sur-Garonne, St-Pierre-d'Aurillac, St-André-du-Bois, St-Martin-de-Sescas, Caudrot, St-Laurent-du-Bois, St-Laurent-du-Plan, Ste-Foy-la-Longue.

The wines of Côtes de Bordeaux-St-Macaire have much in common with those of Barsac and Sauternes. They are made in the same way from the same grapes (Sauvignon, Sémillon and Muscadelle), but they are not so strong, the permitted alcoholic minimum being as low as 11 degrees after fermentation. While never rising to the same heights as the wines of Sauternes they have a distinctive character and are, of course, much cheaper.

Near St-Macaire is the village of St-Maixant where admirers of the novelist François Mauriac will find his home, Chateau Malagar. Two kilometres away at Verdelais lies Henri de Toulouse-Lautrec in the cemetery of the pilgrimage church of Notre-Dame.

7 Ste-Croix-du-Mont
8 Loupiac

Moving back along the right bank of the Garonne towards Bordeaux, we come next to the wine districts of Ste-Croix-du-Mont and Loupiac whose wines are so similar that they are best considered together. They are comparable to those of Sauternes, whose vineyards can be seen on the other

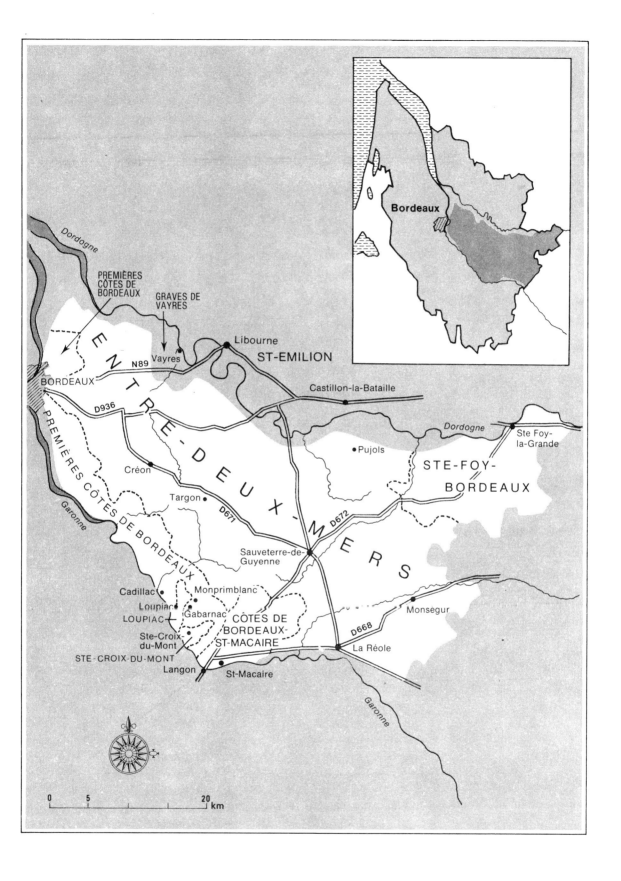

PREMIÈRES CÔTES DE BORDEAUX

GRAVES DE VAYRES

Dordogne

ENTRE-DEUX-MERS

Vayres

Libourne

ST-EMILION

N89

BORDEAUX

Castillon-la-Bataille

D936

Dordogne

Ste Foy-la-Grande

PREMIÈRES CÔTES DE BORDEAUX

Créon

Pujols

STE-FOY-BORDEAUX

Garonne

Targon

D671

D672

Sauveterre-de-Guyenne

Cadillac

Monprimblanc

Loupiac

Gabarnac

CÔTES DE BORDEAUX-ST-MACAIRE

Monségur

LOUPIAC

Ste-Croix-du-Mont

STE-CROIX-DU-MONT

D668

La Réole

Langon

St-Macaire

Garonne

0   5   20 km

Bordeaux

side of the river, but cannot match them in quality. They are, however, not so dear. Like Sauternes the wines of Ste-Croix-du-Mont and Loupiac have a minimum alcoholic strength of 13 degrees, although they sometimes attain 15 degrees (compared with 17 degrees for Sauternes) and are made from the same trinity of grapes: Sauvignon, Semillon and Muscadelle. Ste-Croix-du-Mont is built on a remarkable cliff formed of the fossilized shells of millions of oysters. The terrace on top of this cliff is an ideal place to sit on a balmy summer's evening sipping these excellent wines.

One of the most interesting estates of Ste-Croix-du-Mont is Château de Tastes which dates back to 1230. In 1342 it was exempted from all tolls and taxes by King Edward III of England because he enjoyed its wines so much. There are splendid views of the Garonne and the Entre-deux-Mers from the château. Other estates of repute are: Château Lamarque and Château Loubens, both in Ste-Croix-du-Mont, and Chateau du Cros in Loupiac.

9 Premières Côtes de Bordeaux

This district makes both red and white wines, none of them particularly distinguished. Never more than 6 kilometres wide it stretches from just north of Bordeaux southwards for 48 kilometres on the right bank of the Garonne as far as St-Macaire. Loupiac and Ste-Croix-du-Mont are enclaves contained within the Premières Côtes. The red wines are on the whole found nearer to Bordeaux where the stonier soil is more suitable. The grapes used are Cabernet Sauvignon, Cabernet Franc, Merlot, Malbec, Carmenere and Petit Verdot and the minimum permitted alcoholic content is 10.5 degrees. The best of the communes making red wines are Camblanes, Quinsac and Cambes.

The white wines are grown on the chalkier hills further south from Sauvignon, Sémillon and Muscadelle grapes, with a permitted alcohol minimum of 11 degrees. Here the best communes are Cadillac, Gabarnac, Monprimblanc and Langoiran. The main centre in the white wine area is the old walled town of Cadillac over which there looms the magnificent Renaissance château of the ducs d'Épernon. This is now the headquarters of the Connétablie de Guyenne whose purpose is to promote the sweet white wines of the region. The château is open to the public. Since 1973 the vignerons of Cadillac have been entitled to label their wines 'Premières Côtes de Bordeaux-Cadillac'. Gabarnac and Langoiran are entitled to this *appellation* as well.

10 Entre-deux-Mers

The name 'Entre-deux-Mers' (from the Latin 'Inter Dua Maria') means between two seas and accurately describes this district's position, lying as it does in the triangle formed by the convergence of two great rivers, the Garonne and the Dordogne. It is a very large area, over 60 kilometres long and 40 kilometres at its widest point, between Pujols and Langon, but it is not very well known to tourists. This is a pity, for its countryside is very attractive, green and hilly with winding roads and many interesting villages and monuments, dating from the era of the Hundred Years' War, like the magnificent abbey at La Sauve-Majeure, ruined alas but still impressive, or the old *bastide* of Sauveterre-de-Guyenne, founded by Edward I of England in 1281, with its serene arcaded square. It is ideal country for leisurely touring.

Unfortunately the wine of Entre-deux-Mers is very ordinary. In fact, the prejudice against sweet wines in Britain can largely be attributed the thin, sickly sweet wines once sold under this name, which sadly, were many people's introduction to the sweet wines of Bordeaux. Such wine was quite unrepresentative for at its best an Entre-deux-Mers was a light pleasant wine even if it was never distinguished. Today most *vignerons* of the Entre-deux-Mers make a drier white wine in response to changed tastes and the *appellation Entre-deux-Mers* is now only given to a dry white wine with a permitted minimum of alcohol of 11.5 degrees.

There are no outstanding vineyards in the Entre-deux-Mers and your best bet is to go to any one of the fifteen excellent co-operatives in the area. They are easily found. Nearly all the wine produced in the Entre-deux-Mers is blended and much of it is sold under the simple *appellation Bordeaux Blanc* if it is below 11.5 degrees.

The red wines of the Entre-deux-Mers (about 20 per cent of the whole) are not entitled to the name but must be sold as Bordeaux if they have 10 degrees of alcohol or Bordeaux Supérieur if they have 10.5 degrees. The grape varieties used for appellation Entre-deux-Mers wines are Sémillon, Sauvignon, Muscadelle and Merlot Blanc.

11 Ste-Foy-Bordeaux

The thirteenth-century *bastide* of Ste-Foy-la-Grande is on the river Dordogne. It is the centre of a wine district adjoining the Entre-deux-Mers and at the north-eastern limit of the Bordeaux region. Eastward lies Périgord and the wine district of Bergerac. During the period when the English were in control of Guyenne, Ste-Foy was a frontier town and helped to control the entry of Haut Pays wine into Bordeaux.

Ste-Foy-Bordeaux produces both red and white wines. The reds are full-bodied wines although the permitted minimum of alcohol is only 10.5 degrees. The whites are finer and have a minimum strength of 12 degrees. The wines are made in the communes of St-André-et-Appelles, Les-Lèves-et-Thoumeyragues, La Roquille, St-Quentin-de-Caplong, Landerrouet, Massugas, Pellegrue and Gensac.

12 Côtes de Castillon

This is not an important wine-growing district. The best wines are the reds which are entitled to the *appellation Bordeaux – Côtes de Castillon* if they reach an alcoholic minimum of 11 degrees.

The Côtes de Castillon is situated on the right bank of the Dordogne to the west of Ste-Foy-la-Grande. Just north of the Dordogne, near Castillon-la-Bataille is the site of the battlefield where in 1453 the French finally defeated the English and brought the Hundred Years' War to a close.

13 St-Émilion

The delightful wine town of St-Émilion is built on a small hill 8 kilometres inland from Libourne on the river Dordogne. From the town there are splendid views of the surrounding vineyards, which reach right up to the old walls, and beyond them the river valley.

St-Émilion is believed to be the oldest wine town in France; it certainly has some interesting old buildings, none more remarkable than the Église Monolith, a ninth-century chapel carved out of the very rock on which the town is built. On top of the chapel is the terrace of the Hostellerie de Plaisance from which you can enjoy splendid views over the vineyards while feasting on such Bordelais delicacies as lampreys in red wine or *omelette-aux-cèpes*, accompanied by a glass or two of a good St-Émilion.

The wines of St-Émilion are popular in Britain. They are full, robust wines but less hard than the great Medócs. They also take less time to mature, usually between four and eight years. This is because of the high proportion of Merlot grapes in them. The vineyards are extensive stretching from the lowlands by the river up to the hills surrounding the town. By the river there is a mixture of gravel and sand, but further up the slopes chalk and clay predominate. The grapes used besides Merlot are Cabernet Sauvignon, Cabernet Franc and Malbec.

It is known from the writings of the third-century Gallo-Roman poet Ausonius that there were vineyards in the Bordeaux region in Roman times and tradition associates his name with Château Ausone, which lying just south of the town of St-Émilion is supposed to be on the site of a villa belonging to the poet. True or not, St-Émilion was certainly a wine growing area by the early Middle Ages and there is a record of an agreement with Edward II in 1312 to deliver 50 *tonneaux* (45,000 litres) of wine annually in return for confirmation of the town's privileges.

The greatest of St-Émilion's chateaux is Château Cheval Blanc which commands prices as high as the first growths of the Médoc. The château is sited in the lowlands on the borders of the adjoining wine district of Pomerol. The grapes used at the château are unusual in that there is no Cabernet Sauvignon but a mixture of two thirds Cabernet-Franc, nearly a third Merlot and a tiny fraction of Malbec. The vineyards cover only 29 hectares and production varies considerably year by year, the highest quantity in recent years being 136,000 litres in 1970.

The wines of St-Émilion were not classified until 1955. The best estates were divided into two categories, *Premiers Grands Crus Classés* and *Grands Crus Classés*, with twelve châteaux in the first and seventy-one in the second.

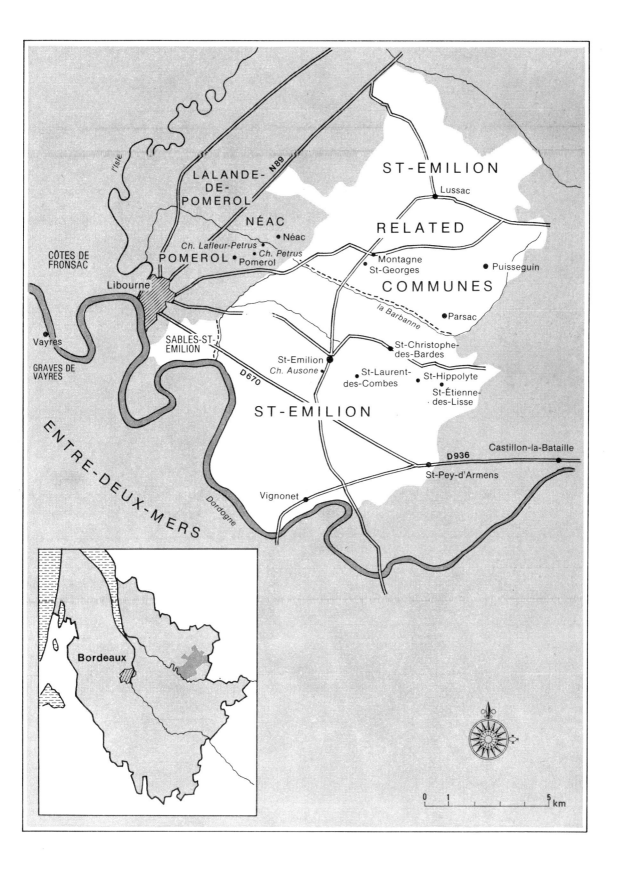

ST-EMILION

Lussac

LALANDE-
DE-
POMEROL

RELATED

NÉAC

CÔTES DE
FRONSAC

Néac

COMMUNES

POMEROL

Ch. Lafleur-Petrus

Montagne
St-Georges

Ch. Petrus

Puisseguin

Libourne

Pomerol

la Barbanne

Parsac

SABLES-ST-
EMILION

St-Christophe-
des-Bardes

Vayres

D670

St-Emilion

Ch. Ausone

St-Laurent-
des-Combes

St-Hippolyte

GRAVES DE
VAYRES

St-Étienne-
des-Lisse

ST-EMILION

ENTRE-DEUX-MERS

Castillon-la-Bataille

D936

St-Pey-d'Armens

Dordogne

Vignonet

Bordeaux

0   1   5 km

To make life more complicated, the twelve *Premiers Grands Crus* châteaux are further subdivided: Château Ausone and Château Cheval Blanc are singled out under a sub-heading A, while the remaining ten appear under sub-heading B. The full list is given in Appendix 5 and we have added our own gloss by marking the châteaux commonly held to be the best (apart from those in the *Premiers Grands Crus Classés* category) with an asterisk.

In addition to the eighty-three classified St-Emilion châteaux, you may well find some whose labels bear the words *St-Émilion Grand Cru*. Any estate not already included in the 1955 classification can earn the right to add these words if its wine meets the approval of the *Jurade* of St-Émilion at the wine tasting of the new vintage held in the spring each year. This distinction only applies to the wine of that particular year, however, and the châteaux concerned have to submit their wines for judgement annually. The *St-Émilion Grand Cru* wines are often good value and indeed St-Émilion is remarkable for having a great many small estates making good quality wine at comparatively modest prices.

East and north-east of St-Émilion are five communes that are allowed to link their names with that of St-Émilion: Lussac-St-Émilion, Puisseguin-St-Émilion, Montagne-St-Émilion, Parsac-St-Émilion, St-Georges-St-Émilion. Here the best known estate is Château St-Georges. South-west of the town, on the shores of the Dordogne, are the associated vineyards of Sables-St-Émilion. Grown in lighter sandy soil, the vines produce a wine lighter in character than the true St-Émilion.

14 Pomerol

The wines of Pomerol have been finding more and more friends in recent years. Supple and full bodied, they are softer than the great reds of the Medoc and they mature sooner. For all these reasons they are amongst the most easily appreciated of all the famous Bordeaux wines, and their prices have unfortunately risen accordingly. Yet before the Second World War Pomerol was not at all well known, even though there have been vineyards here ever since the Middle Ages and perhaps earlier. They cover an area of about 600 hectares on a gravel plateau overlooking the river town of Libourne.

There are few great chateaux in Pomerol and even the most famous estate, Château Petrus, consists of no more than a modest two-storey house, a small *chai* and a small vineyard of only 11.5 hectares. Nevertheless its powerful deep-coloured wine is one of the most sought after in the whole of the Bordeaux region, let alone Pomerol, and correspondingly expensive. The best vineyards of Pomeral are:

Château Certan-Giraud	Château La Croix
Château Certan-de-May	Château La Croix-de-Gay
Château La Conseillante	Clos l'Église

Château l'Église Clinet
Château l'Évangile
Château Lafleur
Château Lafleur-Petrus
Château Le Gay
Château Gazin
Château La Grange

Château Latour-Pomerol
Château Nenin
Château Petit-Village
Château Petrus
Château Rouget
Château Trotanoy
Vieux-Château-Certan

15 Lalande-de-Pomerol and Néac

As the wines of Pomerol became more popular and so more expensive, merchants and shippers began to look elsewhere for bargains. They found them in the adjacent districts of Lalande-de-Pomerol and Néac, which adjoin Pomerol to the north. The country is more rural here and the small vineyards take their place alongside fields planted with crops or given over to grazing cattle, unlike Pomerol where well-ordered rows of vines dominate the landscape.

The wines here are similar to those of Pomerol but heavier with less flavour and less finesse. The whole area is rather a backwater but the wines are becoming better known and at the moment they are still reasonably priced.

The better-known estates in Néac are: Belles-Graves, Chatain, Moncets, Moulin-à-Vent, Siaurac. In Lalande-de-Pomerol they are: Domaine de Anneraux, Bel-Air, Bourseau, La Commanderie, Perron and Viaud.

16 Côtes de Fronsac and Canon Fronsac

Just west of Libourne is the picturesque country known as the Fronsadais. The hills are very steep and from the highest point, Tertre de Fronsac, there are magnificent views of the Dordogne and beyond it the green hills of the Entre-deux-Mers country. The Fronsadais includes two distinct wine districts, Côtes Canon Fronsac near the river and, higher up the slopes, going north, the Côtes de Fronsac. Both make full-bodied fruity wines with a slightly spicy flavour. Now that the wines of the Médoc and St-Émilion are so expensive those of Fronsac are becoming better appreciated and their quality is improving as more sophisticated wine-making techniques are introduced. The finer wines are those of Côtes Canon Fronsac whose vineyards are splendidly sited on a great bluff that overlooks the river.

The best estate is considered to be Château Canon, which should not be confused with the more famous château of the same name in St-Émilion. Other good ones are:

Château Barabaque
Château Canon-de-Brem
Château Comte

Château Coustolle
Château du Gaby
Château Junayme

Château Lariveau   Château Moulin-Pey-Labrie
Château Mazeris   Château Rouet
Château du Pavillon-Haut-Gros-Bonnet   Château Toumalin

17 Graves de Vayres

Across the river from Fronsac is the little river port of Vayres, the centre of a
tiny wine-making district producing only about 29,000 hectolitres annually.
The name 'Graves de Vayres' derives, like that of the better-known Graves
district, from the gravelly nature of the soil. While not outstanding, the
wines are definitely superior to those of the Entre-deux-Mers that
surrounds this little wine enclave, but their limited production prevents
them being better known.

18 Cubzadais

This area is centred on the town of St-André-de-Cubzac 20 kilometres
north-west of Fronsac, near an important crossing place on the Dordogne.
The surrounding communes are Salignac, St-Gervais, Aubie-et-Espessas,
Peujard, Cubzac-les-Ponts, Virsac, St-Laurent-d'Arce and Gauriaguet.
The wines made here are both red and white but they are only entitled to be
called Bordeaux or Bordeaux Supérieur. Some good estates are: Château de
Bouilh, Château La Caussade, Château Timberlay at St-André-de-Cubzac,
Château Terrefort and Château Canada at Cubzac-les-Ponts, and Château
des Arras, Château de Bart, Cru Cantemerle and Château St-Ygnan at St-
Gervais.

19 Bourgeais

The Bourgeais stretches from the north of the Dordogne northwards along
the right bank of the Gironde, facing the southern vineyards of the Haut-
Médoc on the other side of the estuary. It is gentle, rolling hill country
which the French, with typical Gallic exaggeration call the Swiss-Gironde.
The town of Bourg is built high up on a limestone cliff opposite Bec
d'Ambès (the narrow spit of land that separates the rivers Dordogne and
Garonne), and there is a marvellous panorama of the confluence of the rivers
and beyond the vineyards of the Médoc from the town's terrace on the cliff
top.

There were vineyards in the Borgeais long before they were planted in the
Médoc and in the Middle Ages their red wines were often blended with the
wines of the Graves and the Premières Côtes de Bordeaux to give them more
body. The wines of Bourg are full-bodied and fruity, similar in character to
those of St-Émilion, but not as fine. Like those of Fronsac and Lalande-de-
Pomerol, the Bourgeais wines have recently come more into favour because
of the high cost of the better-known Médocs and St-Émilions. The grapes
used are Cabernet Sauvignon, Cabernet Franc, Malbec and Merlot for the
red wine; some white wine is also made here but is not important.

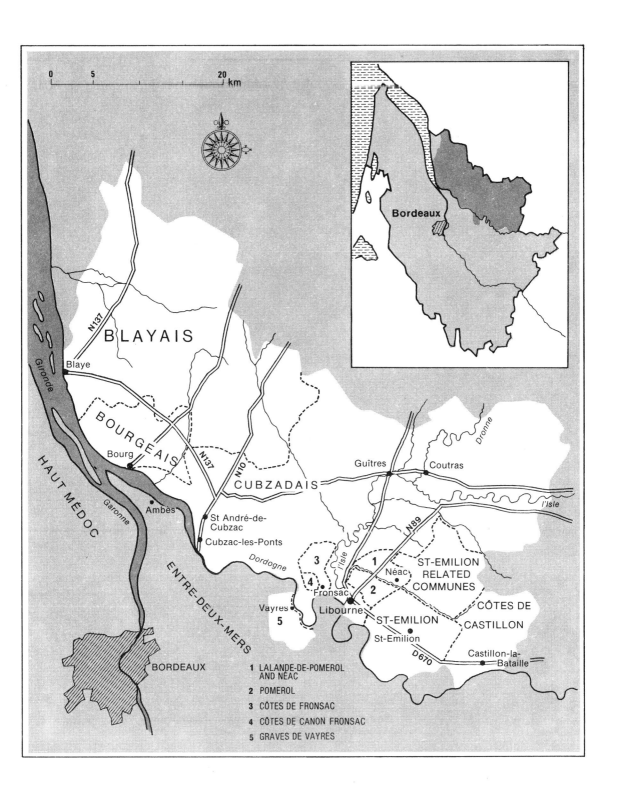

0   5   20 km

BLAYAIS

Gironde

Blaye

BOURGEAIS

Bourg

HAUT MÉDOC

Garonne

Ambès

CUBZADAIS

St André-de-
Cubzac

Cubzac-les-Ponts

Dordogne

Vayres

3

4

5

Fronsac

Libourne

Guîtres

Coutras

Dronne

l'Isle

N137

N10

N137

N89

l'Isle

ENTRE-DEUX-MERS

BORDEAUX

1

2

Néac

ST-EMILION
RELATED
COMMUNES

ST-EMILION

St-Emilion

CÔTES DE

CASTILLON

Castillon-la-
Bataille

D670

1 LALANDE-DE-POMEROL
AND NÉAC

2 POMEROL

3 CÔTES DE FRONSAC

4 CÔTES DE CANON FRONSAC

5 GRAVES DE VAYRES

Bordeaux

Although there are three different appellations in the Bourgeais, 'Bourg', 'Côtes de Bourg' and 'Bourgeais', but all have the same permitted minimum of alcohol of 10.5 degrees and use the same grapes so they are almost indistinguishable, but the wines of Côtes de Bourg we considered to be the best. Among the better estates are:

	Commune
Château de Barbe	Villeneuve
Château de Boucaud	Bourg
Château du Bousquet	Bourg
Château Croûte-Charlus	Bourg
Cru Conilh Haute-Libarde	Bourg
Château Génibon-Blanchereau	Bourg
Château de La Grave	Bourg
Château Greleau	Bourg
Château Falfas	Bayon
Château Eyquem	Bayon
Château Haut-Grava	Bourg
Château Haut-Libarde	Bourg
Château Lagrange	Bourg
Château Landreau	St-Seurin-de-Bourg
Château Laurensanne	St-Seurin-de-Bourg
Château Mendoce	Villeneuve
Château Mille-Secousses	Bourg
Château de la Monge	Bourg
Château Norian la Libarde	Bourg
Château Rebeymont	Bourg
Château Rousset	Samonac

There are also many excellent co-operatives in the Bourgeais that are well worth investigating.

20 Blayais

The pleasant undulating countryside of the Bourgeais continues northwards into the Blayais which faces the more northerly vineyards of the Haut-Médoc but extends further inland than the Bourgeais. The red wines made here are lighter than those of its neighbour; the best of them are sold under the name Premières Côtes de Blaye (minimum alcoholic strength 10.5 degrees). The whites, however, are more important here than in the Bourgeais. As in the Bourgeais there are three separate *appellations*: 'Blayais', red and white wines of no particular merit with minimum permitted strengths 9.75 degrees for the red and 10 for the white; 'Premières Côtes de Blaye', light reds made from Cabernet Sauvignon, Cabernet Franc and Merlot grapes (permitted minimum 10.5 degrees), and good dry and semi-dry white wines from Sémillon, Sauvignon and Muscadelle grapes (minimum alcoholic strength 10.5 degrees); 'Côtes de Blaye', white wines only (regulations exactly as for Premières Côtes de Blaye).

Some leading estates to look out for are:

	Commune
Château Barbé	Cars
Château Bédou	Cars
Château Bellevue	Plassac
Château Les Chaumes	Fours
Château Cantemerle	St-Genès-de-Blaye
Château Grolet	Plassac
Château Lassalle	St-Genès-de-Blaye
Château Peyrebrune	Plassac
Château Segonzac	St-Genès-de-Blaye
Château La Tour-Gayet	St-Androny
Château Virou	St Girons

*   *   *

The cooking of the Bordeaux region is overshadowed by the famous wines. Even so you can still eat very well there, which is hardly surprising considering that the city can draw on the finest products of the South West. To verify the truth of this statement, you have only to visit the central market of Bordeaux, a rotunda of iron and glass called 'aux Grandes Hommes', not as one might think after the creators of glorious local specialities, but after the great men of France whose names have been bestowed on the neighbouring streets: Montaigne, Montesquieu, J.-J. Rousseau and Voltaire. In the market you can buy oysters from Marennes and Arcachon, lampreys from the Gironde, wild doves (*palombes*), from the Landes, baby lamb from Pauillac, *foie gras* from Périgueux, Bayonne ham, Roquefort cheese from the Rouergue, strawberries from the Agenais, asparagus from the Quercy and so on, a veritable cornucopia, all on the Bordeaux housewife's doorstep.

The term 'bordelaise', often found in conjunction with dishes from the region such as *entrecôte à la bordelaise*, refers to a sauce based, of course, on red wine. It goes well not only with entrecôte steak but calves' kidneys (*rognons de veau*) and lampreys. One old version of the sauce uses lemon juice instead of wine; while another suggests dry white wine if the sauce is to accompany fish.

Sauce bordelaise

To make *sauce bordelaise* put the claret, shallots, herbs, salt and pepper into a saucepan and bring the mixture to the boil. Simmer until the wine is reduced by half. Add an equal amount of rich brown sauce (concentrated beef stock mixed with a little roux). Allow to simmer, stirring well. Add a

1 large wine glass good claret
3 shallots, finely chopped
½ teaspoon each thyme and powdered bay leaf
Pinch salt
Good sprinkling freshly ground black pepper
50ml (2fl.oz) rich brown sauce
tablespoon butter
25g (1oz) beef marrow
Chopped parsley

knob of butter and, at the last minute, the beef marrow, diced, poached and drained, and a little chopped parsley.

The old recipe is both simpler and more versatile in that it can accompany a wide range of dishes (veal escalopes, roast beef, mushrooms, egg dishes and even fish) according to the type of stock used: into a thick frying pan put 60g (2oz) of beef marrow, 6 finely chopped shallots and a handful of chopped parsley. Moisten with the meat juices (or fish juices if the sauce is to accompany fish) and heat very gently so that the sauce gets hot but doesn't boil. Stir well until all the ingredients are incorporated. Add salt and pepper to taste. The heat must not be fierce enough to brown the sauce, but warm enough to cook the shallots. You can leave the sauce on one side in a warm place while you prepare the rest of the meal. At the last moment, add the juice of a lemon and serve. The shallots should be slightly crunchy to contrast with the softness of the marrow.

If you are going to make *sauce bordelaise* you will need to be on good terms with your butcher. If he still buys his meat by the carcass, he may be prepared to extract the marrow for you or to saw the marrow bones so that you can extract the marrow yourself. If you are really stuck try sheep's or pig's brains instead of marrow (for meat dishes) or soft herring roes (for fish dishes) mashed and mixed well. It is not true *sauce bordelaise*, but it is an excellent substitute.

Two other versions of *sauce bordelaise* are also worth consideration. Both use shallots but neither depends on beef marrow. Chop a large clove of garlic, 4 shallots and a large, flat field mushroom (better still a *cèpe*). Soften in olive oil for about 15 minutes. Meanwhile, prepare a roux and moisten it with 2 wine glasses of water (150 millilitres or about 5fl.oz) and 1 wine glass of Bordeaux wine (red for a meat sauce and dry white for fish). Add salt and pepper to taste. Stir well until all the lumps have gone. Then add the chopped garlic, shallots and mushrooms and warm gently together for about 5 minutes.

The tomato version consists of chopped shallots browned in olive oil with salt and pepper, moistened with a little *eau-de-vie* (or vodka) and 2 wine glasses of stock. Thicken the sauce with tomato purée, add a crushed clove of garlic, a handful of chopped parsley and simmer gently for 15–30 minutes.

Entrecôte à la bordelaise

Entrecôte in France is likely to be the size of a rump steak in Britain or sirloin steak in the US. Before it is served, garnished with its special sauce, the steak should, according to tradition, have been marinaded in oil with thyme and powdered bay leaves, chopped shallots, salt and some freshly ground pepper for about 4 hours. In some restaurants it will have been grilled on vine clippings (*aux sarments*), a favourite fuel in the South-West. Sometimes it is supplemented by baby onions braised in beef stock.

Here is a simpler version of *entrecôte bordelaise*. Choose your steak carefully and make sure that it is really thick and tender. Grill the steak on a barbecue over vine clippings, sprinkling the steak with salt and freshly ground pepper as it cooks. Just before serving add very finely chopped raw shallots and a tablespoon of parsley butter.

Positioned as it is at the mouth of the river Garonne, its back to the sandy pine-stacked country of the Landes, with its lakes and lagoons, and with the estuary of the Gironde giving easy access to the sea, Bordeaux enjoys a rich variety of freshwater fish and seafood of all kinds.

One of the city's most famous delicacies, found in the waters of the Gironde, is the lamprey. All that most people can remember about lampreys is that an English king died from a surfeit of them. In fact, it was Henry I, who died in Rouen in 1135 and it seems likely that he died of food poisoning rather than greed. Be that as it may, the lamprey is a parasitic, jawless fish, rather like an eel to look at, and there are three kinds: brook lampreys, river lampreys and sea lampreys. The brook lamprey never leaves its home waters, but the other two go to sea and return to fresh water only to spawn. The lamprey's feeding habits are repulsive: it attaches itself to the host fish by its sucker-like mouth, rips off the flesh with its toothed tongue and injects an anti-coagulant to keep the blood flowing.

Considering this unattractive behaviour, it is hardly surprising that lampreys are not favourite eating in Britain, but the real reason is that they are rarely found in our waters, although just occasionally migrating shoals have turned up in Southampton Water and the rivers Trent and Dovey in such numbers that they have been used as pigs' food. Even in Bordeaux they do not often appear on the menu for they are troublesome to prepare and consequently very expensive. Lampreys are best eaten in the spring when they are still tender and the dorsal bones are softer and more manageable. The flesh is fatty, indigestible and something between frog's legs and chicken in consistency and flavour. In most lamprey recipes you could substitute eel and use chicken stock to add flavour.

Lamproie à la bordelaise (also called *lamproie aux poireaux girondine*) This dish consists of chunks of lamprey, cooked with vegetables and red wine.

1kg (2lb) lamprey
8 leeks
4 carrots
3 onions
½ bottle red Bordeaux wine
Small glass armagnac
Slice lean bacon
Bay leaves, parsley, garlic, salt, pepper, thyme

To prepare for cooking, plunge the lampreys in boiling water for several minutes so that you can skin them. You can scrape off some of the subcutaneous fat if you feel it might be too rich. Remove the two back filaments and extract the central nerve by cutting off the tip of the tail, making a cut behind the neck, below the gills and pulling the nerve out through the neck opening.

Cut the lamprey into 5cm (2in) slices and roll in salt and pepper. Put the chopped and sliced vegetables, *except the leeks*, into a saucepan with the herbs and garlic. Moisten with the wine, the armagnac and a couple of tablespoons of water. Cook briskly together for 15 minutes. Add the lamprey pieces, cover and simmer gently.

In another pan gently fry the bacon, cut into pieces, and the cleaned and sliced leeks, with a little pork or goose fat. Thicken with a little flour and moisten with some of the liquid in which the lamprey is simmering. Let the sauce cook gently for 20 minutes. Pour the lamprey pieces, the sauce, the ham and leek slices and any liquid from the lamprey into a fireproof dish and cook over a low flame, uncovered, for about 2 hours.

Another version, with white wine, can also be adapted to eel. Put the lamprey pieces into a bowl and cover with a marinade of dry white wine, thyme, bay leaf, a pinch of ground ginger, powdered celery, powdered fennel, coriander seeds, grated nutmeg, sage leaves, marjoram, oregano and a pinch of tarragon. Add a glass of armagnac or another brandy. Leave the lamprey in the marinade for at least 12 hours, then put the whole lot into a fireproof dish and add 2 cloves, a handful of chopped parsley, 3 chopped shallots and the white parts of 3 fat leeks. Cook on a low flame, for about 2 hours. Just before serving add a desertspoonful of rich olive oil and stir in well. Serve with chunks of wholemeal bread and plain boiled potatoes, and a green salad to follow.

A relatively recent *Bordelais* speciality in the luxury class is caviar. There have always been sturgeon in the waters of the Gironde but before the First World War their eggs were used as bait for sardine fishing. The caviar industry started in the 1920s when the Russian Revolution had made supplies difficult to obtain. Emile Prunier, the famous *chef*, invited a Russian emigré to Bordeaux to show the local fishermen how to convert a sturgeon's eggs into caviar.

Between April and June the fishermen of Meschers-sur-Gironde go out in their boats equipped with heavy nets to find the sturgeon returning to their spawning grounds in the Gironde and the Garonne. The resulting caviar is regarded as excellent. Unlike all but the best Russian caviar, the Gironde variety is treated only with salt, all other preservatives being forbidden. Production is small, most being earmarked for luxury restaurants and special customers, and very little finds its way onto the open market.

If you should be lucky enough to get hold of some caviar, you will probably prefer to savour it spread on thin brown bread and butter with a squeeze of lemon juice; but if you are not too proud to consider lumpfish roe as a substitute here is a delicious egg mousse that looks and tastes very good sprinkled with the little black grains.

8 hard-boiled eggs
1 small carton (150 millilitres) double cream (5fl.oz)
2 anchovy fillets, well rinsed and desalted
or 1 teaspoon gentleman's relish (or anchovy paste)
or 2 teaspoons anchovy butter
300 millilitres chicken stock (10fl.oz or ½ pint)
Powdered gelatine, enough to set ½ litre (1 pint) liquid
Freshly ground pepper to taste
One small jar lumpfish roe, caviar-style
½ slice lemon per person

Egg mousse, caviar-style
Put the shelled eggs, the anchovy fillets and the cream into the blender and

mix until smooth, or mix finely sieved eggs with the cream (lightly whipped) and the anchovies pounded to a mash, picking out any obvious bones. Melt the gelatine in the hot stock and allow to cool. Just as it is beginning to thicken and set, pour it into the egg mixture. Stir well and taste, then add the freshly ground pepper and more salt if necessary. Stir again and pour into small ramekin dishes and leave to set. Just before serving, sprinkle the top of each little mousse with the lumpfish roe and add half a slice of lemon.

The sturgeon itself is a luxury fish. It is in season from March to July. One of the best ways of cooking it is by poaching sturgeon steaks in white wine with mixed vegetables and parsley.

Darne d'esturgeon à la bourgeoise

Season the steaks with salt and pepper and put them in an ovenproof dish on top of a layer of chopped carrots, celery and onions with a sprinkling of parsley. Moisten with dry white wine and stock in equal amounts. Put into a moderate oven and cook covered for about 45 minutes. Remove the sturgeon to a serving plate and keep warm while you reduce the liquid by half. Thicken with a little *beurre manié* and two tablespoons of double cream. Remove the skin of the sturgeon and any bones that you think might worry the guests. Cover with the sauce and serve with little boiled potatoes.

For anyone who is fond of oysters, Bordeaux is the place. Not only can you buy them cheaply in the markets (under 9 francs a dozen in 1980) but they are commonly found in cafés and bistros all over the Bordelais. We well recall a pleasant last hour before catching our plane, spent in a small village café, just outside the airport at Mérignac, chatting to the locals and eating half a dozen oysters each, fresh from the beds at Arcachon that morning, washed down with a glass or two of cool, white Graves: bliss!

Nearly all France's oysters come from somewhere on the Atlantic coast. There are, of course, the famous beds in the Gulf of Morbihan in Brittany, but Bordeaux gets its supplies from two areas closer at hand: Marennes, a few kilometres north of the Pointe de la Coubre at the mouth of the Gironde, and the Gulf of Arcachon on the sandy coast south-west of the city itself.

Flat native oysters or '*plates*', (*Ostrea edulis*), known locally as *gravettes*, have been cultivated in the region since Gallo-Roman times, as we know from the writings of the poet Ausonius, who rapturously extolled their virtues. Much later oysters featured on the royal menus at the court of Louis XIV. Until the eighteenth century, *gravettes* were gathered using rakes and dragnets, a rather brutal method which by 1750 had brought the oysters close to extinction. In that year, these methods were outlawed, but even so the oysters continued to decline until in the 1840s a fishery protection vessel had to be stationed at Arcachon to guard the few that remained. It was finally realized that the oyster beds would have to be restocked: a Monsieur Croste discovered that on Lake Fusaro in Italy oysters were cultivated by suspending oyster traps (a bunch of twigs) from wooden stakes in the lake. The fertilized larvae, called spats or *naissains*, had something to cling to and grow on. In due course, when the traps were raised, the larger oysters were sold, while the smaller ones were transferred to reed baskets to mature. Monsieur Croste brought the method back to France and model oyster beds were started at Arcachon. Unfortunately, the native oysters were virtually wiped out by disease in the 1920s and are now found only in small colonies in both the Marennes and Arcachon beds.

The oysters called *portugaises* (known in some parts as *noisettes*) are larger than the native *plates* and are fleshier with a more irregular and broader, deeper shell. The species was introduced into the area by accident in 1868 when the sailing ship *Morlaisien*, carrying oysters from Portugal to England, put into the Gironde to recover from the effects of a storm. The delay caused by the storm, and the need to repair damage to the ship, meant that the cargo went bad and had to be dumped over the side near Talais, where the *Morlaisien* was anchored. Some of these jettisoned oysters survived their ordeal, started to breed and became the founders of the oyster colonies along the coast. Like the *plates*, or *gravettes*, the original *portugaises* were almost wiped out by disease in 1971 (the variety being cultivated since then comes from Japan and Canada).

Oyster farming is very much a family business and it can be very risky. Apart from being damaged by disease, oysters degenerate quickly and need frequent restocking. They are susceptible to the slightest pollution, to excessive concentrations of salt in the water, to storms and to the cold; they can also become easily choked by sand and mud. As if all that were not enough, they are also prey to marauding crabs, limpets and whelks. Faced by so many hazards, it is a wonder that the oyster survives at all, let alone that it forms the basis of a considerable industry.

The oyster beds, or *parcs*, are found in those parts of the Arcachon Basin and Marennes which are left dry by the retreating tide. The fertilized larvae are washed about by the tides and currents, but many of them manage to attach themselves during the summer to whatever the kindly oyster farmer provides for them: tiles, wooden stakes or large stones. Between twelve months and two years later the adolescent oysters are detached from their refuge and transferred to oyster ponds (called *claires* in the Marennes and *bassins* at Arcachon) where they fatten up and mature. The older variety (*Crassostrea*) needs to grow for four or five years before it is ready to transfer to the *bassins*, but the new Japanese variety (*Crassostrea gigas*) matures much earlier. The *claires* of Marennes are hollowed-out ponds on the shoreline, linked to the sea so that they fill with water at each high tide. The *fines de claires* oysters stay in the beds for two months with ten to fifteen oysters per square metre; the *spéciales*, which are larger and more succulent, stay there for six months with only three to five oysters in the same area. Here they acquire the bluish-green colour by absorbing *marennines*, a microscopic alga covering the bottom of the *claires*, a process that entitles them to be sold as *claires* or *spéciales*.

The final stage in the process is to put the mature oysters into a kind of tank (*dégorgeoir*), where they clean themselves and learn good manners; that is to say they are persuaded not to keep opening their shells every time the tide comes in. Then they are packed into boxes with fresh seaweed for company and despatched by train and plane to grace the tables of ordinary people all over France and the rich abroad. Each crate carries a label from the Institut des Pêches Maritimes, the oyster's bill of health assuring the purchaser of a clean, healthy product. The label also shows the control number of the sender, the date of despatch, where the oysters come from and where they are going.

It would be criminal to buy the best oysters for cooking – a squeeze of lemon is almost too much – but the cheaper varieties can be presented in a number of ways.

Huîtres chaudes girondine

Clean and scrub the oysters and put them on a dish. Cover with foil and put them in a hot oven for about 10 minutes and let them open. Remove the top shell and set the oysters to one side to keep warm. Strain the juice through muslin and use it to enhance a good thick *béchamel* sauce with plenty of nutmeg. Pour the sauce over the oysters and serve piping hot with a quarter of lemon and some chopped parsley.

Huîtres bordelaises

This combination of oysters, spicy sausages (*lou kencous*) and dry white wine seems bizarre, but the Bordelais enjoy the contrasting flavours. Start with an oyster, then eat a piece of buttered bread, then a hot little sausage and finally a sip of dry Graves. Go back to the beginning and repeat the process, and so on until plates and glasses are empty. The cocktail snack of oysters on skewers wrapped in grilled bacon is a variant on the same theme.

Huîtres farcies

Open the oysters under a hot grill or by steaming in a hot oven. Remove the top shells, give the oysters a twist of freshly ground pepper and serve with a mixture of chopped shallots and parsley gently stewed in dry white wine.

Alternatively, you can open the oysters, take them out of their shells and poach them in their own juice for 2 minutes. Drain and save the juice. Chop 4–6 shallots, according to size, and sweat gently in butter (better still goose fat) with 250g (8oz) chopped or sliced mushrooms and a handful of chopped parsley. Add the strained liquid from the oysters, a small glass of dry white wine and thicken with a little flour. Simmer the sauce gently, stirring all the time, for 5 minutes. Add pepper and perhaps salt to taste. Serve the oysters in their deep shells bathed in sauce.

The ways in which oysters can be prepared and presented is almost endless: in little pastry cases with any one of a wide range of sauces; in scallop shells *gratinées* with breadcrumbs and a tablespoon of butter and browned under the grill; poached in their own liquor and grilled on a skewer with cooked baby mushrooms; on a bed of spinach rather like *oeufs florentines*; on a bed of creamy mashed potato covered with white wine sauce; in small earthenware ramekins with a small spoonful of scrambled egg, and so on. If you are on a self-catering holiday in the South-West you can indulge in one of these gastronomic experiences without breaking the bank, but cooked or fresh the oysters of Arcachon and Marennes are not to be missed.

On the west bank of the Gironde, in the neighbourhood of Pauillac, there are extensive salt marshes used for pasturing sheep. Pauillac itself is best known for the superb wines made at its world famous châteaux, Lafite, Latour and Mouton-Rothschild (page 38), but in France it is also renowned for its lamb, whose delicate flesh has a unique flavour imparted by the salty marsh grass. To find the equivalent in this country is well nigh impossible: we seem to prefer our lambs bigger than do the French, who like them small and tender, more of a baby lamb, in fact. On the other hand, while we seldom seem to see a piece of real mutton on the butcher's counter, French mutton has good red flesh and is strongly flavoured.

Gigot de mouton à la girondine

Try to find a large leg of New Zealand lamb (prime grade, in the USA) which will have a stronger flavour and be able to compete with the vegetables and herbs in this recipe. If you can buy English mutton, so much the better.

Remove the skin round the leg of lamb and if you think it might be tough, give the meat a good bashing with the tenderizer. Marinate for 12 hours in a mixture of olive oil, chopped onions, shallots, garlic, chopped parsley, salt and pepper. Transfer to a roasting tin and put in a hot oven for 15 minutes. Then turn the oven down to medium, cover with foil and roast slowly for 20 minutes. Turn the meat, cover again and roast for twenty minutes on the other side. Remove the foil, baste the joint again and turn the oven down low for another ten minutes while you cook the accompanying vegetables or prepare the dressed salad. Do not allow the meat to overcook: it will become grey and lose its flavour. If your guests show a horror of red meat, serve the slices onto very hot plates together with the meat juices from the pan, sizzling hot. This will cook the meat a little more without ruining the flavour.

Snails

In the Bordeaux suburb of Caudéran, it was the custom in the last century to eat snails on Ash Wednesday; the whole city made the annual pilgrimage to the village restaurants of Chez Geille, à l'Étonnoir, Chez Rosette and à la Renommée des Escargots, to eat snails and discuss the merits of that year's gastronomic presentation. Today, Caudéron is just part of the city and the snails and snail-hunters have disappeared. Nevertheless *escargots à la bordelaise* is still a feature of the local cuisine. Any of the recipes for *sauce bordelaise* can accompany them, they can be served in or out of their shells, they may be bathed in sauce or served in their own dish with the sauce separate so that you can dip your snail or bread into it. Snails may not be to everyone's taste but if you do like them, you should certainly try one of these variations as a change from the inevitable garlic and parsley butter recipe.

Anisette

We cannot leave Bordeaux without mentioning Marie Brizard and her famous Anisette. Marie Brizard was born in Bordeaux in 1714 and was the third of fifteen children of a local carpenter. When she grew up Marie became interested in charitable work and devoted much of her time to nursing the poor. On one occasion she looked after a West African native who was so grateful that he gave her a recipe for a cordial, which, he claimed, would cure many complaints, especially stomach upsets. Marie Brizard found that the cordial was indeed very beneficial and soon there was such a demand for it from her ex-patients that she was forced to give up nursing and start the firm that still bears her name. Anisette is an anise-based liqueur and is still Marie Brizard's most famous product, but today the firm makes a wide variety of alcoholic drinks, including a white Crème de Menthe and Apry, a delicious apricot brandy.

Agenais

THE LITTLE market town of Ste-Livrade lies on a crossing of the river Lot between Villeneuve-sur-Lot and Aiguillon. The town is built on a slight rise that would hardly be detectable if the surrounding country were not so flat. The main street climbs gently up to the twelfth-century church and then descends slowly to the Place de la Mairie where there is an imposing Hôtel de Ville whose size and distance from the centre suggests a republican challenge to the church on the hill.

For six days of the week Ste-Livrade basks sleepily in the hot Midi sun like any other small town in the area, but on Friday everything changes: the traffic is diverted and the market takes over. Early in the morning travelling salesmen appear and set up their stalls. Some of them arrive in ingeniously constructed vans, whose sides unfold to reveal well-stocked shops; others have nothing more than a cloth that they lay on the ground on which to display their wares. The vans tour the countryside visiting a new market every day but the smaller stallholders have come from nearby and may have no more than a dozen goats' cheeses to sell.

The easiest approach to the market is from the Place de la Mairie and so the first thing you will see is a display of agricultural machinery and motor bikes. Of more interest is a large mobile stall selling every sort of household equipment with, as this is France, a strong emphasis on the kitchen. This is the place to come if you want to buy a really efficient cook's knife, a chef's whisk, a salad shaker or a garlic crusher. On the other hand you can buy as mundane an object as a washing-up bowl.

At the start of the main street are the clothes stalls. The first carries a range of hats; straw ones for the ladies with pretty ribbons round the crown and for the men sporty check ones with bobbles on top; another has rows of the comfortable-looking carpet slippers that are so popular everywhere in France and are worn out of doors as often as inside. Elsewhere are displays of flowered pinafores, frocks and heavily-boned pink corsets whose styles seem untouched by the march of fashion.

In the square there is plenty of room to move, but once in the main street the pace slows right down, for the street is full of people. Most of them are farmers' wives from the surrounding countryside, but among them you can also see the yellow skins and almond eyes of Vietnamese women wearing wide coolie hats, or the dark faces of Arabs from Algeria and Morocco. They are refugees from former French colonies who have settled in the Agenais.

And now after the stockings, corsets and petticoats comes the olive man's stall, a trestle table bearing wooden half-tubs containing an astonishing range of olives: black ones from Nîmes with an oily skin, pinky-grey ones from Greece and many more, together with tubs of gherkins, small white pickles, peanuts and walnuts, prunes and fat luscious-looking dates.

Next door is the first of a number of cheese stalls and here again there is a temptingly wide selection: three different kinds from the Pyrénées; one made from cow's milk, one from sheep's milk and a third a mixture of the two. They are round with thick, slightly wrinkled orange or black skins. From the Auvergne comes Cantal, a hard cheese rather like Cheddar. Old favourites like Brie, Camembert and Gruyère are side by side with several varieties of local goats' cheeses, all at different states of maturity, and to cap them all the famous Roquefort, cheaper here than in England but still very expensive, although that does not stop the farmers' wives buying 250 grammes at a time.

On the other side of the street there is a stall selling Bayonne ham; it is dark red with a texture nearer to bacon than that of Parma ham, but just as delicious. Here you can also find dishes of home-made *charcuterie*: at one end of the scale there is rough *pâté de campagne*, strongly flavoured with garlic, and at the other duck and goose pâtés, the most expensive of them with a small black core of truffle.

By now the jostling crowd is so thick that it is difficult to move at all, for we are approaching the heart of the market, the square that lies at the east end of the church. But first there are still some more food stalls to pass in the side street that leads up to the church, and the one that sells fish is certainly worth more than a passing glance. Here you will find fish brought fresh from Arcachon on the Atlantic coast that very morning. Sometimes there are enormous blood-red tuna fish steaks, but whatever the season there will be oysters and mussels for sale. The oysters come in three sizes, but even the largest of them cost only 12 francs a dozen and sometimes it is a baker's dozen if the fishmonger likes your face.

Beyond the fish stall, the road turns to the right for a short way along the south side of the church to the market square at the east end. Here the eye is dazzled by a bewildering mixture of colours: above are the strong blues, reds and yellows of the canvas awnings covering the stalls, below the bright hues of the flower market; deep crimson and pink geraniums, blue and white petunias and bright yellow marigolds. Nearby and just as colourful are the fruit stalls piled high with yellow and green striped melons, some cut open to show their deep orange flesh, large yellow peaches, nectarines with their shiny dark-red skins, and crimson strawberries, strangely mis-shapen but fragrant and not at all acid.

From the ground beyond the fruit stalls comes a steady cheeping and glimpses of yellow betray the day-old chicks being offered for sale.

Alongside sit hens, ducks and geese, looking rather uncomfortable and apprehensive, as well they may in view of their likely fates. Live hares and rabbits are also on offer, and it can be disconcerting to see a local housewife bearing a hare off in triumph, hanging down with its back legs looped casually over her arm.

By this time you will probably be feeling tired and hungry. The time has come to retrace our steps until we are back in the Place de la Mairie. Here there is a handy café in which to take a well-deserved aperitif before wandering across the square for a leisurely five-course lunch.

There are many small towns like Ste-Livrade, not only in the South-West but all over France, and their markets are always a great attraction for British holidaymakers, but nowhere is the range and quality of food on offer greater than in the Agenais, whose mild climate and rich soil make it one of the major suppliers of *primeurs* (early fruit and vegetables) to Paris, Bordeaux and Toulouse.

The Agenais takes its name from its chief city, Agen, which occupies a crucial site on the Garonne where major north–south, east–west routes meet and cross the river. To the north the city is dominated by a steep bluff on top of which the Gallic Nitobriges tribe once had their stronghold before the Romans conquered the area. Approaching Agen from the south you have a clear view of the limestone hills, of which this escarpment forms only a part, which stretch eastwards until they meet the granite slopes of the Massif Central although they peter out altogether not far west of Agen itself.

Both Agen and nearby Villeneuve-sur-Lot have large commercial markets specializing in *primeurs* but Villeneuve is much the more attractive. It was founded in the thirteenth century and was one of the biggest and best fortified *bastide* towns in the whole of the South-West. The walls are alas no longer standing but it still retains two remarkably fine towers guarding the northern and southern entrances to the town. The upper parts are built of brick and the lower parts of dressed stone, the whole capped by pointed red slate roofs. Their height is impressive and they give a good idea of how important the town must have been in the Middle Ages.

The Agenais hinges on a triangle formed by the confluence of the rivers Lot and Garonne at Aiguillon. Between Valence d'Agen and Marmande the valley of the Garonne consists of a wide, flat, intensively cultivated plain bounded by distant low hills. The fields are very large and, lacking any hedgerows, the countryside has rather a monotonous aspect, except in early spring when the vast orchards are laced with pink and white blossoms. This is the richest farming area in the South-West and apart from fruit (plums, cherries, peaches, strawberries, apples and melons) it produces big crops of maize, tobacco and all kinds of vegetables, including asparagus. Yet this land of Cockayne is wholly man-made. In the early Middle Ages it was covered by thick forest with only occasional smallholdings in isolated clearings. It was the Benedictines of the nearby abbey of Moissac and the

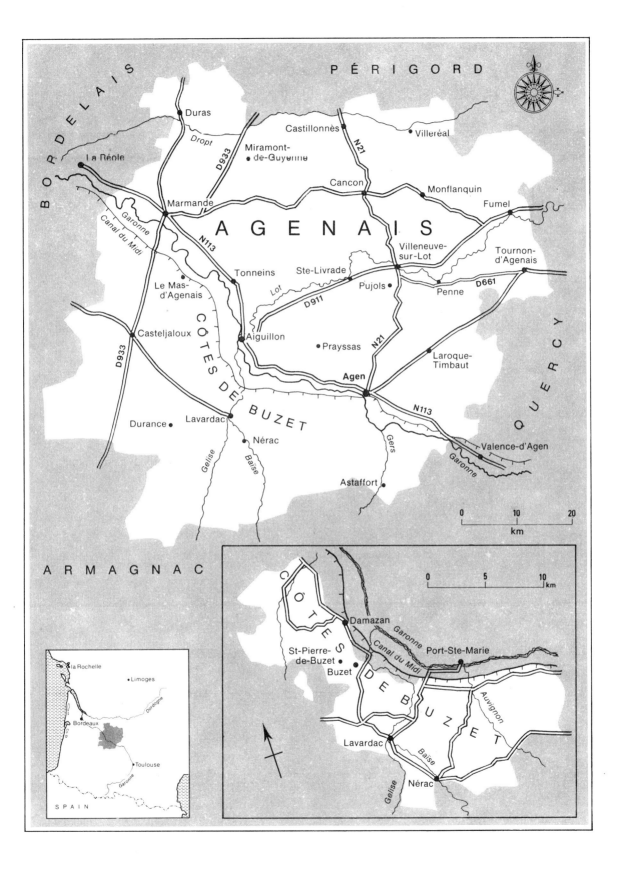

Hospitallers and Templars of Toulouse who provided both the inspiration and the capital to encourage the clearings of the forests and the creation of new settlements. The first fields were planted and hills terraced early in the twelfth century and by the beginning of the thirteenth the area was already prosperous and by the standards of the time densely populated. The main problem after this was, and remains, that the land is very low-lying and prone to flooding, but in the eighteenth century embankments were built and planted with poplars to stabilize them. Today the poplars fringing the Garonne stand out like so many exclamation marks on the blank sheet of the otherwise featureless plain.

Between the rivers, and north of the Lot, you will discover a much more attractive landscape composed of open valleys and low, flat-topped hills, their slopes covered with fields and orchards. The hill-tops are often crowned by impressive castles like the one at Duras or fortified villages like Tournon-d'Agenais or Villeréal, for in the Middle Ages the Agenais lay on the frontier between the territories of the French and English kings and was vulnerable to attack from either side; in fact it changed hands more than once. The north and north-western boundaries of the Agenais adjoin the wine-growing areas of Ste-Foy-Bordeaux and Monbazillac in the Bergeracois and so it is not surprising to find vineyards here in the neighbourhood of Duras. Although the total production is small – about 15,000 hectolitres annually from 2,100 hectares – the standard of the wine is high and it has its own *appellation*, Côtes de Duras. The area embraces fourteen communes but although one or two of the local *vignerons* sell direct to the customer the greater part of the wine is made and distributed by the local co-operative, Les Vignerons de Coteaux de Duras, just outside the village of Duras itself. Both red and white wines are produced. The red is made from Cabernet, Merlot, Malbec and Cot grapes, with a minimum permitted alcoholic strength of 10 degrees, but it is very robust and heady and should be treated with circumspection. The white wine used to be made from the traditional trio of Sémillon, Sauvignon and Muscadelle grapes and some Mauzac, but recently the co-operative has concentrated on making a dry white from the Sauvignon grape. It is one of the best we have found in the South-West, although hardly rivalling the best dry white of an area noted for them, such as the Loire. The minimum permitted strength is 10.5 degrees.

Due south of Duras is one of the major towns of the Agenais, Marmande, which boasts a fine Gothic church, a rarity in the South-West. Marmande is famous for its excellent tomatoes, which, large, misshapen and pale pink, have a much more subtle flavour than the rather acid varieties that we are used to. Served with an oil and wine vinegar dressing they make a satisfying *hors d'oeuvre* on their own. You can also make a delicious jam with the tomato of Marmande.

Tomato jam

You need a large fleshy type of tomato, or if you can find them the Italian plum tomatoes, known as *tomates romains* in France, which are widely grown in the south-west. The fewer the seeds and the more fleshy the tomatoes the better.

Just over 1kg (2¼lb) tomatoes
800g (1¾lb) sugar
Juice of 1 lemon
½ cup water
3 tablespoons rum

Peel and remove the seeds from the fruit so that you have 1kg of pulp. Add to it the sugar, the juice of a lemon and a very little water – about half a cupful is enough because the fruit will give a lot of juice. Heat the fruit, sugar and water slowly together in a thick-bottomed pan, stirring all the time. Allow the jam to simmer gently on a low heat for about 2 hours (remember the jams of the South-West were once made on open fires fed with two or three sticks and twigs to maintain the heat) until the mixture becomes thick and syrupy. There is no pectin in tomatoes and even with the lemon juice, the jam will not give a firm set. At the last moment, add the rum and stir in. Allow to cool slightly before pouring into jars and covering with airtight lids. Watch the jam if you store it in your jam cupboard – it may be better to keep it in the fridge.

Tourin à la tomate

In full summer when tomatoes are abundant our neighbour, Madame Artisié, makes her *tourin à la tomate*, also known as *tourin périgourdin*. Peel the onions and slice thinly. Fry gently in a thick frying pan with a little lard. Take the tomatoes, wash them and cut into pieces. Fry the pieces with a little more lard in a thick saucepan for 15 minutes. Then add the onions, water, and salt and pepper to taste. Cover and cook gently for 30 minutes. You can also add some vermicelli during this time so that it is cooked by the time you want to serve.

2 large onions
Lard for frying
6–7 ripe tomatoes
2½l (4 pints) water
Salt and pepper

Although fruit and vegetables are the chief products of the Marmandais (Marmande also specializes in peaches, both the white and yellow fleshed varieties), some wine is made there as well, but not on any great scale. The Côtes du Marmandais vineyards cover fourteen communes lying both sides of the Garonne. Two co-operatives are responsible for the total production of the area: the Câve Coopérative des Côtes du Marmandais on the right bank of the Garonne at Beaupuy and across the river the Cave Coopérative Intercommunal de Cocument. It has been known for Gallic wits to persuade gullible English wine experts that the wine of Cocument is the 'cuckold's' wine. Cuckolds do of course figure largely in French folk lore but in this case the joke is on the expert, for Cocument is merely the name of the village where the co-operative is to be found. But how the village got such a strange name is anyone's guess. The co-operative at Cocument has a capacity of 8,000 hectolitres and that at Beaupuy about the same. The grapes used to make Côtes du Marmandais are Merlot, Cabernet, Abouriou, Fer Servadou and Syrah for the reds, and Sauvignon, Sémillon and Ugni Blanc for the

whites. The reds are matured for eighteen months in cask and have a
permitted alcoholic minimum of 10 degrees compared with 11 degrees for
the whites.

Good as they are, the Côtes du Marmandais wines are overshadowed by
those of Duras to the north and Côtes de Buzet to the south-east. Côtes de
Buzet wines have a growing reputation in France, accelerated since 1973
when they were promoted from VDQS to AOC status. The vineyards are
planted in a narrow crescent of land not more than 12 kilometres at its widest
point, on the left bank of the Garonne and following the curve of the river
from Casteljaloux to the outskirts of Agen. The principal centres in the
district are Damazan, Lavardac, Nérac, and Buzet itself. Wine has been
made here for a very long time, perhaps since the Roman era, for there are
numerous archaeological remains from this period, including traces of fine
villas with mosaic floors indicating a level of prosperity in which the
cultivation of the vine would have flourished. Be that as it may, there is
documentary evidence of wine being exported from the district in the
Middle-Ages. At that time the wines of Buzet were included amongst the
Haut Pays wines that were not allowed into Bordeaux until after St Martin's
Day (11 November). A tarif agreement drawn up in Bordeaux in 1284 lists
Nérac as one of the wine towns of the Haut Pays, while another document of
1306 lists the following towns and their annual exports of wine (1 *tonneau*
equals 900 litres):

Nérac	281 tonneaux
Buzet	45 tonneaux
Damazan	62 tonneaux
Villefranche du Queyran	71 tonneaux
TOTAL	459 tonneaux

Because of the restrictions placed on their wines by the Bordeaux
authorities, the people of the Agenais were very pro-French during the
Hundred Years' War. Unfortunately the end of the Anglo-French wars in
1453 did not see an immediate disappearance of these restrictive privileges,
which were not finally abolished until 1776 during the reign of the ill-fated
Louis XVI. Even so, the wines of Buzet flourished and more vineyards were
planted, so that by 1757 they covered 1,476 hectares. Forty years earlier the
Intendant of Bordeaux made some interesting comments in a report on the
Agenais, which by then was part of Guyenne. He pointed out that although
the land was very fertile, the roads were very bad indeed and at certain times
of the year they were so muddy that travel was almost impossible. Those
towns and villages that were a long way from the four or five passable routes
were at a considerable commercial disadvantage, so much so that they were
forced to consume most of their own produce, including of course wine.
These remoter parts of the Agenais tended to turn to distilling their wine to

make *eau-de-vie*, as happened on a much greater scale in Armagnac which borders the Agenais to the south. The Intendant went on to say in his report that it was a pity communications in the Agenais were so poor, because some of the local wines, such as those of Clairac, Laparade, Aiguillon, Lafitte, Buzet and Thézac, would otherwise challenge all but the greatest of Bordeaux. High praise indeed.

Despite these and other problems the wines of Buzet continued to increase in importance and by the end of the eighteenth century the district was making 10,000 hectolitres annually. This period of prosperity was brought to an end by the outbreak of phylloxera in 1886. The *vignerons* of Buzet met this disaster, as they had met so many others, with a fierce determination not to be beaten. They started to replant using the same system of grafting their vines onto American stock that saved the Bordeaux vineyards. By 1894 the worst was over, although the vineyard area was much smaller than in its heyday and has remained so.

This revival was not destined to last. In 1911 the local *vignerons* were rocked on their heels by a ministerial decree defining the boundaries of the Gironde (Bordelais) and the wine-growing districts within the region that were entitled to the appellation Bordeaux. For over a century now the wines of Buzet, along with those of the Dordogne (Périgord), had been purchased by the Bordeaux merchants for mixing with their lighter reds to give them more body. Most of the resulting blend was sold to England and Holland where there was a demand for heavier red wines. Under the new legislation this practice was no longer allowed; Bordeaux wines had to come strictly from the Bordeaux region as defined and nowhere else, or lose the name. This legislation was catastrophic for the wine-makers of Buzet who now found themselves deprived of their chief market and producing a wine that did not even have a name.

This setback, the First World War and the economic recession that followed it, all combined to prevent any real progress for the time being. In fact it was not until after the Second World War in 1946 that the next step forward was taken with the founding of the Syndicat de Défense des Vins 'Côtes de Buzet', dedicated to restoring the wine's fortunes and establishing its name. On the one hand the Syndicat began to experiment with different vines and viniculture to improve the quality, and on the other it strove to obtain official recognition. Its efforts were rewarded when in 1953 the wines of Buzet were accorded VDQS status and the name 'Cotes de Buzet' was recognised for the first time. But the sceptical, conservative wine merchants of Bordeaux were still not interested in this unknown wine. So the men of Buzet decided to take matters into their own hands and create their own co-operative, 'La Cave Coopérative des Côtes de Buzet', which opened in 1955. They were extremely lucky to obtain the services of a first-rate manager, Monsieur Mermillod, who had been *régisseur* (manager) at the famous Château Lafite-Rothschild in Bordeaux. Under his energetic management the co-operative has flourished and is now one of the best run in the South-West. In 1973 the hard work of nearly thirty years was crowned by the promotion of Côtes de Buzet wines to full *appellation contrôlée* status, an event that was greeted with enthusiastic civic celebrations in Buzet. Even so the local wine-growers have not rested on their laurels and a new co-operative is even now being built which it is claimed will be one of the most technologically advanced in Europe.

Today the vineyards of Buzet cover 1,000 hectares producing about 65,000 hectolitres of wine, of which roughly 30,000 is of *appellation contrôlée* quality, although there are plans to increase this to 46,000 hectolitres by 1983. Ninety-five per cent of the production is red wine made from Merlot (known locally as Merlau), Malbec (called here Cot-rouge), Cabernet Franc and Cabernet Sauvignon, but Malbec accounts for only 1.5 per cent of the total and is being phased out. In future the wine will be made from one-third each of the remaining grapes. The minimum permitted strength of Côtes de Buzet red is 10 degrees but the Supérieur has a minimum of 11.5 degrees. A *vin du pays* is also sold with 9.5 degrees of alcohol.

A small amount of white wine (about 600 hectolitres) is made from Sauvignon, Sémillon and Muscadelle grapes and a *rosé* from the same varieties as the red. The Vin Blanc Supérieur has a strength of 11.5 degrees and the Rosé Supérieur 11 degrees.

The greater part of the co-operative's production is sold direct to the customer in plastic cubic containers holding 10, 21 or 33 litres, or in *bonbonnes*, attractive glass containers encased in wicker and with a capacity of 10 litres. The rest of the wine is matured in oak barrels for a year before being bottled. The co-operative also sells a small amount of a special wine called Cuvée Napoléon, made from specially selected grapes from the best vineyards. This is matured for eighteen months before bottling. You can also buy a *vin blanc mousseux*, Comte de Noailles, made by the Champagne method, which makes a good Pousse Rapière cocktail (see page 181). Finally there is an *eau-de-vie de marc* made from the pressed skins of the grapes used for the AOC wine. It is called *eau-de-vie-de-marc d'Aquitaine*.

East of Agen the Coteaux de Brulhois produces an above-average *vin du pays* which is worth searching out. It is called *vin du pays de l'Agenais* and is sold direct by the Cave Coopérative de Donzac at Auvillar, near Valence d'Agenais. It is excellent value.

The Agenais is famous throughout France for one product above all others, the *pruneau d'Agen*. Unfortunately, the prune has had a bad press in Britain, having featured so regularly on the menus of unpalatable school dinners. But forget those wizened black gobbets swimming in a sea of tapioca; the plump prunes of Agen are juicy and succulent. Preserved in armagnac they are a gourmet luxury. Most farmers' wives in the Agenais preserve their own prunes and bring them out on special occasions, although they normally use *eau-de-vie de marc* rather than armagnac. The *dégustation* (tasting) of prunes in alcohol is quite a ceremony. On the last evening before we return home to England, we usually make a farewell round of the neighbouring farms. Out come the prunes in their jar, to be served in special small porcelain dishes with matching plates for the stones. These can be bought locally, but coffee cups, liquer glasses or even deep saucers will do just as well. The *dégustation* is often extended to include greengages, cherries or even on one memorable occasion a bottle of apricots in armagnac, found at the back of a cupboard where it had lain for six years! The respective merits of vintages and fruits are discussed with enthusiasm and at last we are allowed on our way. At the next port of call we are met with the same warm hospitality – and so it goes on until we reel home to bed after a delightful but punishing evening.

The bottles of prunes in armagnac sold in the shops are expensive, but you can easily buy your own prunes in the market and a bottle of armagnac: if you can resist eating the one and drinking the other you will be able to bottle your own fruit. If you think good armagnac is wasted on prunes you can buy *eau-de-vie de marc* instead or, cheaper still, use Monbazillac, the sweet fruity wine from the Bergerac area to the north. Buy half-dried prunes (mi-fourrés) and put them immediately into the alcohol or wine.

If however you have to wait until you return home to do the preserving, you will need the fully dried prunes. These should be soaked in the remains of the breakfast teapot for several mornings and then simmered very, very gently until swollen. Drain the prunes well and put them into a glass jar and cover them with the alcohol. Seal with an airtight lid. Six or seven months later the mere sight of the bottle of prunes will confound the sceptics who scoffed at the idea of prunes as a gastronomic delight! If you can wait for a year the results are even better. For those with less patience, a mixture of two-thirds *eau-de-vie* and one-third syrup gives a sweeter less fierce result rather more quickly, say, in two or three months.

The pride with which the *pruneau d'Agen* is regarded locally is shown by the following story which nicely illustrates the difference between our nations. An English rugby club from the home counties was invited to play at Nérac. The whole town turned out to greet the English players and gifts were exchanged. The English gave their hosts club ties which were received politely but with incomprehension. In turn the English team were presented with packets of prunes! Blank amazement was followed by ribald laughter: the French were offended and an international incident was averted only with difficulty. The South-West follows rugby as fanatically as does Wales and actually has a church dedicated to the sport, Notre Dame de Rugby at Larrivière St-Savin in the Landes.

Despite its name, the *pruneau d'Agen* comes in the main from the country surrounding Villeneuve-sur-Lot. The biggest orchards are found in the lowlands bordering the Lot to the west of the town, but there are many smaller ones in the hilly country between the rivers. In early spring when the orchards are sprinkled with white blossom the sunny valleys are a splendid sight. In Villeneuve itself you will find several shops dedicated to the sale of this gastronomic delicacy, their windows offering the kind of magnificent displays associated with superior chocolate shops.

The special variety of plum from which the *pruneau d'Agen* is made, the *prune d'Ente* was first introduced to the Agenais from the Middle East at the time of the Crusades, but it was not until the sixteenth century, when the monks of Clairac near Tonneins planted the first orchards, that plums were cultivated on any scale. By the eighteenth century the prune was a recognized speciality of the area.

The plum harvest begins in September and soon the first half-dried, new-season prunes appear in the markets. The plums are shaken from the trees and sorted according to size and ripeness; then they are put on wire racks which are stacked on trolleys ready for the oven. The ovens are specially constructed concrete bunkers, usually built at ground level to make it easier to wheel the trolleys in and out. In the past they were heated by wood fires but now even quite small farms have oil-fired ovens. The temperature of the oven and the length of time the plums are dried is carefully monitored for if the prunes are to be sold as *pruneaux d'Agen* they are subject to strict quality controls which regulate the moisture and sugar content. The trolleys may be wheeled in and out of the ovens three or four times, according to the size of the plums and their ripeness, and each time they come out the prunes look blacker and more wrinkled. Wasps hum around the trays and at night the odd field mouse might climb in to help himself to the kernels of the stones.

After drying, the prunes are sorted and despatched to the packing plant. Many farms belong to prune co-operatives which collect the dried fruit and sort it to various categories and distribute it. Other farmers send their plums to a factory which handles the whole process. If the prunes have been half-dried they will not need cooking: the flesh is so sweet and the skin so soft that they can be eaten as they are. In the specialist shops you will find prunes covered with crackling sugar, *farcis* (stuffed with marzipan) *fourrés* or plain, and there too you will find last year's prunes preserved in armagnac.

Not surprisingly, the prune figures largely in the local cuisine; in fact you might well say that in the Agenais it is a case of prunes with everything! The range of prune recipes would make a book in itself: steak with prunes and button mushrooms on skewers with pieces of red pepper or tomatoes; roast pork and prune stuffing; goose, turkey, hare or rabbit with prunes; duck or chicken casserole with prunes. . . . Then there are the classic dessert recipes such as prune tart with walnuts, or *clafoutis* with prunes instead of the more usual cherries. The list seems endless and like so many of the specialities of the South-West they depend as much on the ingenuity of the cook as anything else. Here are just a few specialities of the area, not all of them employing prunes!

Goose à l'Agenais

Apart from the goose itself, the main feature of this dish is the stuffed prune stuffing.

Soak the prunes in the red wine for a day. Then simmer very gently so that they swell. Allow to cool and then remove the stones, keeping the prunes as whole as possible. Keep the juice to add to the giblet stock.

Make a stock of the goose giblets, the red wine, a small onion, a bay leaf and a little salt and pepper. Keep the stock to mix the stuffing.

In a covered casserole, cook the chopped onion with the apples, orange, nutmeg, olive oil and stock. The sausage meat should be mashed and mixed well with the above ingredients. Cook for 1 hour and then remove the casserole from the oven and mix the stuffing well. Drain off the surplus liquid, leaving about 300 millilitres ($\frac{1}{2}$ pint/10 fl.oz) in the casserole. Add to the casserole fresh breadcrumbs, sufficient to make a good stiff mixture, and the minced goose liver from the stock, and the armagnac. If necessary, add more breadcrumbs to stiffen the mixture. Allow to stand for several hours or until the next day. Stuff the prunes with the mixture. If there is any stuffing left over, pack this into the goose first. Then pack the stuffed prunes loosely into the bird, and cook according to your usual recipe, allowing 20–25 minutes per pound. Any surplus juice from the giblets or prunes can be incorporated in the goose gravy and thickened if necessary before serving.

Stuffed prune stuffing
750g (1½lb) best prunes
2 chopped onions
1 orange, peeled and chopped
3 apples, peeled, cored and chopped
250g (½lb) sausage meat
Ground nutmeg
3 tablespoons armagnac
2 cups fresh breadcrumbs
Salt and pepper
3 tablespoonsful olive oil
300 millilitres (½ pint/10 fl.oz) red wine

Stock
Goose giblets
1 small onion
1 bay leaf
Salt and pepper
Red wine drained from prunes

Lapin aux pruneaux Serves 6

Soak the prunes in the red wine for several hours. Simmer very gently so that they swell and then set aside.

Fry the onions in the olive oil. Roll the rabbit pieces in the seasoned flour and brown gently in the frying pan. Put the onions, prunes, rabbit, bouquet garni and red wine in a casserole and cook for 2 or 3 hours in a low oven. Thicken the sauce with a little roux before serving if a thicker gravy is preferred.

1.5kg (3lb) best rabbit pieces
12 fat prunes
2 large onions, chopped
1 bouquet garni
2 or 3 tablespoons olive oil
300 millilitres (½ pint/10fl.oz) red wine
Seasoned flour

Clafoutis with prunes

For the hostess who likes to serve a substantial pudding but cannot cope with those that have to come to the table piping hot, the *clafoutis* is useful because it can be served hot or cold, or luke warm or slightly hot, or slightly cold! It is a rich batter custard pudding with innumerable permutations of fruit – prunes in the Agenais, raisins or apricots, peaches or pears, according to what is available. The recipe originates in the Limousin and should really be made with the large black cherries that grow there, but the Agenais has its own variety, known as *flaugnarde*, which is made from prunes.

Prepare the prunes by removing the stones. If you have prunes which have been soaked in *eau-de-vie* or armagnac for a few months, all the better. Arrange them in a buttered ovenproof earthenware dish (avoid using a metal dish as it will cook the *clafoutis* too quickly).

For the batter, mix the flour and sugar together and add a pinch of salt.

250g (½lb) prunes
150g (6oz) flour
125g (5oz) sugar
Pinch salt
1l (2 pints) milk
3 eggs

Warm the milk and beat in the eggs. Mix the warm milk and eggs with the flour and sugar little by little, stirring and beating well. Pour the mixture over the prunes and bake in a moderate oven for about 45 minutes. Serve warm or cold.

Tarte aux pruneaux avec noix   Serves 8

250g (8oz) walnut halves
1kg (2lb) prunes
Cold tea
250g (8oz) Short crust pastry

Soak the prunes in cold tea for several hours and then simmer gently until swollen. Remove stones. Reserve 8 good specimens. Pick out 8 good walnut halves and set aside.

Line a 20cm (8in) flan tin with the short crust pastry. Mash the remaining prunes and chop the remaining walnuts into small pieces. Mix the two together adding a little of the cold tea juice to keep the mixture moist enough to spread easily, and then fill the flan crust.

Bake in a slow to medium oven (Mark 4) for $1-1\frac{3}{4}$ hours. When cooked, decorate immediately with the halves of walnuts and prunes. Serve cold with thick cream.

Stuffed prunes

150 millilitres ($\frac{1}{4}$ pint/5fl.oz)
　brandy or eau de vie
18 fat prunes
125g ($\frac{1}{4}$lb) marzipan
Sweet almonds or walnuts to
　decorate
300 millilitres ($\frac{1}{2}$ pint/10fl.oz)
　hot, stewed tea
Sugar for syrup

This recipe is less complicated than the stuffed prunes of Tours, but the secret of its simplicity lies in advance preparation.

About two months before you need them, take the prunes and pour hot tea over them. We have never found the French housewife so enthusiastic about tea as when she describes the process of swelling the prune! Leave for about 8 hours. Drain the prunes, then transfer them to a large jar and add the brandy. Close the lid securely. Shake and stir every two or three days so that the prunes absorb the alcohol. At the end of the time they should be well 'drunk'.

Drain the prunes for a few hours while you prepare the marzipan. (You can use the brandy again for the next batch of prunes). Remove the prune stones and fill the gap with stone-shaped wedges of marzipan. Make a syrup of another measure of cold tea with added sugar. Boil until it becomes sticky, then baste the stuffed prunes and allow them to dry slightly. You will need frilly paper cases in which to serve the prunes (a good stationer should have these). Decorate with almonds or walnuts. With a glass of sweet wine, port or Monbazillac they make a stupendous finale to a meal.

Jambon de Tonneins

Among the specialities of the Agenais mentioned in a number of books we found *jambon de Tonneins* listed alongside the salt-cured country hams of the South-West, of which the best known is, of course, *jambon de Bayonne*. We asked our neighbours about the Tonneins variety, but although this little town is only 40 kilometres away, no one knew anything about its special ham, so the only thing to do was to go and find out for ourselves. The answer was provided by Monsieur Ponthoreau, *charcutier* of Tonneins, who explained that the '*veritable*' *jambon de Tonneins* is not a cured ham at all, but consists of good-sized pieces of leg and shoulder of pork wrapped in the rind, flavoured with salt, pepper, garlic and spices and cooked slowly in the oven. The exact recipe is Monsieur Ponthoreau's secret. *Jambon de Tonneins* can be eaten hot or cold and is excellent with plain boiled potatoes or *pain frotté*, a slice of bread fried in pork fat and rubbed with a raw clove of garlic.

Until quite recently every farming family had its pig, which was cosseted and pampered throughout the fattening months until the moment arrived for the *coup de grâce* to be administered so that the household could survive the long winter until the new crops sprouted, the *potager* produced fresh new vegetables and the orchards grew heavy with the early fruits. Many families still keep a pig to this day, but in a much less personal fashion than before. Subscriptions are paid to a local pig specialist who cares for a given number of animals. When the pigs are judged to be in their prime, they are killed and each subscriber collects his or her portion. In this way even families that live in towns and villages and lack the space to keep their own animals can own a pig or a portion of one and can thus make their own *pâtés* and *terrines*, *boudins noirs*, *crépinettes*, *saucissons* and cure their own hams.

One December, when our car got stuck in the mud on the steep track leading to our house, we went down to a neighbouring farm to ask for help. No one answered our tentative knock at the door but we could hear voices so we pushed the door open and looked inside. There was the whole family, the five teenage girls and their two younger brothers, sitting round the kitchen table armed with sharp knives of varying lengths, carefully cutting up pieces of pork, supervised by their mother. In front of each of them were two or three mounds of meat or fat, some in tiny pieces, others in larger chunks. Two of the girls were separating the rind from fat, while the elder boy was filleting and boning a piece of loin. All this while their father was collecting the piles of meat at intervals and transferring them either to the salt bath or to the mincing machine that ground away relentlessly in the corner of the kitchen. On the stove an enormous *fait-tout* was steaming gently and a heavenly smell of pork, stock and garlic made us reluctant to broach our problem and drag them away from their task. Everyone seemed to be enjoying himself immensely, even the smallest child, a little boy then aged about four, who was being helped and encouraged by his sister in his important job of cutting up strips of back fat into cubes with a wicked-looking knife. While we waited for the farmer to fetch his tractor, we asked about the pig. We were told that the farmer (a qualified butcher) had killed the animal at the local pig farm, where it had been fattened.

The pig's carcass was going to be turned into all kinds of good things – home-made black puddings, heavy with fat and garlic, were already bouncing gently in a rich stock in the *fait-tout*. Later that week we were given a length, wrapped in greaseproof paper and several layers of plastic bag. We brought it back to England with us, but despite the wrappings, we could still smell *boudin* three years later every time we opened the case! The following year we enjoyed more of the pig in the form of *pâtés* and *terrines*. Talking to Madame Artisié about her recipes, we had the opportunity to look through her notebook which she started while she was still a girl at school. There were all the basic recipes that all French housewives know, such as *poule vieille en sauce* and *lapin sauté à la poele*, and there too was *pâté cochon*. The quantities listed staggered us: three kilos of pig's liver, forty kilos of mixed lean and fat pork and four kilos of eggs! Here is a more manageable recipe that Madame had just given to her newly married daughter who was living in Bordeaux.

Pâté cochon

2.5kg (5½lb) pork (equal parts fresh belly pork and lean pork pieces)
250g (8oz) pig's liver
3–4 large eggs, beaten
1 teaspoon of salt per kg of meat
¼ teaspoonful of pepper per kg of meat

Mince the belly of pork and the lean pieces coarsely. Dip the pig's liver in boiling water for 2–3 minutes and mince when cool. Mix with the minced pork meat, add the salt and pepper and then mix in the beaten eggs. Madame says the secret of good *pâté* is to knead the minced mixture with the eggs by hand, like kneading bread, so that the warmth from your hands starts to soften the fat and helps the meat to absorb the salt and pepper. Madame also adds a tablespoon of her own *eau-de-vie* while she is kneading her *pâté*.

Turn the mixture into greased dishes. The deeper the dishes the better: ideally they should be 8cm (3in) deep by 20cm (8in) across. Cook in a slow oven for about 1½ hours, watching after the first hour to see that the *pâté* is not overcooked. Take the *pâté* out of the oven when the meat comes away from the sides of the dish, for it will go on cooking for a few minutes afterwards.

If you wish to preserve the *pâtés*, put the raw mixture into small kilner or parfait jars and pressure-cook at high pressure for one hour.

Pâté mousse

500g (1lb) pig's liver, sliced
1kg (2lb) pork fat from the back
20 centilitres milk (between ⅓ and ½ pint)
3 eggs, beaten
25g (1oz) salt
Good pinch pepper

Madame Artisié also has her special recipe for a pork liver *pâté*, a *pâté mousse*, which is soft and rich, and like her *pâté cochon* can be preserved or frozen, though freezing and defrosting does make it rather too soft and moist.

Plunge the liver into boiling water for 2–3 minutes. Mince it very finely and then mix in the beaten eggs. Mince the back fat finely and add to the liver mixture. Add salt and pepper. Knead well by hand for about half an hour, mixing in the milk little by little until it is absorbed. The result should be a mushy mixture. Put into greased dishes, again the deeper the better, and cook in a slow oven for 45 minutes to 1 hour, depending on the size of the dishes.

This is a rich *pâté* and the quantities will need to be smaller than for the *pâté cochon*; a dish of 10–12cm (4–5in) diameter, 5cm (2in) deep, will be enough for a substantial *hors d'oeuvre* for six to eight people. If you intend to preserve the mousse, put the raw mixture in kilner or parfait jars and sterilize on high pressure for about 40 minutes in the pressure cooker.

No French housewife will admit that her recipe is inferior to any other. She makes her *pâté* as her mother made it or as her mother-in-law taught her. Her husband and family prefer the familiar flavour and only as a last resort does she buy a ready-made *pâté* from the *charcuterie*.

Another friend, Madame Mercadier, makes a *mousse de foie* which is so fine that it is almost as good as a *pâté de foie gras*. She recommends 1kg (2lb) of pork liver to 1kg (2lb) of pork fat, together with 1 litre (2 pints/40fl.oz) of milk and 2 eggs. Her method is the same as Madame Artisié's. Madame Mercadier also has her own recipe for the *pâté de campagne* or *pâté cochon* consisting of 1.5kg (3lb) belly of pork, 1kg (2¼lb) lean pork pieces, 60g (2oz) pork liver, 25 (1oz) of salt, 1 teaspoon pepper, 5 eggs and a generous glass of *eau-de-vie*.

Madame Mercadier advises us on many aspects of French life and customs. She knows which *charcuteries* make the best *pâtés* and which supermarket is offering the best bargains of the week. If we want quinces and have looked in vain in the local market, she alerts her network and in a few days quinces appear. It was Madame Mercadier who explained to us that when buying pumpkins it is important to have in mind the dish that is to be prepared. The longer, sausage-shaped pumpkins, resembling plump golden marrows, are best for soups and savoury dishes; the round ones are best for sweet pies, puddings and jams. Pumpkin soup makes an interesting and colourful starter, but you need to season it more than you would most soups and you should sprinkle strong, grated cheese over the *croûtons* floating on the surface.

Pumpkin soup

Cut the peeled pumpkin into pieces and put into a large saucepan with the peeled and diced potatoes, chopped onions and the water. Add salt and pepper and cook on a low heat for 45 minutes. Cut the bread into squares and fry until golden in the butter.

When the pumpkin, potatoes and onions are cooked, drain well and then purée them together in the blender. Check the seasoning; you may need more than the normal amount of salt and pepper. Add some milk if you need more liquid.

Pour the soup into the tureen. Float the croûtons on top of the soup and sprinkle the grated cheese over them. Put the tureen in a hot oven for 15 minutes to allow the cheese to brown. As you ladle the *soupe au potiron* into individual dishes, add a dash of single cream and leave your guests to stir it in themselves.

500g (1lb) pumpkin (no need to buy a whole one)
500g (1lb) potatoes, peeled and diced
2 medium onions, chopped
1.5l (3 pints/60fl.oz) water or chicken stock
Salt and pepper
Grated cheese
1 carton single cream (150 millilitres or 5fl.oz)
Bread and butter for croûtons

Terrine de Nérac Serves 8

Terrine here is not so much a rough country-type *pâté* but rather a covered

4 partridges
500g (1lb) chicken livers
1 egg, beaten
250g (½lb) back bacon
250g (½lb) sausage meat
125g (¼lb) mushrooms
250g (½lb) streaky bacon
Seasoning, herbs
2 bay leaves

casserole, the earthenware dish in which meat, game and fish are cooked. Count Austin de Croze recommended red partridges for this dish, but those of us who happen to have a spare bird from a weekend shoot are not disposed to be so particular. Nevertheless a dish from that pleasant town, Nérac, the setting for Shakespeare's *Love's Labour's Lost*, is well worth the effort.

The partridges should be plucked, drawn and trussed. Mince the livers with the chicken livers, the sausage meat, the back bacon and slices of truffle (or *cèpes* or mushrooms). Add salt, pepper, spices and herbs (according to taste but try a pinch of ginger, nutmeg, quatre épices, bay leaf, majoram and parsley) and mix with the livers, binding with the beaten egg.

Split the partridges down the backbone and open flat. Sprinkle with salt and pepper.

Put a layer of forcemeat in the bottom of a fireproof *terrine* then lay the partridges on top. Fill in the spaces with the remaining forcemeat. Cover the whole with a layer of streaky bacon and the bay leaves. Put the lid on the casserole and seal (with aluminium foil), and cook for 3 hours in a slow oven.

Lamb tongues de Guyenne Serves 4

8 lambs' tongues (allow at least 2 per person)
2 large onions, chopped
½ clove garlic, crushed
125g (¼lb) streaky bacon, chopped
1 carrot, diced
1 potato, diced
2 cups red wine
2 dozen black olives
Fresh breadcrumbs
25g (1oz) butter

Cook the tongues in the red wine with one of the chopped onions, the diced carrot and potato, adding water to the cooking liquid if necessary. Pressure cooking will take about 15 minutes at 15lb pressure; or you can poach them gently in the oven in a covered casserole the day before if necessary. Skin and trim the tongues when they are cool enough to handle. Set them on one side until needed, preferably keeping them in their liquid to retain moisture.

Fry gently the remaining onion with the bacon and garlic. Take 16 of the olives and chop in small pieces. Add these to the frying pan. Remove the tongues from their liquid. Blend the juice, carrot, potato and onion together to make what eighteenth-century cooks described as a *cullis* (if you don't have an electric blender, put the vegetables through a sieve or a *mouli-légumes*). Add the *cullis* to the frying pan and let the mixture reduce over a lively heat until it is the texture of thick cream.

Split the tongues and arrange them in a shallow *gratin* dish. Pour over them the contents of the frying pan. A generous layer of fresh breadcrumbs dotted with butter will help to soak up excess liquid. Brown in the top of a medium hot oven (Mark 5) for half an hour. Dot the remaining olives on the top before serving.

Lamb casserole à l'agenaise

1kg (2lb) chump ends of lamb or breast or centre rib, with some extra lamb bones for stock
30 centilitres (½ pint/10fl.oz) dry white wine
30 centilitres (½ pint/10fl.oz) pale stock or water
2 medium onions, chopped
2 aubergines, prepared and cubed
2 cloves garlic, chopped
Salt and pepper
½ teaspoon ground nutmeg
2 tablespoons olive oil

Make a rich stock from the bones, white wine, stock, an onion, salt, pepper and nutmeg. Remove the bones from the stock and make a *cullis* from the liquid and the onion (see above). Cut the meat into 5cm (2in) chunks. Fry in the olive oil. Add the garlic, crushed, and chopped onion. Drain well and transfer to a casserole. Lightly fry the aubergine in the same oil. Drain well and add to the meat. Pour over the stock and cook in a low oven for 2½ hours or until cooked. Thicken the sauce with a little roux – it should be pale and creamy.

The addition of nutmeg helps to balance the strong flavour of the lamb, and brings the aubergine forward.

Oeufs à l'agenaise Serves 4

Slice the aubergine and cut into small dice. Sprinkle with salt and leave to drain. After 1 hour, rinse well and leave to dry in a paper towel. Preheat oven to medium hot.

Fry the onion, parsley and garlic together in the olive oil or goose fat. Drain well and put equal parts in the bottom of four individual fireproof dishes about 4–5cm (1½–2in) deep. Fry the prepared aubergine in the same fat or oil and drain well.

Crack an egg into each of the fireproof dishes. Add a sprinkling of sea salt and freshly ground black pepper to taste. Cover with the cooked aubergine. Top with fresh breadcrumbs and dabs of butter. Place in the top of a medium hot oven for 8 to 10 minutes, or until the eggs are cooked.

This makes a rich *hors d'oeuvre* or, with double the quantities, a substantial supper dish. French bread to mop up the juices and a dish of black olives handed separately complete the course, with a red *vin du pays*. To round off the meal, serve a cheeseboard with fresh fruit as a dessert.

1 large onion
1 tablespoon chopped parsley
4 eggs
1 aubergine, diced
1 tablespoon olive oil or goose fat
Small amount of crushed garlic
Fresh breadcrumbs
25g (1oz) butter
Sea salt and freshly ground black pepper

Brizoles de veau Serves 6

Larousse gives the credit for this dish to a chef in the service of the Marquis of Bresolles. But an English cook book of 1793 (*The French Family Cook*: 'being a complete system of French cookery adapted to the tables not only of the opulent but of persons of modest fortune and condition') lists the dish as *brizoles*, possibly a connection with *briser* (to break) describing the broken nature of the strips of veal.

In a frying pan cook the chopped onions, garlic, parsley and bacon gently with olive oil or goose fat. Add the sausage meat and cook well together, mashing the sausage meat with a fork as necessary to break up lumps. Cook on a very low heat for 5 to 10 minutes.

Meanwhile, prepare the veal, which should traditionally be cut in long thin strips. Use escalopes if you feel very extravagant, but cheaper cuts of veal can be used for this dish. Trim the veal into long fingers and roll in seasoned flour.

Drain the onion and sausage meat. Fry the veal strips quickly in the same fat, adding more oil or fat if necessary.

In a deep casserole put a layer of sausage meat, then a layer of veal strips, then a layer of sausage meat, then another layer of veal. Season with freshly ground nutmeg as you go. Moisten with the dry white wine.

Cover and cook for 2 hours (for braising veal) or ¾ hour (for fillet) at Mark 3. Then turn the oven up to Mark 5 or 6. Remove the lid and cover the veal

1.5kg (2½–3lb) braising veal
Seasoned flour
2 medium onions, chopped
1 clove garlic, crushed
250g (½lb) streaky bacon, chopped finely
1 tablespoon olive oil or goose fat
250g (½lb) sausage meat
Ground nutmeg
3 tablespoons chopped parsley
Fresh breadcrumbs
25g (1oz) butter
250ml (½ pint/10fl.oz) dry white wine

with fresh breadcrumbs and dabs of butter. Allow to cook briskly without the lid for another $\frac{1}{2}$ hour until the top is brown and crisp.

300 ml ($\frac{1}{2}$ pint/10fl.oz) milk
125g ($\frac{1}{4}$lb) flour
4 eggs
2 tablespoons armagnac
1 dessertspoonful orange flower water (or use 2 or 3 drops of vanilla essence)
Caster sugar
Butter or lard for frying

Crêpes agenaises For 18 pancakes

At the entrance to the covered market at Agen is a pancake stall which sells sugary *crêpes*, waffles and sweet batter *brioches* in rings: just the thing to sustain the flagging *ménagère* as she negotiates prices and quantities, or tackles the perennial and ubiquitous parking problems.

Mix the batter well. It should be liquid and the pancake should be thin. As soon as each pancake is done, sprinkle with caster sugar and roll before putting on a warm plate.

Périgord

IT IS FOUR O'CLOCK on a hot Sunday afternoon in Périgord. We are sitting on a vine-covered terrace overlooking the river Dordogne. On the far bank, behind a line of poplars, there is a patchwork of open fields and beyond, a wooded crag surmounted by a formidable-looking castle. We have just finished lunch and what a lunch! *Pâté de foie gras truffé*, fresh trout with almonds, *côte de veau* and *sauce Périgueux*, a crisp fresh green salad dressed with wine vinegar and walnut oil, a *tarte périgourdine* and a choice of cheeses. Now we sit stupefied by such gastronomic riches, drowsing in the shade over our glasses of *crème de noix*.

In Périgord the cuisine reaches heights that, if sometimes equalled in other parts of the South-West, are never surpassed. Its gastronomic reputation in France, and indeed in the world, stands very high, enhanced by the number of famous chefs who have made their mark in Paris or even further afield. The most remarkable of them all, Eugene Noël, was summoned to the court of Frederick the Great of Prussia and was his head chef for many years.

The reasons for this pre-eminence are not far to seek: the Périgord produces the finest ingredients a cook could wish for. The rich alluvial soils of the river valleys are a source of a variety of excellent vegetables and fruits, the woods yield walnuts from which a refined oil is made that is very good in salads. Everywhere there are geese from which so many delicacies are made, the most famous of them being, of course, *foie gras*. And then there is the most precious of them all, that remarkable tuber that Brillat-Savarin called the diamond of cuisine: the truffle. Périgord's cuisine is thus firmly based on the region's natural resources which, in the fertile river valleys at least, encouraged the creation of a flourishing traditional peasant cuisine.

Edward Harrison Barker, who spent two years in the area in 1892 and 1893, gives a vivid picture of this good life in his book *Two Summers in Guyenne*. Here is his description of a mower's feast on the banks of the river Isle:

> At about ten o'clock the big bell that hangs outside the château is rung, and the mowers, dropping their scythes, leave the field and troop into the great kitchen which has changed so little for centuries. The pots and pans hanging against the walls, and the pieces of bacon from the beams, have

been renewed, but not much else. There is the same floor paved with stones, now much cracked and worn into hollows, the same hearth and broad chimney with hanging chain; and the long table and benches stretching from end to end, although their age is uncertain, were certainly fashioned upon the exact model of others that preceded them. Richard Coeur-de-Lion when campaigning in Guyenne, may have sat down many a time to such a table as this, and to just such a meal as the one that is about to be served to the mowers, with the exception of the coffee and rum.

Let us take a look into the great cauldrons, which appear to have come out of Gargantua's kitchen. One contains two full-sized turkeys and several fowls, another a leg of pork, and a third a considerable portion of a calf. Then there is a cauldron of soup, made very 'thick and slab'. Home-baked loaves, round like trenchers, and weighing 10lb each, are on the side table, together with an immense bowl of salad and a regiment of bottles filled with wine newly drawn from the cask.

In the evening, when all the grass has been cut, there is another and a greater feast. The work being done, the men linger long at the table. Then all the household is assembled in the great kitchen, including the *châtelain* and *châtelaine*, and the young men who are known to have voices are called upon to sing. They do not need much pressing, for what with the heat of the sun during the day, then the wine, the coffee and rum, their blood is rushing rather hotly through the veins. One after another they stand up on the benches and give out their voices from their sturdy chests, which are burnt to the colour of terra-cotta. They make so much noise that the old warming-pan trembles against the wall. Although they all speak *patois* among themselves, they are reluctant to sing the songs of Périgord in the presence of strangers. The young men are proud of their French, bad as it is, and a song in the café-concert style of music and poetry fires their ambition to excel on a festive occasion like this, whilst their *patois* ditties seem then only fit to be sung at home or in the fields. At length, however, they allow themselves to be persuaded, and they sing in chorus a 'Reapers Song', composed long ago by some unknown Périgourdin poet, who was perhaps a jongleur or a troubadour. The notes are so arranged as to imitate the rhythmic movements of the reaper; first the drawing back of the right arm, then the stroke of the sickle, and lastly, the laying down of the cut corn. There is something of sadness as well as of joy in the repeated cadences of the simple song, and it moves the heart, for now the old men join in, and the sound gathers such strength that the little martins under the eaves must be pressing troubled breasts against their young. . . .

Harrison Barker's idyllic picture should not blind us to the fact that life on the limestone plateaux and in the forests was hard and the peasants were

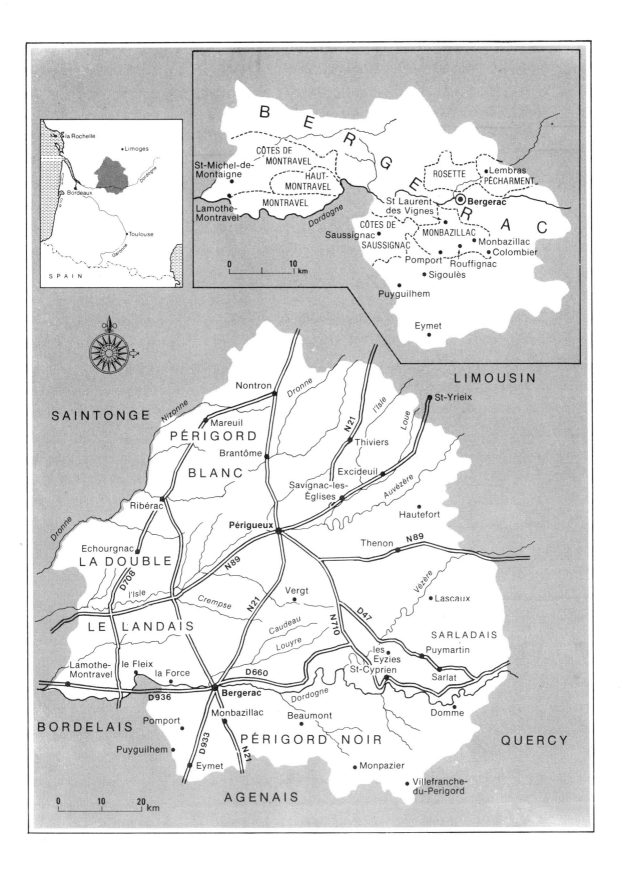

BERGERAC

CÔTES DE MONTRAVEL
St-Michel-de-Montaigne
HAUT-MONTRAVEL
MONTRAVEL
Lamothe-Montravel
Dordogne
ROSETTE
Lembras
PÉCHARMENT
St Laurent des Vignes
Bergerac
CÔTES DE SAUSSIGNAC
Saussignac
MONBAZILLAC
Monbazillac
Colombier
Pomport
Rouffignac
Sigoulès
Puyguilhem
Eymet

0   10 km
1 km

la Rochelle
Limoges
Dordogne
Bordeaux
Toulouse
Garonne
SPAIN

LIMOUSIN

SAINTONGE
Nontron
Dronne
St-Yrieix
Nizonne
Mareuil
PÉRIGORD
BLANC
Brantôme
l'Isle
N21
Thiviers
Loue
Excideuil
Savignac-les-Églises
Auvézère
Ribérac
Périgueux
Hautefort
Dronne
Thenon   N89
Echourgnac
LA DOUBLE
N89
Vézère
Lascaux
D708
l'Isle
N21
Vergt
D47
les Eyzies
SARLADAIS
Puymartin
Crempse
LE LANDAIS
Caudeau
N710
St-Cyprien
Sarlat
Louyre
Lamothe-Montravel
le Fleix
la Force
D660
Dordogne
Domme
D936
Bergerac
Pomport
Monbazillac
Beaumont
BORDELAIS
Puyguilhem
D933
PÉRIGORD   NOIR
QUERCY
N21
Eymet
Monpazier
Villefranche-du-Perigord
AGENAIS

0   10   20 km

often on the verge of starvation. The misery of these wretches, eking out a meagre existence on stony, barren land was in complete contrast to the lives of the noble families who lived in the great châteaux. During the Middle Ages, when the power of the central government was at its weakest, the barons of Beynac, Biron, Bourdeilles and Mareuil divided Périgord between them. Their rivalry was intense and their imposing castles testify to this day to their wealth and power. It was in the kitchens of these great nobles that their chefs created the refined cuisine that has made Périgord famous. The chefs were supported by the *traiteurs*, middle men from Périgueux, Sarlat and other towns, who catered for their patrons, cultivated tastes by providing the *pâtés* and conserves that are always associated with the Périgourdin table. This sophisticated cuisine reached its apogee in the eighteenth century. After the French Revolution, however, it was the local bourgeoisie who inherited the tradition and have maintained it to this day.

Crossing Périgord from north to south, the traveller has a superficial impression of a succession of rounded, well-wooded hills, punctuated by river valleys whose fertile bottoms are covered by a patchwork of interlocking fields where not an inch of the rich soil is wasted. Like most first impressions, this picture has an element of truth: over a quarter of the region is forest and in some areas, north-west of Sarlat for example, the percentage is even higher. It is also true that this is a well-watered land. Four river systems flow through the Périgord: the Dordogne (from which the modern department takes its name) with its tributary the Vézère; the Isle, on whose banks stands the capital Périgueux; the Dronne, a smaller and very attractive river in the north of Périgord; and to the south, and much less important than the other three, the Dropt. All these rivers, together with their confluents, run roughly speaking on parallel courses from north-east to south-west, while their smaller tributaries, running north–south, provide numerous valley routes, which, before the coming of the railways, were the only highways. On these routes there grew up the many small market towns where produce from different parts of the region was interchanged.

But, of course, there is more to Périgord than just woods and water: the region lies between the lower slopes of the Massif Central to the east and the lowlands of the Bordelais to the west. To the north and north-west lie the modern departments of the Limousin and Charente, while the south-eastern and southern parts are bordered by the Quercy (Lot) and the Agenais (Lot-et-Garonne). Most of the ancient County of Périgord is included in the modern department of the Dordogne, although a small south-eastern portion now falls within the department of the Lot.

The landscape naturally reflects Périgord's transitional position. The highest land (551 metres) is in the north-east and from here the land slopes very gradually in a generally south-western direction until in the lower reaches of the river Dordogne, below Bergerac, it is not much above sea level. Between these extremes lies a variety of landscapes.

The Nontronnais, to the north-east of Nontron, is a continuation of the Limousin. The climate is damp and the soil acid and siliceous, conditions unsuited to good farming, although in one or two places where soil erosion has broken down the hard rock, resulting in a workable soil, there are small farms growing wheat and potatoes; otherwise dairy farming is the main occupation. In the past, however, the peasants depended on the chestnut forests for their sustenance and their income (the place of the chestnut in such poor rural economies is discussed at greater length in the section on the Quercy). The Nontronnais is still one of the poorer areas of Périgord but modern farming methods are making it a better place to live. Apart from Nontron itself, the chief market centre is Thiviers, near which you will find one of the largest goose farms in the South-West where *foie gras* is produced for export all over the world.

South-east of the Nontronais is the start of the Causse de Périgord. This is an arid limestone plateau occupying the triangle between Périgueux, Thiviers and Thenon. Lack of water has meant that the *causses* have never been able to support a large population, although before the outbreak of phylloxera in the late 1870s vines were grown in the area.

The *vignerons* were saved from disaster by the truffle which, it so happened, was abundant at this time. The astute Périgourdins were able to exploit the situation and during the next thirty years or so the truffle reached a height of popularity in France that it has never known before or since. Now, of course, truffles are so expensive that most people consider buying them out of the question; indeed it is fashionable to sneer at these luxuries and pretend that they are not worth the high price demanded. But do not be deceived: if you have never tasted a fresh black truffle you cannot judge what you are missing. Those little black bits of rubber encased in soggy liver *pâté* are worlds apart from the fresh truffles that you buy and cook yourself. If you are interested in sampling the flavour, you can buy truffles much more cheaply in Périgord than at home, especially if you purchase them at the right time of the year, between November and March.

If you don't want actually to buy a truffle then you can certainly find out what they taste like by eating a dish flavoured with *sauce Périgueux* or garnished with truffles at a local restaurant, but don't do what is reported to have happened at an expensive restaurant at Domme, on the Dordogne, where an English visitor allegedly carefully extracted all the little black bits from a roast duck cooked with truffles and placed them at the side of his plate! Such a dish will be a little more expensive than usual but it certainly won't bankrupt you.

Truffles are sold in the markets of Périgueux, Sarlat, Thiviers and Excideuil in December and January. Much of the harvest is bought up by local firms and is destined to end up in *pâté de foie truffé* and other preserved meats and sauces. Since truffles do not stay fresh indefinitely most of the remainder is also preserved either whole or in other ways.

The best place to buy truffles is the capital of the region, Périgueux, which lies to the west of the Causse de Périgord on the river Isle. This small provincial town (population approximately 38,000) has two very interesting Romanesque churches, both domed, but its most remarkable features are its market and food shops. It is an amazing experience in a town of this size to find delicacies like *foie gras truffé*, *confit d'oie* and truffles displayed for sale on trestle tables in the market square behind the cathedral of St-Front. Nearby there is the retail shop of the famous *foie gras* firm Champion selling a range of luxury foods that even Fortnum and Mason would find hard to match. There is a permanent market open every day in the Halle de Coderc and here you will find the stall of Monsieur J.-C. Brusle. He will advise you on truffle buying, how long and under what conditions you should keep that precious black nugget. Monsieur Brusle also has on offer his own tinned *foie gras truffé*, *confit d'oie* and *de canard* and *rillettes d'oie*.

The truffle is a fungus that grows on the roots of trees, just below the surface of the ground. It is dark brown in colour and can be as small as a hazel nut or as big as your fist. The exterior of the truffle is rough and knobbly while the inside is veined like marble. There are some thirty varieties of underground fungi belonging to the truffle family or nearly related but only a few are used in cooking. The best truffle, with the finest perfume, is the black truffle of Périgord, *tuber melanosporum*. Its flesh is white in the summer, turns grey in the autumn and finally becomes black, with white veins in November when it is harvested.

Only a few of the remaining varieties of truffle are edible and their sale is strictly controlled. You may come across a dark brown truffle called *brumalée* in Périgord. It looks a little like *tuber melanosporum* but is not as dark and has a strong, musky perfume (*musquée*) which many people find quite unpleasant. The *brumalée* cannot be offered for sale as *truffe du Périgord*, this appellation being reserved solely for *tuber melanosporum*. There is also a white truffle (*tuber aestivum*), which is also found in the south of England, but this is much inferior to the black *truffe du Périgord*. Another variety is the *terfez*, known in Périgord as *nez de chien*: it is small and brown, smoother than the black truffle and has white flesh. The *terfez* always appears a year before the true black truffle and has earned the name 'false truffle'.

The appellation '*truffe*' or '*truffe du Périgord*' has been regulated since 1973 by the Centre Technique Interprofessionel des Fruits et Légumes (CTIFL) and the Centre Technique Interprofessionel des Conserves de Produits Agricoles (CTICPA). It can be applied to *tuber melanosporum* only if the truffles are sold fresh. The truffles must have been gathered in the prescribed manner using a pig or a truffle dog and the earth must have been carefully brushed off before they are sold. Over-ripe or soggy truffles must not be offered for sale as *truffes du Périgord*, while those that are broken, partly damaged or smell musty or stale have to be sold separately as *deuxième choix*, along with those that weigh less than 5 grammes. Dyeing, colouring or varnishing truffles is illegal, as is the trade in *chevillées*, truffles that have been broken and stuck together again.

Equally strict rules apply to preserved truffles, whether tinned or bottled, but batches of *tuber melanosporum* sold commercially for use in conserves are permitted to contain 2 per cent of other dark varieties. The lighter-coloured *tuber aestivum* is not allowed, however. No preserved truffle may be artificially coloured and all must be clean and washed before they are sold to the factories or shops that make the conserves. They must also be either brushed (*brossée*) or peeled (*pelée*) and even the parings that are sold must be clean and sound with no dirt or foreign bodies attaching to them.

Whole truffles, whether brushed or peeled, fall into three categories: *surchoix* are black truffles which must be ripe, but not over-ripe, with firm flesh and a round uniform shape; *extra* denotes truffles that are less black than the *surchoix*, but still of superior quality, although they may be less regular in shape; *premier choix* indicates a lighter-coloured truffle and even grey truffles are tolerated in this category (but this still does not include *tuber aestivum*). These categories apply to both fresh and preserved truffles but their importance is greatest when you are buying tinned truffles because here the label is your only guide to what you are buying, whereas when they are fresh you can see for yourself the quality on offer.

If the whole truffles are too expensive it is possible to buy small pieces: *truffes en morceaux* are prepared from dark-coloured truffles and the pieces must be at least 0.5 cm thick; *pelures* are truffle peelings and may include up to 3 per cent of varieties other than the black Périgord truffle; *brisures* are tiny bits and pieces and may contain other varieties than the black truffle up to a maximum of 5 per cent of the drained weight.

Additional information that may appear on the label is an indication of how often the preserved truffles have been boiled. *Première ébullition* means that the truffles have been cooked or boiled once only, thus ensuring a good strong flavour. It is possible to boil the truffles several times, the flavour declining correspondingly. Surprisingly, the two regulating bodies have not ruled on this practice.

Truffles are so expensive (a walnut-sized truffle cost over 30 francs in January 1980) that they should not be squandered on dishes that are good to eat on their own. If you are thinking of including truffles in a special menu you will need to allow at least 6 grammes per person and that is only sufficient for sauces or for a garnish; for omelettes you should allow 12.5 grammes per person, but if you have delusions of grandeur and wish to serve truffles on their own you will have to have 25 grammes per person and a healthy bank balance.

Magret truffé
A delicious recipe that uses truffles sparingly is breasts of duck with thin slices inserted into them. Breast of duck or goose is known as *magret* or

maigret in the South-West. It is considered the best portion and most good restaurants will ensure that anyone ordering *confit de canard* or *confit d'oie* gets a piece of *magret* as well as bits of the legs.

For *magret truffé* you should allow one breast or fillet per guest. As there are only two fillets per duck a big dinner party will use up a lot of birds, but you can spread the cost by buying the odd duck from time to time, slicing off the fillets and putting them in the freezer wrapped in an airtight plastic bag. The wings, legs and other bits and pieces can be served in a casserole to the family. The carcass should be boiled in a mixture of water and red wine to make a rich stock.

Start the preparations a day in advance. First make sure the duck is completely thawed out and then insert a slice of truffle under the skin in the centre of the fillet. Put the *magrets* in the fridge overnight in an airtight plastic bag so as to retain the fragrance of the truffle. Do not waste the juice in which the truffle is preserved but add it to the reduced stock to make a thin but flavourful gravy.

To cook the *magrets*, fry them quickly on both sides in goose fat (or lard) and arrange them in an ovenproof dish, skin-side uppermost. Cover with foil and cook in a low oven for between 30 minutes and 1 hour, or longer depending on how you like your fillets.

In a restaurant in the Pyrénées we have been served *magret* rare (*au bleu*) like steak; elsewhere it has been medium or well cooked. It is best not to overcook the *magret* for if you do both duck and truffles will lose flavour. Serve the *magrets* as a course on their own with perhaps some boiled new potatoes and salad to follow.

For the mirepoix
*500g (1lb) knuckle of veal or
  veal bones*
2 carrots
2 onions
2 sticks celery
500g (1lb) bacon, diced
*250g (½lb) fresh belly pork,
  diced*
Pinch thyme
2 bay leaves
*250ml (½pt/10fl.oz) Madeira
  or medium Cyprus sherry
  (which seems to work just
  as well)*
1l (2 pints/40fl.oz) beef stock
Cornflour for thickening

Sauce Périgueux

A relatively inexpensive way of introducing your friends to the flavour of truffles is to make a *sauce Périgueux*. You start by making what is known as a *mirepoix*. This is a sauce made from knuckle of veal or veal bones and a selection of vegetables. (If this sounds expensive remember that you can fish the pieces of meat out of the stock when cooked and serve them dressed with a *béchamel* sauce in vol-au-vent cases.)

Put all the *mirepoix* ingredients (except the cornflour) in a large saucepan and cook for at least 4 hours on a low heat. Strain. Put the stock in a saucepan and reduce by about half by boiling quickly. When you judge there is about $\frac{3}{4}$ of a litre left (about $1\frac{1}{4}$ pints/25fl.oz), thicken with cornflour and you have a classic *mirepoix* sauce, rich and brown. *Mirepoix* is an excellent standby; it will freeze well in small quantities and because it is so rich it can be diluted with thinner stock, water, red or white wine or even milk.

For the *sauce Périgueux* you will need one whole truffle the size of a large walnut sliced thinly. Alternatively you can use an equivalent amount of preserved truffles *en morceaux* or even the parings. Wash and slice the mushrooms and fry gently in butter or lard. Add the sliced truffles and simmer for another 10 minutes. Set the pan aside while you complete the sauce. Boil the Madeira and *mirepoix* sauce together until reduced by a quarter. At the last moment add the truffle and mushroom mixture, stir well and serve. It is important that the truffles are not overcooked or they will become rubbery and quite tasteless.

For the sauce
1 truffle, sliced thinly
250g (½lb) button mushrooms
100g (4oz) butter or lard
250ml (½ pint/10fl.oz)
  Madeira
250ml (½ pint/10fl.oz)
  mirepoix

There is no shortage of recipes for truffles in many good English and French cookery books but many of them seem over-rich as well as being prohibitively expensive. In fact the truffle's attraction lies in its unique perfumed aroma, which transforms a simple dish like roast chicken and is lost in more complicated concoctions. Nothing could be more delicious than a new-laid egg from a basket in which a truffle has been left for a few hours. The truffle scent will have permeated the egg through and through.

Truffles are harvested in November in the time-honoured manner using pigs, whose sensitive noses can detect the aroma of the fungus, even though it is below the surface of the ground. The animals become adept at finding the delicacy, which they enjoy as much as do their masters, and in the early days of their training they have to be forcibly restrained from eating them, but they soon learn to give up the truffles in return for a handful of maize.

The best truffles are found on the roots of oak trees. These grow well on limestone soils like those of the Causse de Périgord or the more extensive *causses* that lie to the south-east in the Quercy.

Because demand for truffles far exceeds supply, efforts have been made in recent years to increase production by planting fresh oak trees in these areas. The French Institute of Agronomical Research and a number of in-dependent researchers are working on the symbiotic relationship between truffles and oak trees; it seems that certain oaks provide the truffles with hydrocarbons, while the fungi provide the trees with mineral salts. It is now possible to buy truffle oak seedlings in plastic bags or pots grown from specially treated acorns from truffle-bearing trees. Planting them is an act of faith for it is impossible to predict for sure whether truffles will appear on the roots of the new trees or not. Even if they do it will not be for ten years, and it will be fifteen before there is a reasonable yield. The IFRA claims a high success rate; one can only hope that they are right and that larger harvests will eventually bring down the present exorbitant prices.

Périgord Blanc, which lies to the north of Périgueux, has more open countryside than the rest of Périgord and derives its name from the chalky hills and frequent limestone outcrops. The valleys of Périgord Blanc are green and lush, often with streams and rivers running through them lined with poplars. The rivers and streams were once full of freshwater fish but pollution and overfishing have reduced the stocks so much that fish farms are being established not only in Périgord but all over the South-West. At La Rochebeaucourt-et-Argentine, near Ribérac, the fishponds and the terracing of the fine Renaissance château have been made into a farm for écrevisses, the freshwater crayfish that is much sought after in this part of the world.

There are a number of classic *écrevisse* recipes, of which the best is probably *écrevisses à la bordelaise*: the crayfish are fried in butter with chopped carrots, onions, shallots and parsley, flambéed in armagnac and served with the juices and vegetables from the pan.

For *écrevisses à la nage* it is the *nage* that is important. Finely chop 1 large carrot and 2 onions and simmer in 250ml ($\frac{1}{2}$ pint/10fl.oz) of dry white wine and the same amount of water with a bouquet garni, a pinch of salt, 6 peppercorns, a crushed clove of garlic and a handful of chopped parsley. Let this simmer for about half an hour, before adding the crayfish. Allow to simmer for another 8–10 minutes. Serve as a soup with plenty of bread to mop up the *nage*.

Écrevisses à la marinière are browned in butter over a hot flame with finely chopped onion and celery and moistened with a little dry white wine. Add salt and pepper to taste and cook for about 10 minutes. Drain the *écrevisses* and arrange them on a plate while you reduce the liquid by about half. Add a knob of butter and pour over the *écrevisses* and serve decorated with a little chopped parsley.

The valleys of Périgord Blanc are for the most part given over to mixed farming, cereals and livestock predominating. The north-east of the area is another source of truffles. The delightful river town of Brantôme, with its fine Romanesque church, is one of the chief local markets for them, and its shops, although less sophisticated than those of Périgueux offer a formidable range of *pâtés* and conserves as well as fresh truffles at the right time of the year. Brantôme has a number of good hotel restaurants on whose menus trout, *écrevisses* and truffles have pride of place.

In striking contrast to the gentle landscapes of Périgord Blanc is the region of extensive forests known as Périgord Noir, so called because of its dark forbidding aspect. Périgord Noir stretches southwards from Périgueux to just east of Bergerac on the river Dordogne and south-east towards Sarlat. The soil here is infertile and in the past supported only a few isolated smallholdings in occasional clearings. The peasants, like those of the Nontronnais, depended chiefly on the byproducts of trees for their livelihood. They also gathered mushrooms for sale in the local markets, the *cèpe* being especially popular. It was a miserable existence, but since the last war things have improved: large areas of the forest have been cleared and given over to the growing of strawberries. This has proved to be a most successful cash crop and Périgord now supplies 15 per cent of France's total production. The chief centre is Vergt, just south of Périgueux. The strawberries start to appear in the markets in May and are amongst the first fruit and vegetables (*primeurs*) supplied to Paris and other parts of France.

The area around Sarlat, on the other hand, has always been famous for walnuts, although walnut trees are found all over Périgord, particularly in the valley of the Dordogne and east of the *causse* between Thiviers and Terrasson. In recent years plantations have been established south of Bergerac and further east in the Fôret de Belvès. Sarlat, however, has always been the chief market and as long ago as the seventeenth century was exporting walnut oil downriver to Bordeaux, and thence to Holland and England. Walnut oil is highly prized in France. It is very expensive but makes the most delicious salad dressing. It is too dear to waste in cooking.

The walnut harvest is in September and the Périgord produces between 6,000 and 8,000 tonnes a year, more than any other part of France. Most of the walnuts are sold direct to the merchants to make into oil. First, however, the shells have to be cracked: the merchants employ local women and in the autumn they are often to be seen sitting in the sun at the front door or on the porch cracking the nuts with mallets on wooden boards resting on their knees. They know just how hard to hit so that the shell falls into two parts.

The walnut grown in the Sarladais, the *corne*, has a soft shell which makes it relatively easy to crack without damaging the kernel, and so from the middle of the nineteenth century an ancillary trade in kernels for eating developed alongside the one in oil, the principal export market being Britain. Whole nuts are also exported, the *Grandjean* hard-shelled variety, found chiefly in the area east of the Causse de Périgord, being popular in Germany. *Grandjean* nuts are also sold to confectioners for decorating cakes and tarts.

The nuts that the farmers have not sold are spread out on wooden slats to dry in the sun and are then stored for the winter. Some, however, are cracked for eating or for pressing to make walnut oil. Many of the farmers have their own small presses; otherwise a local mill will oblige. Shelling the nuts is a good excuse for an evening get-together called the *énoisement*. The neighbours converge on the farm bringing their wooden mallets with them. The work of cracking, separating the kernels from the shells and sorting good from bad goes on to the accompaniment of roasted chestnuts, the new season's wine, gossip, songs and tall stories. The broken shells are good for lighting the fire but have no commercial value – friends of ours who moved into a farmhouse south of Sarlat found the cellar ankle-deep in them, presumably the result of many years' *énoisements*.

Nothing is ever wasted in France and the farmers' wives make all kinds of delicious drinks, not only from the nuts but the husks and leaves as well.

Our neighbour, Madame Artisié, has a recipe for using green walnuts with *eau-de-vie* and sugar. If you have no *eau-de-vie* you can use vodka instead. You must pick the nuts when they are green, towards the end of June or early July in England. You have to crush the nuts, no easy or clean task but made easier if you chop roughly by hand and grind the chunks in the mincer until the whole is a dark-brown mass of pulp. It is advisable to wear rubber gloves while doing this because the walnut juice will stain your fingers black. Using one part of the pulp to three parts *eau-de-vie* or vodka, put the quantities into a large stone jar and leave to macerate, closely covered, for at least three months. Filter the liquid and then mix in sugar to taste. Madame Artisié suggests that there are three degrees of sweetness: very sweet needs about 1kg (2¼lb) of sugar to 1 litre (2 pints/40fl. oz of the liquor; medium sweet needs 800g (1¾lb) per litre, and slightly sweet only 500g (1lb). You should allow a day or so for the sugar to melt in the liquid, stirring the mixture frequently. You can melt the sugar in water first and then mix this solution with the liquor, but Madame Artisié thinks this dilutes it too much and prefers to keep stirring. When the sugar is melted, bottle the liquor and leave for at least another six months in a cool dark place.

One evening when we were visiting her, Madame Artisié produced with great excitement a bottle of *eau-de-noix* that she had discovered in a cupboard in the loft; it was from the 1974 vintage, a very good year we were assured. When we left some of the treacly black liquid was poured into an empty sauce bottle for us to drink as a *digestif 'après la soupe'*.

Another delicious liqueur called *crème de noix* is made from fresh walnut husks. The husks are crushed in a mortar and the pulp emptied into an earthenware jar until it is nearly full. *Eau-de-vie* is then added until the pulp is covered. The mixture is left for a fortnight when the contents are poured into another similar jar through a muslin filter. The resulting black liquor is poured into bottles until they are three-quarters filled. The remaining quarter is filled with a syrup made by heating sugar and a little honey in *eau-de-vie*. The bottles are then corked and left to mature for at least six months. This liqueur is also called *brou de noix*.

Madame Barde, who has a *ferme-auberge* near Monflanquin, also has a recipe, this time for *liqueur de noix*: you need 20 tender green walnuts, cut into small pieces, 600g (1¼lb) of sugar, 2 cloves, ½ litre (1 pint) of *eau-de-vie*, 2 litres (4 pints) of a good red or *rosé* wine. Mix the whole lot together and make sure that the sugar melts. Allow it to macerate for two months before you filter and bottle.

An aperitif called *quinquina* can be made from walnut leaves. The leaves are dried for a few days in the sun until they are brittle enough to disintegrate when rubbed between the hands. Wine bottles are one-third filled with rubbed leaves and *eau-de-vie* is poured over them so that they are slightly more than covered. The bottles are left for a fortnight in a cool place and then the liquid is strained through muslin into new bottles which are topped with mulled wine and to which twelve lumps of sugar are added.

Many of these *apéritifs* and *digestifs* made from walnuts are on sale in the expensive shops that sell specialities of the area, but it is probably more sensible to try them out at a restaurant before buying a whole bottle.

You can also make a very good cake using walnuts. Here is Madame Barde's recipe:

Walnut Cake

For the *cake*: whip the egg yolks with the sugar until white and creamy. Add the potato flour, rum and crushed and chopped walnuts. Mix well. Beat the egg whites until firm and incorporate carefully into the yolk mixture. Turn into a buttered and floured cake tin and cook in a moderate oven for 45 minutes.

For the *cream*: mix the eggs, egg yolks and sugar in a basin. Add the flour. Moisten with hot milk and put on a low heat, stirring all the time until the mixture thickens and remove from heat. Melt the chocolate in a *bain-marie* with the butter and incorporate the still warm cream.

Cut the cake in two and spread the cream between the halves and all round the sides and the top. Decorate with walnut halves.

For the cake
6 eggs, separated
250g (½lb) caster sugar
2 tablespoons potato flour
1 tablespoon rum
200g (6oz) walnuts

For the cream
3 whole eggs and 3 yolks
200g (6oz) caster sugar
75g (3oz) flour
1 litre (2 pints) milk
200g (6oz) plain chocolate
tablespoon butter
Butter and flour for the mould
Walnuts for decoration

West of Périgueux is another heavily wooded region, the Double. Today this stretch of forest, studded with lakes, is a popular tourist centre for holidaymakers who like camping and caravanning and outdoor sports such as fishing, boating and horse-riding. Up to the last quarter of the nineteenth century the Double was a fever-infested area of stagnant lakes and marshes. It was not until the Trappist monks decided to found the monastery of Notre Dame de l'Espérance at Echourgnac in 1863 and began to show the few wretched peasants who lived there how to drain the land and improve their farming methods that this sad part of Périgord began to come to life Among the other contributions made by the monks of Echourgnac to the welfare of the Double was the production of cheese and this is still to be found today selling under the name of Echourgnac. It is made from cows' milk and is a mild flavoured cheese similar in appearance to St-Paulin, having a smooth orange or yellow rind and an ivory-yellow interior.

Bordering the Double to the south is the Landais which, like the Landes (see pages 161–171), has extensive pine forests, planted in the early years of the century when resin was in great demand.

The south-west of Périgord, in the neighbourhood of Bergerac, is altogether different. It is an attractive country composed of low rolling hills given over mainly to policulture: wheat, maize, tobacco, hay and above all vineyards. This is a very fertile part of Périgord and has a distinctly arcadian feeling to it, the farmhouses, fields of crops, vineyards and occasional cypresses all blending to produce a landscape reminiscent of Tuscany.

In this idyllic setting Périgord's finest wines are produced, amongst them one that is outstanding: Monbazillac. This sweet white wine is virtually unknown in Britain, although its reputation in France itself is high and it is also greatly appreciated in Holland and has been since the seventeenth century. Indeed, if we are to believe local tradition the wines of Monbazillac were highly thought of even in the Middle Ages. The story is told of a band of pilgrims in Rome who were presented to the Pope. 'We come from Bergerac,' said their leader, and when he saw that this awoke no response in the Pope added, 'from Bergerac near Monbazillac.' Immediately the Pope's face lit up. He raised his hand in blessing, murmuring as he did so, 'Ah, Monbazillac – an excellent wine.'

Monbazillac is made in the same way as Sauternes and, at its best, equals, all but the very finest of them. However this is difficult to prove for the best Monbazillacs are not easy to find. The ones readily available in Britain are usually not good examples, and even in Périgord it is not easy to find a really good bottle. Nevertheless it is worth the effort and the best thing to do is to go direct to one of the local *vignerons* for a tasting – you will not be disappointed. In fact there is every reason to suppose that the *vignerons* of the Sauternes learned the method from those of Monbazillac, for there is evidence to show that the fine sweet wines of Sauternes date only from the period of the Second Empire while those of Monbazillac can be traced back to the Renaissance. Sweet wines unfortunately have a bad reputation in Britain, being associated in people's minds with thin, sickly-sweet, straw-coloured wines with no particular flavour. These wines have been degraded by the indiscriminate addition of sugar. Nothing could be further removed from the smooth, mellow, aromatic wines of Monbazillac which, when they have matured, take on a deep orange tint.

Monbazillac is made from three grapes: Sémillon Blanc, Muscadelle and Sauvignon in the proportions two-thirds Sémillon, one sixth Sauvignon and one sixth Muscadelle. The Sémillon helps to make the wine mellow and gives it in part its unusual bouquet. The Muscadelle adds a scent of musk, while the Sauvignon also contributes to the aroma and adds finesse.

Making Monbazillac is a protracted and difficult business requiring great skill on the part of the *vignerons* combined with extreme patience and almost religious faith in the success of the outcome, for the grapes are left very late before harvesting. The *vendange* does not begin until 10 October at the earliest and can go on until the early days of December. By this time the grapes are over-ripe and begin to dehydrate, leading to a greater concentration of natural sugar. The process is accelerated by the presence of a mould on the skin of the grape called *Botrytis cinerea*, which produces a condition known as *pourriture noble* or 'noble rot'. The skins of the grapes become mottled with grey spots and then split and wither. At the same time chemical changes take place in the grapes themselves resulting in an increase in their pectin and glycerin content. It is these transformations that help to give Monbazillac its peculiar unctuous quality.

The *vendage* is not only very late but very slow. The grapes cannot be harvested until the *Botrytis cinerea* has done its work, but because the 'noble rot' does not attack all the grapes at the same time there have to be repeated pickings over a long period. To make the very finest wine the grapes have to be picked individually, a long, back-breaking business. And yet at the end of it all the yield is bound to be low because the *pourriture noble* reduces the quantity of juice that can be extracted from the grapes. Even in a good year the amount of wine produced is small, no more than 35 hectolitres per hectare. For this reason Monbazillac can never be a cheap wine, but it compares very favourably in price with Sauternes.

When the grapes are pressed the juice has the consistency of oil, hence the cry *pisso l'oli!*, meaning the wine will be of good quality. After pressing, the juice ferments furiously producing a frothing surface scum that looks like dirty snow. Frequent racking from barrel to barrel is needed to control the intensity of the fermentation and to keep the alcoholic and sugar content in balance. The wine begins to stabilize in February or March but even after this, unceasing care is needed if the quality is to be maintained right up to the time the wine is bottled. No wonder Monbazillac is not cheap.

The wine is made in the communes of Monbazillac, Pomport, Rouffignac, Colombier and a part of St-Laurent-des-Vignes. The vineyards run northward from an escarpment that overlooks the river Dordogne and Bergerac can be seen in the distance. On top of the escarpment is the Château de Monbazillac, a beautiful piece of Renaissance architecture commanding a superb view northwards over the Bergeracois. The château is maintained by the Coopérative de Monbazillac. You can have wine tastings there and buy bottles of wine, but alternatively you can visit one of the nearby domaines such as that of Cabaroque, where Monsieur and Madame Yourassovski-Cabane will be delighted to offer you some of their very fine wines and to show you their interesting seventeenth-century *chai* which they are busy restoring.

Sweet wines are usually served with a dessert in Britain, but the locals recommend Monbazillac as an aperitif, preferably taken with *pâté de foie gras*. It should of course be served chilled.

The other wines made in the Bergeracois are not in the same class as Monbazillac but are nevertheless certainly worth trying. We particularly like the wines of Montravel, which are light and fruity whites with a quite distinctive earthy tang. The Montravel area lies 40 kilometres west of Bergerac and just north of the Dordogne. Immediately next door are the Bordeaux districts of St-Émilion, Entre-deux-Mers and Ste-Foy-Bordeaux. The country here is very pretty, a gently undulating green landscape of small fields and vineyards. The wine is made in fourteen communes, amongst them St-Michel-de-Montaigne where the château of Montaigne, the famous essayist, still stands and still makes wine, just as it did in Montaigne's own day. Montaigne, who liked his glass of wine, once wrote: 'It is not right to enjoy wine in moderation; it makes it look as though you take this gift from God for granted!'

The vineyard area is 4,000 hectares, producing 180,000 hectolitres, but only 50 or 60,000 hectolitres are actually sold as wines of Montravel. These include Haut Montravel and Côtes de Montravel, both having a minimum alcoholic strength of 11 degrees and Montravel with a minimum of 10 degrees. All three make dry, semi-sweet and sweet wines from the usual trio of Sauvignon, Sémillon and Muscadelle grapes. We like the semi-sweet (*demi-sec*) best. Montravel also makes a *vin de l'année* called Vin de Maccadam, which like a Beaujolais *nouveau* is intended for drinking only a month or so after fermentation has finished.

Another unusual wine, Rosette, is made just north of the Dordogne in five communes on the fringe of Bergerac; Lembras, Creysse, Maurens, Prigonrieux-la-Force, Ginestet and in the commune of Bergerac itself. Confusingly, Rosette is a straw-coloured, semi-sweet white wine with a distinctive flavour of the Muscat grape, although the Sémillon and Sauvigon grapes are also employed. It is also quite heady having an alcoholic content of at least 12 degrees.

The Côtes de Bergerac–Côtes de Saussignac vineyards lie just to the west of those of Monbazillac. They produce a sweet white wine made from the same trio of grapes but with a lower permitted alcoholic minimum (12.5 degrees). The vineyard area is very small and production is limited. Nevertheless it is a good-quality wine with a growing reputation, but inevitably it is overshadowed by those of its illustrious neighbour.

The Côtes de Bergerac *môelleux* are sweet white wines made throughout the Bergeracois. The grapes used are the Sémillon, Sauvignon and Muscadelle and the strength varies between 12 and 15 degrees. Although similar in character to a Monbazillac they are not so full-bodied and lack the same finesse.

At one time Bergerac *sec* was as near as the Bergeracois ever came to producing a dry white wine. It is made from Sauvignon, Sémillon and Ugni Blanc grapes and must have less than 3 grammes of natural sugar per litre to qualify as *sec*. The minimum permitted alcohol content is 10.5 degrees. Nowadays, the local *vignerons* are meeting the demand for a drier wine by making a Bergerac Blanc Sauvignon. This wine is quite popular and is to be found in nearly all the local shops and supermarkets but it is not yet one of the recognized *appellation contrôlée* wines of the region.

The Bergeracois also makes a small amount of red and *rosé* wine (about 30 per cent of the total), using the Cabernet Sauvignon, Merlot, Cabernet Franc, Cot, Périgord and Fer grapes with Malbec predominating. These wines have much in common with the ordinary reds of Bordeaux, being light table wines without the high tannin content that makes for a long life. Much of it is sold in the local restaurants as house wine and as such it represents very good value. To qualify for the appellation 'Bergerac' the wine must have an alcoholic minimum of 10 degrees.

North-east of Bergerac, in the communes of Bergerac, Lembras, St-Sauveur and Creysse, are the vineyards of Pécharmant where the best red wine of the region is made. It has a considerable local reputation but so little is produced (only 4,000 hectolitres from 100 hectares) that it is hard to find and quite expensive when you do. It is made exclusively from Cabernet Sauvignon, Merlot and Malbec grapes and needs four years in the bottle to mature. It is a full-bodied wine having a minimum alcoholic strength of 11 degrees. We may have been unlucky but so far we have not been impressed by the odd bottle we have tried.

All the wines of the region may be sampled at the special tasting booth on the corner of the Place Docteur-Cayla in the heart of what is left of old Bergerac. It is next door to the headquarters of the CIVRB (Conseil Interprofessionnel des Vins de la Région de Bergerac), a very interesting old building with two beautiful first-storey wooden galleries dating back to the fourteenth and fifteenth centuries. Here you can obtain all the information you need about the wines of the Bergeracois. Below is a list of the leading estates in the area and the wines they offer:

Château de Monbazillac	Monbazillac
Domaine de Cabaroque	Monbazillac, Bergerac rouge, Bergerac rosé
Domaine de la Truffière et Tirecul	Monbazillac, Bergerac rouge Bergerac rosé, Pécharmant
Domaine de Fontdoules	Monbazillac (old vintages)
Domaine de Libarde˙	Haut Montravel and Montravel
Domaine de Jolis-Bois	Côtes de Montravel
Château le Roy	Haut Montravel Moelleux
Clos des Ganfards	Côtes-de-Bergerac–Cotes de Saussignac
Clos les Donats	Côtes de Bergerac
Château la Jaubertie	Bergerac blanc sec, Monbazillac, Bergerac rosé
Domaine de Maison-Neuve	Côtes de Bergerac moelleux
Domaine de la Barde	Côtes de Bergerac
Clos du Poncet	Bergerac, Monbazillac
Château de Planques	Bergerac
Chartreuse de Pécharmant	Pécharmant, Bergerac rouge and rosé Côtes de Bergerac, Monbazillac
Château de Tiregand	Pécharmant, Bergerac blanc sec de Sauvignon
Domaine de Haut Pécharmant	Pécharmant
La Rose de Tourmantine	Rosé
Château le Pontet	Sauvignon Côtes de Bergerac

There are also a number of good local co-operatives: Cave Coopérative de Monbazillac, Cave Coopérative de St-Vivien-de-Velines, Cave Coopérative Vinicole de Lamothe-Montravel, Cave Coopérative de Moncaret, Cave Coopérative de Sigoulès and the Cave Coopérative de Port-Ste-Foy.

During the period of the *vendange* in the Bergeracois meals are large and have many courses: picking grapes is no job for a weakling. The day begins early, as soon as the dew has gone, but first the pickers are fortified with the *sagranada* or *saugrenée*, a bean stew with tomatoes and potatoes and garnished with chopped garlic, parsley and salt belly of pork. At midday there is the *soupe des vendangeurs*: this consists of a mixture of cheese, toast and onions simmered with the stock from a *pot-au-feu*.

Soupe des vendangeurs

Peel and chop 500g (1lb) of onions and fry until brown in a good thick frying pan using goose or pork fat. Moisten with stock from the *pot-au-feu* and simmer gently for at least half an hour, strain and set aside to keep warm. Prepare several slices of toast with really stale bread (you should have enough slices to half-fill your soup tureen), grate 500g (1lb) of strong cheese and put in the tureen a layer of toast, a layer of cheese, a layer of toast and so until the tureen is half full, Pour the onion stock over the bread and allow it to soak in. Cover with a layer of grated cheese and some knobs of butter. Put the tureen in the oven for 40–45 minutes until the top has formed a good crust. Just before serving take one egg yolk per person, beat well in a serving bowl with the same number of glasses of red wine, a pinch of salt, some freshly ground pepper and nutmeg. Both the tureen and the serving bowl are placed in front of the head of the house who mixes the *soupe* and the egg-yolk mixture into each person's bowl as he serves them.

All over the South-West it is the custom to finish off the last dregs of *la soupe* (for more about *la soupe* see page 142) by pouring some red wine into the bowl raising it to the lips and draining it straight off. This practice is known as the *chabrol* or *chabrot*, although in the Rouergue it is called *lou sabrot*. No one seems to know the origins of the word; some say it is derived from the Limousin dialect *beure a chabro* (*boire comme les chèvres*) or it may be from *sabrous* (*savoureux*) or even from another similar dialect word *sabros* or *soubro*, meaning 'leftovers'. There are also those who think the word is derived from the mediaeval *saburra*, a nasty granular sandy deposit in the stomach, the theory being that the *chabrol* helped to dissolve it. If this is true it adds a whole new meaning to St Paul's injunction, 'take a little wine for thy stomach's sake'.

When the pickers have finished work for the day they can indulge in two or three helpings of *la soupe des vendangeurs*, followed by *charcuterie*, thick slices of home-cured ham, perhaps an *enchaud* (see page 121), various kinds of *daube*, cheese, salad and of course some of the best grapes. The last meal of the *vendange* is something special: it is the *gerbe-bande*, *gerbande* or *lou gargabande*, a kind of farewell similar to a harvest-home supper. *Pot-au-feu* is followed by *fricassée* of chicken or rabbit with a rich sauce, roast chicken or leg of mutton with garlic and haricot beans, followed by cheese and a *tourtière* to finish with. The constituents of the meal naturally vary from farm to farm but there are always plenty of courses and generous helpings to

Château d'Yquem in the
Sauternes (Bordelais) where the
greatest sweet white wine of
France is made

The grape harvest, Côtes de
Buzet (Agenais)

Truffle-hunting with a pig in Périgord
Below A goose farm in the Quercy

The market at Villeneuve-sur-Lot
Below Plum orchards in the Agenais   *Overleaf* The tourtière-maker (Agenais)

Distilling armagnac. Unlike Cognac, France's other great brandy area, there are few big firms in Armagnac, but hundreds of small ones, each jealously guarding its independence
Overleaf Garlic on a farm in Armagnac

Making cheese from ewes' milk in Béarn. Much of this cheese is sent to the caves at Roquefort to mature.
Below Curing a country ham in the Rouergue
Overleaf Peppers drying in the sun at Espelette in the Pays Basque

satisfy the gargantuan appetites of the pickers. Similar meals are provided during the *vendange* on farms or at châteaux all over the South-West. Unfortunately labour costs are now so high that there is a growing tendency to bring in machines to do the work so the hearty grape-pickers' supper may soon become a distant memory in all except the poorest parts of the region.

Although the Bergeracois is best known for its wines, it does also have a famous local dish, the *enchaud*. This is a loin of pork, boned, rolled and roasted and served hot or cold, either with juices from the roasting pan or with cold jelly. A number of restaurants in the area offer *enchaud* as a speciality, but should you wish to try it you are advised to book both the restaurant and the *enchaud* a couple of days in advance for the pork needs to stand for at least twelve hours before roasting. The Conseil Inter-professionnel des Vins de la Région de Bergerac in the Place Docteur Cayla at Bergerac has a list of the restaurants specializing in the *enchaud* with a useful map to help you track it down. The *enchaud* is usually served with fried potatoes or whatever fresh vegetables are in season. At the Hotel Le Cyrano in Bergerac you might find *pommes sarladaises* (potatoes with truffles) as an accompaniment, while at the Restaurant La Grillade, also in Bergerac, the *enchaud* is served with *pommes forestières* (diced potatoes with morels fried in butter.

Enchaud

To cook an *enchaud* for six to eight people you need 1.5kg (3¼lb) of loin of pork, boned and with the rind removed. Make sure your butcher lets you have both bones and rind to help you make the pan juices rich and succulent.

The previous day, peel and cut into slivers four cloves of garlic. Lay out the pork on a flat surface and insert the slivers of garlic into the meat using a sharply pointed knife to make the incisions so as to help the garlic penetrate the meat. Sprinkle with salt and freshly ground pepper and roll the loin on itself, tying it securely. Set aside overnight in a cool place, covered with a damp cloth. The next day melt two tablespoons of pork fat or lard in a roasting pan and brown the pork loin on all sides for about 25 minutes. When the *enchaud* is nicely brown, add a cup of water to the pan, together with the bones, a sprig of thyme, the rind, a pinch of salt and some freshly ground black pepper. Cover with cooking foil and roast in a slow oven for about 1½ hours. The cooking should be slow but regular.

When the *enchaud* is cooked take the dish out of the oven and remove the bones, the sprig of thyme and the rind. Remove as much fat from the juices as you can before serving the pork hot with the juices as gravy. If you want to have the *echaud* cold with salad, then remove the pork from the pan and pour the juices into a small dish. Allow both joint and juices to cool thoroughly before slicing the pork and chopping the jellied juices.

If you are presenting your *enchaud* cold and you have time to prepare the jelly in advance, try cooking the bones with a pig's trotter, a bay leaf, salt, pepper and a little pinch of ground cloves with enough water to cover. Allow this to simmer gently for 4–5 hours, then remove the trotter and bay leaf and let the juice set to a jelly. The next day when you are cooking the *enchaud*, you can use this jelly instead of water to moisten the roasting process, and the trotter you can eat with a spicy *vinaigrette* sauce to sustain you during the preparation and cooking of the *enchaud*. If you are feeling really rich and just happen to have a truffle to hand, you can dispense with the garlic and substitute slivers of truffle.

In the south of Périgord, quite near the fine *bastide* town of Monflanquin, is the *ferme-auberge* run by Madame Barde and her daughter. *Ferme-auberges* are a relatively new category hotel, consisting of working farms with one or two guest rooms and sometimes a restaurant as well. Conditions are strictly regulated by the government and the proprietors must stick to the rules or lose government approval. The *fermier-aubergiste* must welcome the guests simply and naturally in the true spirit of the countryside, 'thus enhancing and improving the image of the peasant's life style'. The food served to the guests must as far as possible be based on the best produce of the farm itself. It is no good looking for lobster or caviar in a *ferme-auberge*, but you can rely on getting authentic local cooking served to order. In most cases a *ferme-auberge* will not have a menu and you will have to order in advance, but going over the menu of your choice with the *patron* is half the fun!

Madame Barde is in her seventies and yet still copes with a busy summer season of guests and *pensionnaires*. In her parents' days ten or twelve geese were all that the farm could support; now Madame Barde has 270 geese, 250 ducks and some guinea fowl as well. With her daughter Madame Serres she makes all her own *pâtés* and *terrines*, preserves her own *foie gras*, makes her own puddings for her guests and has a fine selection of home-made wines and liqueurs.

Our first visit to Madame Barde's *ferme-auberge* was for one of her glorious meals. We started with *tourin périgourdine* (described by Madame Artisié in the chapter on the Agenais as *tourin à la tomate*) served in an enormous tureen – of course it was so good we had second helpings and one of the party even managed a third. Then home-grown melons appeared, a whole melon each, filled with port wine. Before we were even half-way through, another dish was brought to the table: a large portion of home-made *pâté de foie truffé*.

For the next stage we had ordered *omelette aux cèpes*. It came hot and creamy to the table, stuffed full of *cèpes*. We took some time to savour fully the taste and texture of the omelette and the *cèpes*, mopping up the juices left on the serving dish with fresh crusty bread. Home-made *confit de canard* was the main item on the menu. After some discussion we had decided our *confit* should be grilled, and served with the traditional fried potatoes. The portions were generous – was it two or three each? By this time we had begun to lose count of who had eaten what.

From the beginning of the meal we had been drinking the farm wine, light and red and the ideal accompaniment to the excellent local produce. As each carafe was sunk, another took its place. A green salad followed the *confit*, the dressing and crispness of the lettuce contrasting with the richness of the *confit* and fried potatoes. Then there was the cheese board, with a range of six or seven local cheeses including two varieties of goats' cheese – a flat round creamy *petit chèvre* and a more mature roll with a layer of rich creamy cheese inside the crust.

The grand finale was the *tourtière* (more fully described in the chapter on the Armagnac). The art of making and rolling the rich flaky pastry as thin as a *voile de mariage* is one which few practice nowadays. Fortunately, in a nearby village lives one of the few tourtière-makers in the area: we bit into the crusty, succulent, prune-filled, armagnac-flavoured pastry and sipped more armagnac in tiny glasses. The bottle was left on the table in case we should feel able to cope with a second round, and Madame Serres hovered round as our plates grew emptier, hoping that we would take more *tourtière*, but alas, we had no more room except for coffee. At last we shuffled into the moonlit garden and listened to the quiet cackles and squawkings of the geese and ducks in their enclosure.

Our autumn visit to the farm was a sequel to that marvellous meal, but this time we went to find out as much as we could about the secrets of *foie gras de canard* and *d'oie* and Périgourdin cooking.

It was a quiet period in Madame Barde's life: because of poor summer weather the maize was late and would not be harvested for another three weeks. Until then Madame could not start fattening the ducks and geese. Afterwards she would be occupied boiling the maize and feeding her chosen birds three times a day. This process is known as the *gavage*, the overfeeding of a duck or goose so that its liver grows large and fat, out of all proportion to the bird's size; this is the famous *foie gras*. The practice of *gavage* is very ancient and goes back at least to the Romans, who fed their geese on figs.

If you are beginning to wonder whether the *gavage* is a form of cruelty and how normally sensitive human beings can maltreat birds for their own depraved tastes, you will be in the company of many other doubters. French animal welfare organizations keep a close eye on the practice and in 1975 a special enquiry was mounted into the whole business, but the investigators were unable to find any proof of cruelty. Indeed they had to confess that the birds appeared to enjoy being overfed; the boiled maize seems to act like a drug and the birds become addicts. Madame Barde herself rejects any idea of cruelty. She maintains that only certain birds are suitable for *gavage*: they need to be temperamentally and physically adapted to take the food three times a day from the same person in a quiet calm atmosphere. The birds will not accept food from a stranger; even a member of the same family cannot be a substitute when it comes to the daily *gavage*. Madame Barde feeds her special geese for three weeks or a little longer; she needs at least four weeks for the ducks. After that the birds are killed and opened. There is no guarantee that the liver will be worth the trouble, but a careful choice of bird in the first place and astute judgement about the exact day when the liver will be at its peak are part of the instinctive knowledge of the *foie gras*-producer.

Once the *foie gras* are laid out in the farm kitchen, Madame selects those most suitable for processing. Some will be preserved whole in tins or preserving jars; others will be split up into chunks and then surrounded with minced pork and fat to make a *pâté de foie gras*. The best livers are those weighing about 600–800g ($1\frac{1}{4}$–$1\frac{3}{4}$lb). Although some reach 1kg ($2\frac{1}{4}$lb) or more, these are generally considered to contain too much moisture and to have less flavour and a more spongy texture.

A series of local and regional fairs are held throughout the South-West in December at which prizes are presented for the best *foies gras*. Stalls are set up in the local markets at which the farmers' wives display their achievments alongside those of specialist producers like Delpeyrat of Sarlat or Champion. Housewives move from stall to stall, carefully scrutinizing the colour, size and price of each liver. The best *foie gras* is generally held to come from the Toulouse goose, a handsome bird, with beautiful subtle light-brown plumage on its back and wings and white feathers underneath. It is the largest and heaviest of the three kinds of geese from which *foie gras* is obtained in the South-West, weighing on average 11kg (about 24lb). The smallest goose is the one found in the Landes which only weighs about 7kg (15lb); in between comes the Masseube goose from the Armagnac country (the Gers) which is about 8–9kg (about 18–20lb). All three produce excellent-quality *foie gras*.

Despite assurances about the health and happiness of the geese, you may well feel qualms about buying a whole fresh liver: if nothing else the price is likely to deter you. The answer is to buy tins or jars of preserved *foie gras* which, while still not cheap, will mean that you can buy a smaller quantity. However, it is important to read the labels so that you know exactly what you are buying. If the label says '*foie gras au naturel*', this means that the liver is in one piece or several pieces unmixed with any other kind of meat. It may or may not be flavoured with truffle; if it is, the word '*truffeé*' will also appear. The label will also tell you whether the liver comes from a goose or a duck. You will also find mixtures of whole pieces of liver encased in a covering of minced pork or veal. This casing must not amount to more than 25 per cent of the total weight. Such a mixture may be variously described as a *bloc, lingot, massif, parfait, pâté, pavé, rocher, rondeau, roulade, suprême, terrine* or *tombeau de foie gras d'oie* or *canard*. There is a less rich *pâté de foie d'oie* or *de canard* which may include a minced meat filling amounting to 50 per cent. The clue is the omission of the word *gras* on the label. *Crêmes, purées* and *mousses de foie gras* consist of mashed and pounded liver to which is added not more than 25 per cent of forcemeat. *Crêmes, purées* and *mousses de foie d'oie* or *de canard* can have up to 50 per cent of forcemeat. If truffles are included the percentage will be given '*truffé à 5 pour cent*' and so on.

Many French people prefer the half-preserved (*semi-conserve*) *foie gras* which must carry the date on which the liver was processed, but you must keep it in a refrigerator. These particular *foies gras* are often sold in attractive porcelain or earthenware *terrines*.

Although the production of *foie gras* plays such a major part in the economy of Périgord and other parts of the South-West, France as a whole produces only 40 per cent of her needs; livers are imported from Hungary (33 per cent), Israel (13 per cent) and a number of other countries. Although the French naturally claim that their *foies gras* are the best, those from Hungary are excellent and command the same high prices.

As with the pig, no part of the goose is left unused: the skin of the neck is stuffed with a good mixture of minced pork and veal, enriched with minced goose, flavoured with garlic and herbs and cooked in broth as sausage. It can be eaten hot or cold. The gizzard, heart, wings and feet are delicacies which can be stewed in an *alicuit* (from *ailes cuites*), while the head forms the basis of a good stock. The blood is made into flat round cakes (*sanguettes*) which can be sliced and fried in goose fat. You may well see them for sale in the local markets and *charcuteries*.

But the best parts of the goose, other than the liver, are usually made into another of the South-West's best known specialities, *confit d'oie*. Once the goose has been killed and plucked, the blood is drained into a bowl, the bird cut into manageable pieces and as much fat as possible trimmed off. The meaty parts, including the neck and the giblets, are put in layers in a box of rough salt, about 25g (roughly 1oz) of salt to a pound of goose. At this stage you can add a sprinkling of powdered thyme and bay leaves, although Madame Barde disapproves of the practice. The goose pieces are left in salt for about thirty-six hours, after which they are shaken and brushed well to remove the surplus salt.

The fat is put into a large cooking pot (a *marmite*), hanging over the open fire in the hearth, with a little water and left to melt and sweat over a low heat. Once the fat is simmering the pieces of salted goose are added. The meaty parts of the breast and legs will need to cook over a moderate heat for at least two and a half hours, but the stuffed neck, the wings, gizzard and giblets should be taken out earlier. The way to tell if the goose is done is to take a straw and try to pierce the flesh: if the straw goes in easily the goose is ready. Remove the *marmite* from the fire and take out the pieces. Put them into a tall earthenware pot, packing them well in and keeping the giblet bits in a separate pot from the breast and legs. The gizzards are usually packed together as are the hearts, the wings and the rest. Pour the top fat off into a thick saucepan and set aside for later. The rest of the fat with the juices, the bits of fat (the *grillons* and *grillettes*) and the other bits left in the bottom can be poured over the giblets to seal the pots from the air. The better fat that was set aside is reserved for the leg and breast pieces and the gizzards. First, however, you must boil the fat again in the pan until the surface is covered with thick bubbles and the fat below is clear. Remove from the heat and allow to cool a little, then pour over the pieces of goose in their pot. When quite cold cover with clean greaseproof paper and store in a cool place.

Removing a piece of *confit* from its pot is simply a matter of putting the pot in a warmish place and allowing the fatty covering to melt very slightly so that you can fish out as many pieces as necessary for the particular dish you are preparing. But about May the following year you will need to boil the whole of what remains of the *confit* again for about twenty minutes, which will ensure that it lasts through to the next autumn, if necessary. *Confit* may be eaten fried, grilled or cold. It is an excellent accompaniment to a picnic.

All the while that we sat discussing the cooking of Périgord with Madame Barde, she was pouring out a succession of tiny glasses of home-made liqueurs. Apart from her *liqueur de noix*, mentioned above, Madame Barde has two more favourites: *liqueur des îles* and Anisette or *liqueur d'anis*. The islands of the *liqueur des îles* are those of the French Caribbean, Martinique, Guadeloupe and other French territories in the Antilles, which have become synonymous with citrus fruit (*les agrumes*).

Liqueur des îles

1kg (2lb) sugar
1l (2 pints) eau-de-vie (45 degrees) or vodka
130ml (⅓ pint) boiled, cooled milk
1 orange
1 mandarin
1 lemon
2 sticks vanilla

Cut the fruit into rough pieces, add sugar and mash with a fork. Stir well so that the sugar melts. Add the milk and *eau de vie* and let the whole mixture macerate, covered, for about a fortnight in a large earthenware pot. Then filter and bottle. Allow the bottles to stand for about a year if you can in a cool place. The liqueur will be clear and golden and have a marvellous fruity fragrance.

Liqueur d'anis

2l (4 pints) eau-de-vie (45 degrees) or vodka
1kg (2lb) sugar
60g (2oz) aniseed grains
30g (1oz) coriander
½ teaspoon powdered cinnamon
Good pinch mace

You can obtain the aniseed grains from the oriental spice section of good food stores or, if you are in France, from the *pharmacie*. Put all the ingredients into a large earthenware jar or pot, cork firmly and allow to infuse for a month; then filter into bottles and cork securely. It should be ready for drinking in four to six months. A liqueur d'anis makes an excellent end to a meal – and to a chapter!

Quercy

IF YOU DRIVE eastwards from Villeneuve-sur-Lot towards Cahors, taking the D661 south of the river Lot, you will pass first through a broad fertile valley with rich fields of crops stretching up the hills on either side and beautiful farms often with imposing pigeon towers proclaiming their owner's prosperity. After about twenty minutes you will see ahead of you a hill town called Tournon d'Agenais which commands splendid views of the surrounding lush valleys.

East of Tournon the road climbs and suddenly the landscape changes: you are now on an undulating plateau covered with small oak trees, blackthorn and juniper bushes. The soil is thin and in places barely conceals the white limestone that lies beneath. There are farms here and there but they are smaller and the stony fields are clearly harder to work. This is the Quercy where limestone in one form or another dominates the landscape. The limestone was laid down during the second geological era, about 200 million years ago, when this part of the South-West was covered by the sea. Limestone is porous and much of the Quercy consists of arid plains, known as *causses*, where the water has sunk straight through the limestone to form underground rivers and streams that find their way to the surface many miles away. Some of these underground systems are accessible from the surface and have become tourist attractions. The most famous of them is the Gulf of Padirac, north of Rocamadour, where after a descent by lift you can take a boat voyage through a series of spectacularly beautiful caves.

For the most part, the *causses* lie east of a line roughly defined by the Route Nationale 20 and running from Souillac in the north, southwards to Cahors, the capital of the Quercy, and on over the river Lot to the small town of Caussade, north-east of Montauban. The thin topsoil and lack of water on the *causses* has meant that they have never been able to sustain a large population but, inhospitable though the landscape may appear to be, the many ruined farmhouses and collapsed dry stone walls of numerous small fields are ample evidence that the land was once worked and produced a reasonable living. In fact until the coming of the railways in the 1870s the *causses* had a reputation for prosperity that seeing them today it is hard for us to understand. The area was known as the 'Pays Fromental' because the soil was good enough to grow wheat, from which white bread could be made. This was in contrast to the Ségala of the Rouergue, to the east, whose sour soil produced only rye. The *causses* grew vines, some fruit as well as wheat, and there were also large flocks of sheep. But this apparent prosperity was only enjoyed by a few well-off farmers and was based on the unremitting hard work of the peasant labourers. So long as the *causses* remained cut-off from the rest of France, with the rivers as the chief means of communication with the outside world, their enclosed economies worked. The area was self-sufficient and many small market towns grew up serving local needs. But as soon as the railways were built the temptation to leave and seek easier pastures was irresistible and the population declined rapidly. The process was accelerated by the spread of the phylloxera, the disease that killed off the vines in nearly all of France during the 1870s, and more farms were abandoned and fell into ruin while the woods and scrub began to take over the hard-won clearings once more. In recent years many of these farms have been bought as holiday homes, for to urban man the wildness of the landscape of the *causses* has a strong appeal.

The *caussenards* who remained took advantage of the *fin-de-siècle* truffle boom, grubbed out the diseased vines and planted truffle oaks (the fact that truffles could be induced to grow in areas where the soil was known to be suitable had been discovered as long ago as 1810 by Joseph Talon a native of the Vaucluse who did not share his secret, however, until 1851). As a result the Quercy, although not so well known for truffles as Périgord, became a major producer of this rare delicacy. In Sauzet near Cahors there is even a truffle co-operative. Where truffle trees were not planted the areas previously devoted to crops became pastures for sheep and goats. There are still large flocks of the hardy sheep, the famous Caussenards du Lot, although their number has declined from 500,000 head in 1850 to 150,000 today.

The Causse de Martel, which lies north of the river Dordogne and stretches into the Périgord and the Limousin, is a little more fertile than *causses* further south. Cattle are raised here as well as sheep and a popular cheese, Bleu des Causses or Bleu de Quercy, is made from skimmed cow's milk and matured in local caves. It is blue-veined, wheel-shaped and strong-smelling, with a savoury flavour and is similar in character to the better-known Bleu d'Auvergne. The capital of the Causse is the small market town of Martel which is a centre for truffles and walnuts. The liqueur *eau-de-noix* is made and sold there and it is well known for conserves, especially *foie gras truffé*. Martel is an interesting old town with a sixteenth-century town hall and a fine fortified church which has a beautiful sculptured porch depicting the Last Judgement, an appropriate theme perhaps, since it was in the near-by Maison Fabri that Henry Court-Mantel, the rebellious son of Henry II of England, died in terror for his soul, having come here immediately after sacking the sanctuary of Rocamadour, one of the great pilgrimage centres of the Middle Ages.

The shrine of Rocamadour clings precariously to a sheer cliff face 120

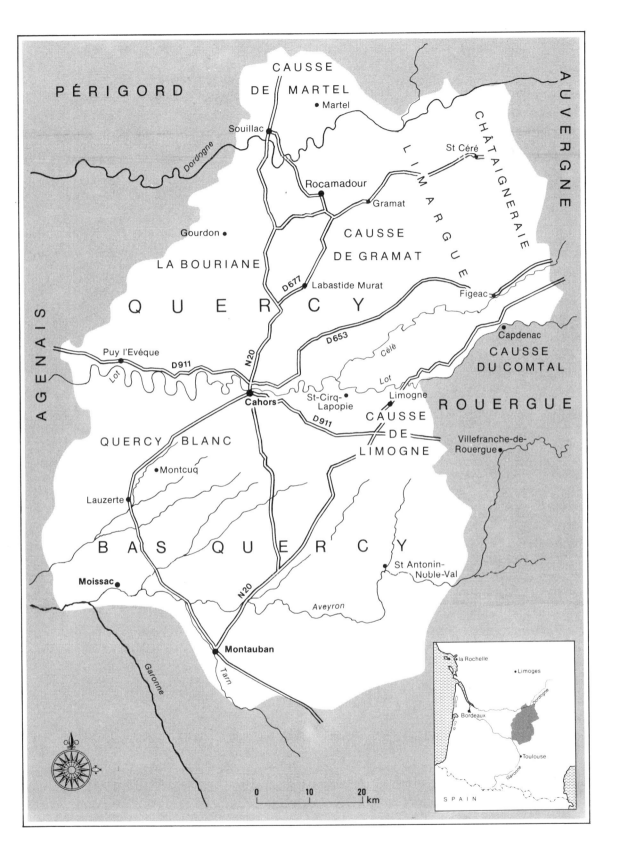

CAUSSE DE MARTEL

Martel

Souillac

Rocamadour

Gramat

St Céré

CHÂTAIGNERAIE

L I M A R G U E

Gourdon

LA BOURIANE

CAUSSE DE GRAMAT

D677

Labastide Murat

Figeac

Q U E R C Y

D653

Célé

Capdenac

CAUSSE DU COMTAL

Puy l'Evéque

D911

Lot

N20

Lot

Cahors

St-Cirq-Lapopie

Limogne

R O U E R G U E

D911

CAUSSE DE LIMOGNE

Villefranche-de-Rouergue

QUERCY BLANC

Montcuq

Lauzerte

B A S   Q U E R C Y

St Antonin-Noble-Val

Moissac

N20

Aveyron

Montauban

Tarn

Garonne

P É R I G O R D

Dordogne

A U V E R G N E

A G E N A I S

0   10   20
km

la Rochelle

Limoges

Bordeaux

Dordogne

Toulouse

Garonne

S P A I N

metres above the small village which straggles along the cliff foot. It is a superb site that makes Rocamadour one of the great tourist attractions of the Quercy. The surrounding country is barren and sparsely populated for this is the Causse de Gramat, the largest of the *causses* of the Quercy and, for those who crave solitude, the most spectacular. It stretches from the river Dordogne in the north to the river Célé, a tributary of the river Lot which it joins just east of Cahors. The Causse de Gramat is not a place to look for gastronomic delights but it produces a cheese known as Cabecou de Rocamadour, of which we are very fond. It is made from sheep or goat's milk and has a nutty flavour that is more pronounced in the goat's cheese. It is small, not more than 5cm (2in) in diameter, and weighs about 25g (1oz). It should be eaten as fresh as possible, which should not be difficult since it will be easy to find, sold by the local farmers themselves in the market of Rocamadour and elsewhere. If left too long the cheese becomes dry and unpleasantly strong. Sometimes it is sold wrapped in chestnut leaves, when it is called Picadou. South of the river Lot, is the third of the great *causses* of the Quercy, the Causse de Limogne. Large stretches of this *causse* have been planted with lavender, a cash crop which is sold to the makers of toilet waters.

In contrast to the inhospitable landscape of the *causses*, the river valleys are often fertile and intensively cultivated. The Quercy is crossed from east to west by three major rivers, the Dordogne, a short stretch of which cuts through the north of the region, the Lot, from which the modern department derives its name, and the Aveyron in the south. Of these by far the most important is the Lot (the 't' is pronounced as in the English word 'hot'). In its upper reaches the Lot flows through narrow gorges with occasional castles perched on sheer crags at vantage points where their garrisons could command the river traffic. Just upstream of Cahors is St-Cirq-Lapopie, an attractive old village built on the steep cliffs on the south bank of the river.

Not far west of St-Cirq-Lapopie the river Lot leaves the confines of the gorges and begins to meander from side to side of the widening valley in a series of gigantic horseshoe loops. Tucked tidily inside one of them is Cahors, the ancient capital of the Quercy. In the thirteenth century, Cahors was one of the great cities of Europe, its wealth largely derived from commerce and usury, the latter practice earning its citizens a place in the seventh circle of Dante's Inferno wearing purses round their necks. Cahors' preeminence was lost when England defeated France at the battle of Poitiers and took control of the Quercy for a time. But Cahors remained an important local capital, situated as it is at a crucial river crossing connecting Brive in the north with Montauban and Toulouse in the south and with the river Lot itself forming a major route to Bordeaux in the west. With the coming of the railways, however, Cahors found itself isolated from the main traffic routes and today it is no more than a provincial town.

Nevertheless, Cahors is well worth a visit. It has the finest mediaeval bridge in France, the Pont Valentré which dates from 1308 and is fortified with three formidable towers. There is also a domed Romanesque cathedral with a fine sculptured north porch depicting the Ascension. Hard by the cathedral is a good covered market selling chiefly fruit and vegetables and where at the right season you can buy excellent strawberries and asparagus.

Cahors is hemmed in to the north and the south by bleak limestone hills, but despite their inhospitable appearance they produce one of the best wines of the South-West, the famous 'black' wine of Cahors. It is, as the name suggests, a dark red robust wine, high in tannin which gives the wine a touch of astringency and means that it takes several years to mature. At least, that was its traditional character. Unfortunately the *vignerons* of Cahors, like those everywhere else in France, can no longer afford to wait for their wine to reach its peak and have changed the constituent grapes to help the wine mature earlier. The chief grape variety is, and always has been, the Auxerrois, which in the Gironde is called Malbec. Cahors wine must contain at least 70 per cent Auxerrois grapes.

In the past the Auxerrois was mixed with a grape called Jurançon Noir, but in recent years this has not been planted because it is rather prone to rot. Instead a hardier grape, the Tannat, which is the chief constituent of Madiran (a robust red wine made near Pau), is now used, together with Merlot which tempers the harshness of the Auxerrois and helps the wine to mature earlier. The *vignerons* have also reduced the minimum alcoholic strength of Cahors to 10.5 degrees, although most of the bottled wine has a strength of 11.5 degrees. As a result of these changes the character of Cahors has been subtly altered. Like the best clarets the old Cahors wines had amazing longevity and sometimes did not reach their peak for twenty years or more; a bottle of 1945 Clos de Gamot that we opened in 1970 was magnificent. All the astringency had disappeared leaving a mellow, still fruity wine, the equal of all but the finest clarets.

Clos de Gamot is owned by Monsieur Jean Jouffreau who in 1971 acquired Château du Cayrou, a vineyard of 37 hectares which at that time was lying fallow. Monsieur Jouffreau is a firm believer in quality before quantity and has replanted 30 hectares of Château du Cayrou according to traditional methods. Each vine is laboriously trained on seven wires in such a way as to give all the grapes an equal amount of sun and so that those at the bottom are not hidden in the shade. This method also helps to aerate the vines and to prevent mildew and other diseases. The mixture of grapes is also close to traditional usage with 70 per cent Auxerrois, 20 per cent Merlot, $7\frac{1}{2}$ per cent Tannat and $2\frac{1}{2}$ per cent Jurançon. The methods employed by Monsieur Jouffreau are painstaking and laborious but his reward is a really excellent wine in the traditional manner.

At the other end of the scale is the Cave Coopérative de Parnac, also called La Cave des Côtes d'Olt. This was founded in 1947 at a time when the local *vignerons* were at a low ebb; for many of them a co-operative venture like this meant the difference between abandonment of the land and survival. The venture proved extremely successful and now over half the growers in the region belong to the co-operative, which markets its wine under the label of Les Côtes d'Olt. It is possible to buy the wine in plastic containers holding 10, 26 and 32 litres, or, if you prefer, you can take your own barrel or some other container to be filled. There are various grades of wine: the cheapest is a *vin ordinaire* for everyday drinking, but the most expensive, the *supérieur*, is suitable for laying down. Good vintage years such as 1971 or 1975 need at least five years to show their true worth. If opened too early the wine will still taste bitter.

Cahors wine has a long history. The vines were originally brought from Italy by the Romans. During the Middle Ages, Cahors was one of the Haut-Pays (the highlands) wines that competed with those grown in Bordeaux. After the marriage of Eleanor of Aquitaine to Henry Plantagenet, later Henry II of England, had added the Duchy of Aquitaine to the crown of England, the shrewd *Bordelais* merchants took advantage of the English connection to build up a flourishing wine trade with large fleets sailing to England each autumn loaded with the new season's wine. It was discovered, however, that the full-bodied Haut-Pays wines travelled better than the lighter clarets and were preferred to the Bordeaux wines. In fact there are records of Cahors being imported into England as early as 1225. As has been said the Bordelais used their influence with the English court to protect their interests and obtained a charter preventing wines from outside the Bordeaux region from being brought into the city between 8 September and St Martin's day (11 November); in other words the Haut-Pays wines were deliberately excluded from the city until after the Bordeaux vintage had been harvested and shipped to England. To counter this *Bordelais* monopoly, the Haut-Pays wine-growers were forced to ship their wines down the Garonne to St-Macaire (which was outside the control of Bordeaux) and thence across land to the free port of Bergerac on the Dordogne, which flows into the Gironde below Bordeaux. In this way the Haut-Pays wines bypassed Bordeaux, but the route was longer and the Haut-Pays producers were at a definite disadvantage. Even so the popularity of the heavier Haut-Pays wines forced the *Bordelais* to purchase them to blend with their own lighter product.

After the end of the Hundred Years' War in 1453, the black wine of Cahors became better known in France itself, especially when Francis I chose to plant vines from the Quercy in the grounds of his palace at Fontainebleau, under the supervision of *vignerons* from Cahors. By the seventeenth century the fame of Cahors wine had spread as far as Russia, and Peter the Great kept some in his cellar. The painter Ingres, who was born in Montauban, helped to make the wine of Cahors better appreciated in Paris by insisting that a daily supply was essential for his good health.

Ingres died just ten years before the arrival of the destructive aphid, the phylloxera, which in 1877 wiped out the vineyards of the Quercy. The vineyards were replanted once the remedy had been discovered (see page 30), but the total area was much reduced from the original 25,000 hectares, producing a million hectolitres of wine a hundred years ago, to a mere 4,000 hectares today, of which only 1,200 produce *Appellation Contrôlée* wines. This is not necessarily a great loss, since many of the vineyards before the arrival of the phylloxera must have been tiny and the wine they produced of inferior quality. Nowadays quality control is very much stricter. The best vineyards are situated, as they always were, on the slopes immediately south of Cahors itself, but good wine is also made further west near Puy l'Évêque, another cliff-top village commanding a fine view to the south over a well-farmed stretch of the Lot valley. Cahors was generally regarded as the senior VDQS wine in France until it was promoted to full *Appellation Contrôlée* status in 1971.

The reputation of Cahors wine is well established and you will find it on sale throughout the South-West. *Vin de paille*, by contrast, is so rare that it is difficult to find even in the Quercy itself. In fact, we had given up all hope of ever tasting it when an English friend, Peter Holt, who lives near Gourdon, gave us the tip that it is still made at Queyssac-les-Vignes, a hamlet in the extreme north of the Quercy, about 20 kilometres north east of Martel. Despite its name, there are few vineyards to be seen at Queyssac, the area having never fully recovered from the phylloxera blight, and it took some time to find anyone who knew where *vin de paille* was made. At last, after several false starts, we tracked down Monsieur Soursac. Even now our troubles were not over for Monsieur Soursac spoke a dialect so thick that we had great difficult in understanding him at first. He explained that a number of local farmers made the wine but on a very small scale and purely for their own use. The name derives not as we had supposed from the colour of the wine but from the fact that at one time the grapes were spread out on straw to dry. *Vin de paille* is made from a variety of local grapes and according to Monsieur Soursac it does not matter very much which are used – this after all is not an *Appellation Contrôlée* wine. They are picked late, from towards the end of September up until the end of October. Instead of the wine being made right away, the grapes are spread out to dry, but nowadays shallow fruit trays are used rather than straw. The grapes remain in the trays until they are quite dry before they are pressed. In practice this means the New Year, sometimes as late as February. By then the sugar content is very high and the fermentation takes a long time, perhaps as much as six months. The wine is matured in the cask for two years before it is drunk. *Vin de paille* is a strong, sweet red wine that reminds one distantly of port, although it is not fortified of course. In most years it reaches a strength of 15 degrees, but a really good vintage can be as high as 20 degrees. We were lucky enough to be able to buy a bottle from Monsieur Soursac's small stock. Drunk like a port at the end of a meal we found it very good. *Vin de paille* also goes very well with the delicious orange-fleshed charentais melons.

West of Cahors, the river Lot continues to loop its way through a fertile valley full of prosperous-looking farms. The alluvial soil here is rich and the farming has much in common with that of the Dordogne valley to the north, as does the cuisine. Mixed farming holds sway and cereals, fruit, vegetables and tobacco are all grown as well as some excellent asparagus, which is well worth looking out for in the local shops and markets.

South of the river, between Cahors and Puy l'Éveque, lies Quercy Blanc, a region of limestone hills, intersected by lush valleys, which stretches south-westwards towards the rivers Aveyron and Tarn. Quercy Blanc, together with the Lot valley itself, is the most fertile part of the Quercy and its mild climate means that here, as in the nearby Agenais, fruits of all kinds ripen well. Cherry, plum and peach orchards are common and a wonderful sight in the spring.

Near Moissac you will find a delicious dessert grape called the Chasselas. Over 40,000 tonnes of Chasselas grapes are produced every year, most of them finding their way to Paris where their lightly perfumed flavour is much appreciated. If you are in the area, Moissac is not to be missed: the abbey church of St-Pierre has what is probably the most famous Romanesque cloister in France, while the main porch contains some of the greatest Romanesque figure sculpture.

In the extreme north-east of the Quercy is the Châtaigneraie, so called because of its extensive chestnut forests. This fragment of the Massif Central consists of a plateau of between 400 and 600 metres in height, but with outcrops of over 700 metres in places, sloping towards the south-west and riven by the deep gorges of the rivers Lot, Célé and Cère. Until the end of the nineteenth century the tiny population lived a miserable existence. The acid soil and humid climate meant that the only cereal that could be grown was rye. Before the introduction of potatoes at the end of the eighteenth century chestnuts were an important part of the peasants' diet, replacing even bread when times were hard. The nuts were collected and soaked for two or three weeks in large barrels and then taken out and dried in the sun; if the weather was bad they were dried in ovens. After this they were piled up in the granary where it was dry and where they would keep for several months. The chestnuts that went bad were used to feed the pigs and chickens and the rest were ground to make flour or used in soups or stews.

Eugène le Roy gives a vivid description of a peasant's frugal main meal in his novel *Jaquou le Croquant* which is set in the Fôret Barade in Périgord, where, in the early years of the nineteenth century, conditions were much the same as in the Châtaigneraie:

> After putting the soup tureen on the table my mother served my father and me first and then herself and we began to eat with relish, all three of us

being very hungry, especially my father who had spent nearly the whole night out in the open. When he had drunk his two large plates of soup, mixing the last of it with some wretched thin wine, my mother removed the brown earthenware plates, took the pot that the chestnuts had been cooked in off the hook and strained the steaming chestnuts onto the coarse grey linen tablecloth. Cooked chestnuts are good while they are still fresh, but once they have been dried it's not the same thing at all. But there it is! You have to eat them dried because it is impossible to keep them fresh for ever. So we ate them all the same with root vegetables cooked in the same pot as the chestnuts and picked out the worst to feed the chickens.

The chestnut tree is not native to France. It comes originally from Asia and was cultivated in Italy by the Romans who introduced it to France. Until the arrival of the potato from the New World, the chestnut was one of the principal resources of the South-West, but potatoes were a more convenient vegetable and cereals, especially maize, also became important in the rural economy. In the last century blackspot and a canker infection ravaged the chestnut trees. A systematic destruction of the chestnut woods then took place, transforming the countryside. In many areas the old forests have given way to the open country where machines can be brought in to cultivate the soil or plantations of quick-growing pines have been introduced to meet the heavy demand of modern industry for soft woods.

Thanks to the *marron glacé*, however, chestnut trees are beginning to be planted again. Close enquiries among our French friends about the real difference between a *châtaigne* and a *marron* drew puzzled frowns: surely a *marron* was the fruit of the horse chestnut, the *marronier*, (*Aesculus hippocastanum*) and everyone agreed this was inedible; the *châtaigne* was the fruit of the *châtaignier* (*Castanea vesca*), the sweet chestnut, and very good to eat. What about *marrons glacés* we asked and the frowns increased: the *marron* was only a name for the very large sweet chestnut it was explained. Both answers were probably right; some varieties of the chestnut tree are prone to septate (*cloissonier* in French) which means that several little nuts form inside the prickly shell instead of the single large fruit so prized by the food industry. The single large nut is much more the shape and size of the *marron*, the fruit of the horse chestnut, and hence the likely transfer of the name to *marrons glacés*.

France imports 65 per cent of her chestnuts for *marrons glacés*, but although consumption is increasing French production declines year by year. The gap is now so great that there are hopes that chestnut-growing may revive and have a future in France. Apart from the value of the nuts, however, the chestnut tree had many other uses: the leaves were spread as winter feed and litter for the cattle, while the wood was used for pit props, barrel hoops, stakes for vines and furniture; resin was extracted from it and finally it could be burned as charcoal.

The new chestnut plantations were started for the sake of the wood, for no one thought at the time there would be a demand for the nuts themselves. Two of the new varieties are M15 and AW74, both of which produce excellent wood, but also give good-quality nuts as big as the Italian variety which are imported to make *marrons glacés*. The smaller chestnuts which you may see in the markets are likely to be wild chestnuts with several little nuts inside one spiny case compared with the single large nut in the cultivated variety. One ten-year-old tree will yield 12–15kg (27–33lb) of nuts; a hundred trees can yield 1.5 tonnes fetching 4.5 francs a kilo. Even allowing for the cost of gathering, this can make a sizeable income. Machines are being introduced which will cut the costs of labour and there are high hopes that the decline of the beautiful chestnut forests of the South-West has been arrested.

Preparing chestnuts is always a tiresome task and we have had all kinds of different suggestions for the best way of getting rid of the brown skin and bitter inner layer (the tanin) while keeping the nut itself in one piece.

One traditional solution is to take off the outer brown skin with a knife and put the chestnuts in boiling water for ten minutes. Take them out, put them in a plastic bucket and stir them with an implement called the *bouiradour*, an ingenious device made of two pieces of notched wood fixed together in the middle to make a cross. You won't have one of these, of course, but you could try two wooden spoons tied together with stout thread instead. If this does not work, then you will need to risk burning your fingers for the bitter inside skin has to be removed while the chestnuts are still hot. Another method is to tie them up securely in an old piece of sheeting and let them revolve in the washing machine for a few minutes! In any case you need to pick each one over by hand to ensure that the nuts are free from tannin. If, as seems likely, you do not have the time to peel your own chestnuts, try stocking up with a few tins; you can buy canned whole chestnuts as well as chestnut purée.

If you are lucky enough to be in Quercy in the autumn you might well find chestnuts on sale in the markets, already prepared and ready for use. In that case it would be an idea to put some in a *bocal*, a preserving jar with a rubber flange and metal clip. Take care not to fill the jar too full or to squash the nuts. Use a new rubber flange, close the jar and sterilize in boiling water for a good half hour. If water has got into the jar, open it within a day or two as the chestnuts are probably spoiled.

Chestnut garnish

250g (½lb) potatoes per person
1 small carrot
6 peeled chestnuts per person
Goose fat or lard for frying
1 clove garlic, finely chopped
Handful chopped parsley

One of our favourite recipes is whole cooked chestnuts mixed with pieces of cooked potatoes, rounds of carrot and garnished with garlic and parsley. Cook the vegetables slowly until they are almost done. Drain well and put a generous amount of goose fat (or lard) into a deep frying pan. Add the cooked vegetables and allow them to brown in the fat. Drain again and arrange in an ovenproof dish. Mix in the garlic and chopped parsley. Stir round well and put in a warm oven to allow the flavours to mature. Serve with plain roast or grilled meat.

Gâteau de marrons au chocolat

This is another delicious recipe and was given to us by Madame Athannassoff, a Parisienne married to a Bulgarian now retired and living in the Quercy near some English friends. We went to see her after we had sampled her *gâteau* at our friends' house. She thinks the recipe is an old one. Prepare the chestnuts by removing the skins as described above. Do not worry if they break up. Put them into boiling water and simmer gently until they are cooked but not too soft. Drain well and put them into a bowl which will fit on top of a saucepan of hot water. Crush the chestnuts while they are still hot (but do not mash to a pulp) and add the butter. The exact quantity of butter depends on how stiff the mixture is; Madame Athannassoff insists it must be very stiff.

1kg (2lb) chestnuts
125g (4oz) soft butter
4 tablespoons sugar
½ cup hot milk
Vanilla essence
Melted chocolate or chocolate cream
Walnut halves to decorate

Stir well with a wooden spoon or fork and keep the bowl over the hot water to ease the stirring. You will find that the chestnuts absorb the butter and it becomes a nutty paste. Mix the sugar with the hot milk (if you have vanilla sugar that is best, but if not add a couple of drops of vanilla essence). Stir the milk and sugar into the chestnut paste and mix really well. Butter a soufflé dish or a charlotte mould and pour in the mixture, piling it well into the dish and giving it a cake shape – slightly higher in the middle than at the edge. Leave in a cool place or in the fridge overnight.

Next day unmould the cake and arrange it on a flat plate. Cover the cake with melted chocolate or chocolate cream (see page 115) and decorate with walnut halves.

Monsieur Athannassoff thinks the cake would be all the better for a spoonful or two of armagnac, but Madame sniffs disapprovingly.

Châtaignes blanchies

Cover the bottom of a thick saucepan with a few fig leaves and then a layer of peeled chopped potatoes mixed with peeled chopped turnip. Add a cupful of water and the peeled chestnuts wrapped in a clean cloth. Cover the saucepan closely (make sure it is quite airtight) and cook very slowly for half an hour. The chestnuts can be served as they are, with poultry, or you can make a white sauce using the water they have been steamed in. Try them mixed with brussels sprouts.

If they have broken up mash them and mix well with the cooking liquid, some fresh breadcrumbs, salt, pepper and a beaten egg together with either the juice of half a lemon or the grated rind of a whole one; this will make a stuffing for chicken (add a little milk if you need extra liquid). You can use the potato and turnip blended with a little milk to add to the stuffing or as the base of a white sauce.

Life in the Châtaigneraie has improved since the days when chestnuts were the staple fare. Better farming techniques and the use of lime and chemical fertilizers have resulted in good harvests of hay and other fodder, as well as crops of corn and potatoes, and this is now cattle country. Even so, the area has suffered from depopulation; there are no large towns in the area but Sousceyrac (population 1,044) has a famous restaurant, Au Déjeuner de Sousceyrac, which rates a Michelin star and offers among its specialities truffled sweetbreads.

Sandwiched between the Châtaigneraie and the *causses* to the west is a narrow strip of land called the Limargue. It runs slightly east of south from Bretenoux on the river Cère to Capdenac on the Lot. It is the most fertile part of the Quercy north of the river Lot itself, for the soil is enriched by the alluvial deposits of four rivers as they emerge from the confinement of the gorges of the Châtaigneraie into the plain. St-Céré, with its winding mediaeval streets full of half-timbered houses and the imposing ruins of a feudal stronghold dominating it from the hill above, is one of the most attractive towns of the area. It lies on the Bave, a delightful trout river which is a tributary of the Dordogne. Further south is Figeac on the river Célé, an important market centre for the area which, although it has some old buildings, has suffered more than St-Céré from development. The Limargue has rich fields growing a mixture of crops and tobacco alongside orchards, vineyards and walnut plantations.

The hills round Figeac used to be covered with vineyards before the phylloxera aphid arrived on the scene. Wine was so plentiful in those days that the local innkeepers charged a standard two sous to passing travellers for as much as they cared to drink. Afterwards the land was desolate for many years and although some vineyards have been replanted, the wine production is only a tiny fraction of what it once was. However, a man of Figeac told Edward Harrison Barker, when he visited the town in the late 1880s, that the phylloxera had probably saved many lives because previously the locals drank wine at all hours of the day and afterwards when water became the common beverage the death rate dropped noticeably!

The Bouriane, a hilly well-wooded region that lies in the north-west of Quercy borders the Sarladais region of Périgord. Oaks, chestnuts and pines cover much of the land and forestry plays an important part in the local economy, although mixed farming is also carried on in the narrow winding valleys and occasional clearings.

The largest town of the Bouriane is Gourdon (population 5,000) which in the Middle Ages had a much greater importance than it does now as is shown by its imposing Gothic cathedral of St-Pierre. Today Gourdon is no more than a small rural market centre specializing in the sale of cattle, walnuts and chestnuts. The town is built on a small hill giving extensive views northwards towards the Sarladais.

The Bouriane has a cold damp climate that encourages the growth of fungi, and local tourist signs proudly display a picture of a mushroom to remind visitors that this is a good place to look for *cèpes* and other delicacies of this kind.

In France the *cèpe* (*Boletus edulis*) is the most celebrated of all the edible fungi and its appearance in the early autumn is as eagerly awaited as the strawberry season in England. The first *cèpes* usually arrive in the markets at the beginning of October and are easily identifiable by their brown skins, fleshy caps and yellowish-beige spongy undersides instead of gills. (The name, by the way, comes from the patois *lou cep*, 'the cap', meaning the floppy beret that is worn throughout the South-West.) If you are buying *cèpes* in the market, choose those with round dark caps and thick stalks; small ones are also preferable to large ones since these tend to be spongy and are more likely to have little white worms in their tubular undersides. The sister of a French farming friend always took part in the family *cèpe*-hunting expeditions and consumed with great enjoyment the *cèpe* dishes her mother cooked, until one day she saw an elderly *cèpe* in the saucepan being skimmed of the little white worms that can infest the underside of the flesh. This put her off *cèpes* for life, but the reader need not worry; the worms can easily be dealt with by plunging the mushrooms into boiling water with the juice of a lemon and a pinch of salt, poaching them gently for a few moments and skimming off not only the worms but also the bits of leaves and grass which might be sticking to them. If the *cèpes* are young and fresh, all you need to do is to scrape them clean of the bits of leaves and twigs. However if the idea of the worms still worries you, then scrape off the underside and just use the caps and stalks; it seems a pity to waste any part of the *cèpe* but better that than miss the experience of tasting *cèpe* for the first time.

Authorities are divided about the need to blanch the *cèpes* before cooking them; some say that this spoils the flavour, but blanching makes them more tender and also shortens the cooking time. You can of course strain the liquid through muslin and reduce it to a few 'spoonsfull' for use as a moistener in the cooking of the *cèpes*; or you could use it as a *court-bouillon* for poaching fish, or in soups.

Cèpes à la bordelaise

The most famous *cèpes* recipe is *cèpes à la bordelaise* which, despite its name, is not exclusive to the Bordeaux region but will be found, with many variations, throughout Guyenne, wherever *cèpes* grow in fact. It is usually served as an accompaniment to roast meat dishes instead of a vegetable.

Prepare your *cèpes* by cleaning and blanching them in 500ml (1 pint/20 fl.oz) of boiling water to which you have added the juice of a lemon and half a teaspoonful of salt. Simmer gently for 5 minutes, drain well and pat dry with a paper towel. Remove the stalks, and chop the tender inside with the stalks.

Up to this point most recipes agree but Alcide Bontou in his book *Traité de cuisine bourgeoise bordelaise* (1921) describes how he introduced *cèpes* to Paris restaurants in the 1880s and how the Parisians could not get used to the classic Bordelais mixture of oil and garlic. Butter was substituted for the oil and many recipes now replace the chopped garlic with chopped shallots. The classic recipe, however, should contain several cloves of garlic, finely minced, mixed with the chopped stalks of the *cèpes* and fried gently in hot olive oil with a handful of chopped parsley. Add the caps of the *cèpes*, cut crosswise to make large slices, and cook slowly in an earthenware dish in a medium oven for at least an hour. Before serving mix in the juice of a lemon and thicken with some fresh breadcrumbs.

Cèpes gasconnes

This is an alternative recipe which comes from a delightful book called *La Bonne Cuisine Méridionale de Tante Gracieuse: de Bordeaux à Menton*. Tante Gracieuse was a great Bordelaise character who cooked and served *la cuisine méridionale* for over forty years. Her book, which appeared soon after the war, was based on a series of famous broadcasts that she made on Radio Luxembourg from 1935 up to the outbreak of war.

To make *cèpes gasconnes*, clean and prepare the *cèpes* as before. Mix the chopped stalks with small pieces of lean ham or bacon and fry gently in olive oil. Slice the caps and add to the mixture. Simmer gently for about an hour. Serve very hot.

Tante Gracieuse also gives a recipe for *cèpes au gratin de la girondine*. This is the same as the *cèpes gasconnes* recipe but with the addition of a glass of dry white wine incorporated in the cooking and, a few minutes before serving, some breadcrumbs sprinkled on top and the dish browned under the grill.

Madame Léon Daudet (Pampille) in her book *Les Bons Plats de France* describes the idea of substitutes for the oil/garlic mixture as a *monstrueuse hérésie*! If, however, you find the idea of *cèpes* and garlic repellent, then by all means try the more genteel recipe with shallots. For 500g (1lb) of *cèpes* allow 2–3 small shallots. Chop the shallots finely and sweat in oil with the chopped stalks for 5–10 minutes in a covered pan. Serve hot with chopped parsley as a topping. This is a good dish which allows the flavour of the *cèpes* to come forward.

However, with *cèpes*, you really do not need either garlic or shallots. Try cleaning them carefully with a dry cloth and separate the caps from the stalks. Put the whole caps under a hot grill, first one side then the other: this will help dry them and make them less slimy and will also bring out the worms, should there be any, in the tubes. Cut up a piece of ham (*jambon de Bayonne* or a piece of green bacon) and fry gently in oil. Add the whole heads of the *cèpes* and the sliced stalks and cook for 20 minutes. Add salt and pepper to taste and chopped parsley. Turn off the heat and cover the pan. You should prepare this dish as long in advance as you can; the flavour will improve and you can reheat the pan gently about 10 minutes before you need to serve. You can cook the whole amount of *cèpes* together in one go and keep what you don't eat until the next day: it will be even better next time.

One word of warning about *cèpes*, they do not seem to like pepper, nor should you add more salt than is necessary. Let people add their own at the table.

Salade aux girolles

The *girolle* or *chanterelle* (*Cantharellus cibarius*) is a beautiful mushroom, apricot in colour and with a large curving trumpet, something like an old gramophone horn. The underside is finely ribbed in a manner reminiscent of Gothic fan vaulting. The name *girolle* seems to be interchangeable with *chanterelle*.

Girolles have a fine flavour. Try them in a *salade aux girolles*: you need a crisp heart of lettuce, cleaned and chopped. 300–400g ($\frac{3}{4}$lb) of *girolles*, 1 shallot, a few chives, 150g (5oz) of sweetbreads, about 100g (3$\frac{1}{2}$oz) of butter, 1 tablespoon of olive oil, 1 tablespoon of vinegar, and salt and pepper. Prepare the sweetbreads by blanching and removing the veins and membranes; press the water out and then slice the sweetbreads. Cook the blanched sweetbreads with half the butter in a frying pan; cook the *girolles* separately with the rest of the butter in another pan. Put the chopped lettuce in a salad dish, arrange the sweetbreads and *girolles* in the centre and cover with a good *vinaigrette* mixture using the chopped shallot, the vinegar and the oil. Season to taste and serve.

Morels (*Morchella esculenta* and *Morchella vulgaris*) are also much sought after in France. They can be easily recognized by their brown, cone-shaped, honeycombed cap with its spongy texture.

Apart from the common field mushroom, which is exactly the same as our own variety, these are the best of the edible mushrooms, and all of them can be bought dried in packets and tins. There are, of course, many other varieties, all of which are assiduously hunted by the French. However it would be tedious to list them all and anyone who wants to pursue the matter further is advised to read Jane Grigson's admirable book *The Mushroom Feast* which describes the main edible varieties and how to cook them. The classic botanical book on the subject is James Ramsbottom's *Mushrooms and Toadstools*.

Each autumn the local pharmacies display lurid colour photographs and charts of the toxic species and the *pharmacien* himself will always give advice on doubtful cases. The local library will usually have a book on mushrooms which will give the French names as well as the Latin and this also helps in identification; but if you are not an expert the best advice is to buy your mushrooms in the market. The trade, like that in shellfish, is strictly regulated and the gruesome accounts of poisoning encountered in the local papers always concern people who have picked wild mushrooms in the woods and, through lack of knowledge or carelessness, chosen poisonous varieties. It is really a matter of commonsense.

The peasants of the Quercy traditionally ate four meals a day, starting with *lo soupo*, a bowl of soup and a glass of wine, for breakfast. At ten came *l'esprontina*, which was soup again. At four o'clock they stopped work for *los quatre ouros* or *le gouter*. This was the main meal of the day with soup as the first course followed by a main course of chicken or ham and then cheese, fruit or nuts. Finally, at the end of a long day in the fields, they sat down to *lo soupo*, soup yet again and perhaps some ham or a boiled egg. The exact times varied of course according to the season of the year and so did the content of the meals, depending on the part of the Quercy where the peasant lived and how well off he was. In a very poor area like the Châtaigneraie the meals would consist of soup and little else and malnutrition was a serious problem. The inhabitants of the river valleys, on the other hand fared much better and had more substantial meals.

Today, *lo soupo* matches the *petit déjeuner* at about eight in the morning. The principal meal of the day is now *l'esprontina* which starts about midday or soon after and lasts a good two hours. This is a point to remember if you are in the Quercy, for not only must you be prepared to have your lunch earlier than perhaps you would in Britain but the meal itself is usually a copious four or five courses; what is more you may well find it difficult in country areas to dine out in the evening, the midday meal being the time the restaurants can expect a regular clientele. *Los quatre ouros* and the final *lo soupo* have been merged in some families into *le souper* eaten at a time to suit the work in hand, which could mean six o'clock in the winter when the animals have been attended to, or at nine or ten at night in the summer months. One of our farming friends in the Agenais was working late in the fields one July when we called. He came in at 10.30pm and sat down to a large bowl of soup, full of bread and vegetables, followed by a boiled egg into which he carefully chopped two cloves of garlic; he then rubbed a third clove of garlic on to a piece of bread, carved a good portion from a round black-skinned cheese from the Pyrénées and ate it with the *pain frotté*. Liberal glasses of his own rough red wine washed down his *souper* and then he turned in straight away: he had to be up at four next morning.

Clearly soup played an important role in the peasants' diet, not only in the Quercy but throughout the South-West, but it was not what we think of as soup. It consisted of a bowl of meat stock or vegetable water thickened with stale bread. *La soupe*, the bread, was an essential ingredient because it was a main source of calories and filled the stomach quickly. Bread was usually baked once a fortnight and soon went stale but it was too precious to waste, however old, and even if it went mouldy it all ended up in the soup. No wonder then that *la soupe*, that precious slice of bread, came to be synonymous with the steaming bowl of stock thickened by bread, potatoes or chestnuts. It formed the simplest of meals: '*Fenno, trempo la soupo*' ('*Femme, trempe la soupe*') was the peasant's instruction to his wife as he came in for his breakfast after a good two hours' work with the animals or in the fields. The *soupe* was quickly ready and his wife would have made enough for it to be served again at lunchtime. What was left in the earthenware pot was slipped into the great box-bed under the eiderdown to keep warm until the family came in from the fields for the evening meal.

Our English trifle, with its cream, sherry, sponge cake and custard, might seem far removed from the French peasant's *soupe* but the idea is the same. Trifle is known in France as *la soupe anglaise* (*zuppa inglese* in Italy) because the cake is soaked in fruit juices and sherry, just as the stale bread (*la soupe*) is soaked in stock.

A more nutritious meal than *la soupe* is *potage*. This is stock thickened with puréed and mashed vegetables and is closely related to the *pot-au-feu* and the *potée* and other stews, casseroles and stocks with a meat or fish base. *La soupe* and *potage* nowadays form a separate course at the start of the meal; the *pot-au-feu* and *la potée* are complete meals in themselves. The *garbure* of Béarn and the *poule-au-pot* are other examples of the meal-in-a-soup type of cooking. Today most of our soups come from packets but we could do worse than revive the old custom of the stockpot. With the new style crockpots and slow cookers (new only because they depend on electricity instead of the low steady heat of the coal- and wood-burning stoves and open fires) even the working wife and mother can produce economical and nourishing meals without being tied to the cooker; if you have a 10–12 litre saucepan, or one of the really big French *faitouts*, try this *plat complet*.

Pot-au-feu aux quatre viandes Serves 4

Put 2 litres (4 pints/70–80fl.oz) of water in a large cast-iron casserole or an enamel *faitouts* and bring to the boil. Add the shin of beef with salt and pepper and skim when the water has started to boil again. Reduce to a simmer and add the pigs' tails and the herbs, cloves and bay leaf. Cook for about 1 hour in a slow oven or on a slow heat on top of the stove. Now add the veal and the belly pork and continue cooking for another hour. Then add the chicken and the chopped vegetables and cook for another hour. At this stage you can leave the whole lot to cool and heat it again just before serving. If you are using a slow cooker or a crockpot, you need to cook everything except the chicken for 8 hours on a slow heat. Fry the chicken pieces and cook in the frying pan, covered for half an hour, before adding to the *pot-au-feu* for a further hour at high heat. Warm a large serving plate and a soup tureen (or you can use the cooking pot as a tureen if you ladle the meat and vegetables onto a deep serving plate). Serve the liquid to start the meal with croûtons or toasted bread sprinkled with grated cheese; then follow with meats and vegetables served with gherkins and mustard and sprinkled with freshly

500 g (1lb) shin or shank beef in a piece
1 knuckle veal, chopped
1 pig's tail per person
1 chicken cut into quarters
125g (4oz) salt belly pork
2 cloves
Salt and pepper
Mixed herbs
1 bay leaf
4 carrots
4 leeks
2 small turnips
1 onion
1 stick celery
2 cloves garlic

chopped parsley.

This *pot-au-feu* is also known as *bouillon de noce* and once formed an essential part of the wedding-day meal, but the quantities would have been much larger and the chicken would be stuffed with forcemeat of minced ham or bacon, fresh breadcrumbs, chopped shallots, parsley, tarragon, chives, garlic, the minced chicken liver, salt and pepper, mixed together with two beaten eggs and perhaps a little milk.

Cooking in the Quercy has much in common with that of the Périgord. Both are famous for truffles, a fact that is the cause of some acrimonious comment in the Quercy because the Périgourdins swear that their truffles are the best although, according to the Quercynois, a high proportion of the truffles sold in the markets of Périgord actually come from the Quercy. All the dishes garnished with truffles mentioned in the section on Périgord will also be found in the Quercy, as are most of those using walnuts. Chestnut and mushroom dishes also belong to both regions as does the *mique*, a kind of dumpling made with flour and semolina (or polenta) and boiled in stock or *bouillon* from the local cabbage soup. Each cook has her own recipe but one favourite is to take the *miques* when they are cooked, drain them in a piece of kitchen paper towel, slice or chop them and fry with pieces of the local country ham, mixing in a couple of beaten eggs at the last minute to make a kind of omelette.

The Quercy has a number of its own specialities and one of the best of these comes from Cahors. It is a casserole of tripe, highly spiced and with a great deal of garlic and tomatoes. One of the favourites from the Causse de Limogne is the *daube aux morilles*, a rich beef stew with bacon, wine and morels, the edible fungus described above on page 141. Further east on the borders of the Quercy and Rouergue there are dishes as strange as the country. *Mourtayrol* (also *mourtaidol* or *morteyrol*, from the French meaning the soup *du mort* because it was always served at funerals) is made by mixing stale bread with chicken stock and saffron and simmering in a slow oven for half an hour or so until it becomes thick and creamy, adding more stock if necessary. For the *mourtayrol de fêtes* the stock is enriched with minced beef, chopped turnips and chestnuts. *La soupe au saffron* is another variation of the *mourtayrol:* a layer of bread, a layer of saffron; a layer of bread, a layer of saffron and so on until the tureen is full and then the whole is moistened with chicken stock

The *alicuit* is a stew of chicken or turkey giblets (not to be confused with the *aligot*, see page 153). Finally there is *tripoux*, which consists of pieces of tripe wrapped round a stuffing mixture of minced pork and veal with herbs. It is simmered slowly for twenty-four hours in a white wine stock with onions, carrots and spices. *Tripoux* is sometimes made with sheep's tripe, sometimes with calves', but always with a good rich stuffing, often with minced or chopped ham added to the other minced meats. *Tripoux* is

common to both the Quercy and the Rouergue and appears under a variety
of names: *petitos d'Espalion, trenels, tresses, manouls* and *fardels.*

Rouergue

UPON THE Causse du Larzac a bitter struggle has been going on for years between the local farmers and the French army – and all over a cheese! Surely only in France could a cheese cause so much trouble, but then this is no ordinary old mousetrap: it is the world-famous Roquefort that is at stake.

The Causse du Larzac is a barren, windswept, limestone plateau where little grows except some scruffy grass, juniper and one or two aromatic plants like thyme. But since time immemorial it has served as grazing land for sheep from whose milk is made the cheese that will eventually be sold as Roquefort. The Causse never supported a large population but for a hundred years it had been steadily declining in numbers until in 1965, with the help of the government, sheep farmers began to resettle the land and increase the production of ewes' milk.

But in 1971 the same government, acting on the advice of a local deputy who thought it would help to bring work to the area, decided to increase the local army camp about 3,000 hectares to over 16,000 – at the local farmers' expense. The farmers reacted quickly and in 1972 they formed a 'Committee of 103' to resist the appropriation of their land. Since then they have waged a well organized campaign to publicize their cause, including lighting beacons on the clifftops above Millau, the main town of the area, driving tractors in convoy all the way to Paris to lobby the government and loosing a swarm of bees at an officer's ball! The public has been very much on the side of the farmers but the military cannot afford to lose face and at the time of writing there is still a stalemate.

Roquefort is made from ewes' milk cheeses which come not only from the Causse du Larzac but also from Corsica and a part of the Pays Basque where the same grazing conditions are found. The cheeses are sent to be matured in the caves of Combalou in the limestone cliff that looms over the small town that gives its name to the cheese. The maturing process turns the ordinary ewes' milk cheeses into one of France's gastronomic glories.

The story is that the secret of the caves was discovered by a local shepherd who was exploring the caves. He had taken some bread and a ewes' milk cheese with him and inadvertently left some of it behind him when he left. Visiting the same caves some time later he found the remains of his meal and saw to his surprise that the cheese was covered with blue veins. He was so hungry that he tried the cheese and found it delicious. True or not the story makes the point that it is the combination of the climatic conditions in the caves, the mould *Penicillium Roqueforti* and time that gives Roquefort cheese its distinctive character.

A visit to Roquefort is a unique experience. For a start the surrounding countryside is strange and bleak. Approaching from the west, across the Plateau du Lévézou, one is struck by an abrupt wall of cliffs that bars the way east of the R N 9 that runs from Sévérac south to Millau. The country looks as bleak and empty as the moon. At the top of these cliffs is an extensive plateau riven by the spectacular gorges of the Tarn and the Dourbie. To reach Roquefort from Millau one would normally take the N 592 towards St Affrique and turn left to Roquefort after 20 kilometres, but we chose to drive a little way up into the Gorges of the Dourbie to see the fantastic rock formations of Montpellier-le-Vieux, a bizarre landscape full of grotesquely shaped and giant rocks that long ago wandering shepherds gave its strange name because they thought it looked like a ruined city. From here we turned south and then west across the Causse du Larzac itself. It was every bit as forbidding as we had imagined and yet here, as on the Causses de Quercy, there were once prosperous farms and the main crop was wheat in contrast to the Ségala, further west, where only rye could be grown. Just as in Quercy, however, the opening up of the Rouergue led to a steady decline in the population. Even so, there are still one or two large farms on the Causse and it is their land that will become a training area when the Army takes over. One cannot envy the lot of the hapless soldiers who find themselves stationed in the middle of this empty landscape where the only signs of life that we saw were the occasional large flocks of sheep guarded by a solitary shepherd.

Roquefort itself is a curious town. It is built on a ledge half way up the cliff of Combalou and consists of one long street up and down which thunder enormous lorries full of cheeses. The caves extend back into the cliff both above and below the town and altogether there are fourteen different firms producing between them 17000 tonnes of cheese annually. The largest producer is a cooperative, the 'Société Caves & Producteurs Réunis', which accounts for 60 per cent of the total production.

The remarkable thing about the Caves de Combalou is that the temperature inside them never varies more than a degree or so. This is because the great limestone cliff of Combalou is porous and contains a labyrinthine network of fissures, known locally as *fleurines* that allow air to circulate freely, maintaining a constant temperature of about 9° C winter and summer. This makes the caves an ideal place to store the cheeses: the very high humidity encourages the growth of the penicilium mould, and the unvarying climactic conditions mean that, provided there is no reduction of quality in the ewes' milk and the making of the cheeses is strictly controlled, the matured Roquefort will always be of the same high standard.

A number of the Roquefort caves are open to the public. We visited Le Papillon, where, after seeing an interesting background film, we were taken on a conducted tour of the caves themselves. This included a glimpse of one of the *fleurines*, in this case a narrow gallery the height of a man that we were told could be followed many metres into the depths of the cliff.

The cheeses stored in the caves have not actually been made there, but in dairies on the Causse du Larzac from the milk of local ewes. The milk is collected at dawn each day during the season and taken to the dairies, where it is warmed in large open tanks and the curds separated from the whey. The curds are drained, using hemp or linen cloths, according to local tradition, and then put in standard-sized metal moulds to produce a cheese 2.8kg (6lbs) in weight made from 10–12 litres (20–24 pints) of milk. At this stage a little *penicilium glaucum Roqueforti* is added to the cheeses, using what looks like a pastry cook's flour sprinkler. These days most of the *penicilium* mould used in Roquefort is made in the laboratory but at Le Papillon they still bake enormous loaves of rye bread, 9kg (20lb) in weight, which are stored in the caves for 70–80 days so that the mould can develop. Each loaf furnishes 400 grammes of *penicilium* powder.

The cheeses in their moulds are now placed on tables in the *salle d'égouttage* which is kept a constant temperature of 17°C. They remain here for four days during which time each cheese is turned four times a day and washed every morning in warm water. They are then transferred to another room where the temperature is 10°C to await despatch to the caves.

Le Papillon takes delivery of fresh cheeses twice a week. The first stage in the maturing process is the salting. Seventy grammes of salt are rubbed into one face of the cheese and the circumference; the cheeses are then left for a day, turned, and salt rubbed into the opposite face and circumference once more. Two days later the cheeses are put through a simple machine that pierces them all over with thirty-two stainless steel needles, three millimetres in diameter. This is to facilitate the spreading of the mould.

Now at last the cheeses are put into store on oak racks in a series of caves, each one ventilated by its *fleurines*. They remain here for two to five months while nature does its work. At the end of that time the fully matured cheese with its characteristic blue veining is ready to eat. We found the new matured cheese much more to our liking than that usually sold in the shops: the texture is still crumbly and the flavour creamier and milder. As Roquefort grows older the texture becomes smoother and the taste sharper and saltier.

It is not known how long cheese has been made in this way at Roquefort, but it could date from Roman times, for Pliny the Elder mentions an excellent cheese imported from the region of Mons Lesura (Mont Lozère) and there is good reason to suppose that this was Roquefort. In 1411 King Charles VI gave a charter to Roquefort, granting it sole rights to mature this cheese 'as it has been practised from time immemorial in the caves of the aforementioned village'. Roquefort is one of the few distinguished cheeses that, like the best

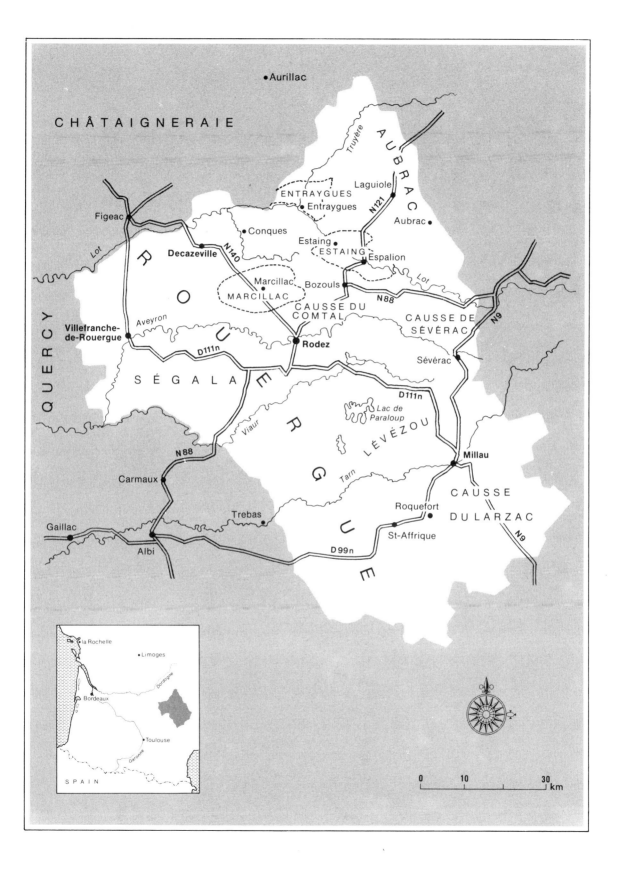

• Aurillac

CHÂTAIGNERAIE

AUBRAC

Truyère

Laguiole

ENTRAYGUES
• Entraygues

Aubrac •

N 121

Figeac

Lot

R
O
U
E
R
G
U
E

Conques •

Estaing •

ESTAING

Espalion

N 140

Decazeville

Lot

Marcillac •

MARCILLAC

Bozouls •

N 88

CAUSSE DU
COMTAL

CAUSSE DE
SÉVÉRAC

QUERCY

Aveyron

Villefranche-
de-Rouergue

D 111n

Rodez

Sévérac •

N 9

SÉGALA

Viaur

Lac de
Paraloup

D 111n

LÉVÉZOU

Tarn

N 88

Carmaux •

Millau

CAUSSE
DU LARZAC

Trebas •

Roquefort •

Gaillac •

St-Affrique •

N 9

Albi •

D 99n

• la Rochelle

• Limoges

Dordogne

Bordeaux •

• Toulouse

Garonne

SPAIN

0   10   30
km

wines, has an *appellation d'origine controlée*, designed to prevent imitations.

The Causse du Larzac lies at the extreme south-east of the Rouergue. Further north is the smaller Causse de Sévérac in a triangle formed by the river Aveyron and its tributary, the Serre. Like the Causse de Larzac, the Causse de Sévérac is largely deserted except for occasional flocks of sheep, and here too the ewes' milk is made into cheeses and sent to the caves at Roquefort.

West of the Causse de Sévérac is the Causse du Comtal, so called because it was part of the territory of the powerful counts of Rodez, the capital of the Rouergue, which lies immediately to the south. The altitude here is lower and the climate less severe than on the uplands of Sévérac, and in former times the Causse du Comtal was one of the richest agricultural regions of the Rouergue, for like the Causses of Quercy to the west it was a *fromental* whose limestone soil produced good crops of wheat.

By contrast, most of the rest of the Rouergue to the south consists of an undulating, hilly plateau composed of hard, crystalline rock, covered with thin, acid soil, much of it heavily wooded. This part of the Rourgue is known as the Ségala because formerly only rye (*seigle*) would grow there. The sour soil of the Ségala could only support a scanty population, in whose diet chestnuts played a large part, and it was for long one of the poorest and most backward parts of France. Slowly, however, conditions changed for the better. The first advance was the introduction of the potato in 1817, which did much to improve the peasants' diet and became the basis of one of the Rouergue's most famous dishes, *aligot*; but the most important development was the building of the railway line between Carmaux and Rodez which was completed in 1902. This meant that fertilizer could for the first time be transported cheaply to the area, and as a result it became possible to grow hay and thus raise cattle instead of sheep. More recent improvements in agriculture have led to the introduction of cereals such as barley and maize, at the expense of the potato. Even so the highest parts of the Ségala, like the Plateau de Lévézou and the Forêt de Palanges in the east, remain empty and sterile.

The most attractive parts of the Rouergue are the river valleys of the Lot, Truyère, Dourbie and Aveyron, and the lowlands in the neighbourhood of Villefranche de Rouergue on the borders of the Quercy. The rivers are often confined in narrow gorges and even where they do widen out there is nothing to compare with the rich alluvial valleys of the lower reaches of the Lot and the Dordogne; but the stretch of the Lot between Entraygues and Espalion, hemmed in as it is by mountains, is very picturesque, and Entraygues in particular is a delightful town with a thirteenth-century bridge, a small Renaissance Hotel de Ville and the interesting Romanesque chapel of St Hilarion.

The steep slopes above Entraygues were once covered with vines, for there have been vineyards here for a very long time. The name 'Entraygues' is occitane for *entre eaux* 'between the waters'. The earliest reference to vines is in two documents in the archives of the abbey of Conques which show that the local *vignerons* made donations of vines to the Abbey in 902 AD and again in 997 AD. In the Middle Ages most of the wine was sold to the bourgeoisie of Aurillac to the north or the mountain farmers of Aubrac. At one time the vineyards covered more than a 1000 hectares and there was no nook or cranny where a vine would grow that was not planted; but the area has never recovered from the devastation caused by the phylloxera in the 1870s and today the cultivated area comprises a mere thirty or so hectares.

The picturesque village of Fel stands on a high ridge giving magnificent views of the Lot winding in its narrow gorge five hundred metres below, and of the mountains of Aubrac to the east. The dark grey stone houses are roofed with the attractive fish scale stone tiles that are a feature of the Rouergue and other parts of the Massif Central, where hard rocks like granite predominate. The slopes at Fel are so stony and steep that it is a wonder that anything can grow here at all, but there are indeed a few vines straggling up the warm south-facing side of the ridge from which is made a light red wine, some of it entitled to carry the VDQS label 'Vin d'Entraygues et du Fel'.

For the most part, however, the vineyards are to be found lower down on a hillside immediately above Entraygues, where the contours are kinder and the soil sandier. The largest vineyard belongs to Emile Viguier, whose son is the only one of Entraygues' younger generation who wants to follow in his father's footsteps and who has plans for future expansion. He told us that there are only five local producers, including those of Fel, making about 1,350 hectolitres of wine between them. Of this quantity just over 300 hectolitres is sold under the VDQS label. The 'Vin d'Entraygues et du Fel' is in fact one of the smallest *appellations* in France.

At Fel only red wine is made but the vineyards below also produce *rosé* and white wines. When the VDQS regulations were first introduced in the 1960s many of the old varieties of grape were abandoned in the search for quality. The red wines are now made from a mixture of Cabernet Franc, Gamay, Mansoi, the local name for Fer, and a local grape called Negret de Banhars. The white wines are made from Chenin Blanc and a very little Baroque. The red and *rosé* wines have a permitted minimum strength of 9.5 degrees and the white 10 degrees. In a good year they can achieve strengths of 11 and 12 degrees respectively.

We found the red wine a little astringent for our taste and we were told that it is best served cool like a Beaujolais. The white wine however is very good and has much in common with a dry white Loire wine such as Muscadet: it is well worth trying if you are in the area.

Further up river is Estaing, which also has an old bridge, dominated in this case by a fine castle built on a granite outcrop. Estaing gives its name to another local VDQS wine; it is, in fact, the last place on the river Lot where wine can be made for, although further south than Entraygues, it is higher in the mountains and colder. The vineyards of Estaing, like those of Entraygues, are of great antiquity, the earliest reference to them occuring in an inventory found at the nearby monastery of Cabrespines dated 1399. The vineyards comprise about 100 hectares producing 5000 hectolitres of wine. Twelve local producers between them make 400 hl entitled to a VDQS label, the rest is *vin courant*. As at Entraygues red, *rosé* and white wines are all made: for the red, Pinotou d'Estaing, Gamay and Fer Servadou grapes are used, for the *rosé* Pinatou and for the white Chenin Blanc and Mauzac. The minimum permitted levels of alcohol are 9 degrees for the red and 9.5 for the *rosé* and white. The character of these wines is very similar to those of Entraygues. Both are very local and only to be found in this limited area.

East of Estaing and Entraygues lies the highest part of the Rouergue, the mountains of Aubrac. Over a distance of less than thirty kilometres, as the crow flies, the land climbs a 1000 metres, culminating in a height of 1,471 metres at the highest point, the Signal de Mailhebiau. High though the mountains are, the landscape looks more like an immense rolling prairie than anything else, for here the crystalline rock of the Massif is covered with waves of basalt, dating from a period of high volcanic activity. These grasslands have been used since time immemorial as summer pastures for the long-haired, fawn cattle of the Rouergue. The grazing period traditionally begins on the 25th of May when the great herds, wearing garlands on their horns, are driven up to the highlands. Each herd is looked after by a team of herdsmen who live together in a small stone cabin, where most of their time is spent making cheeses to be sold at the end of the summer.

The cheeses of Aubrac are almost indistiguishable from the better known ones of Cantal, further to the north. They are pressed into great wheels 46cm in diameter and are very similar in texture and flavour to our own farmhouse cheddar. One of the best is Laguiole, which is named after one of the local villages. It is a mild cheese, but the flavour is quite individual and it has a distinct after-taste.

South-west of Estaing the country is totally different. The soil consists of red sandstone, and here is to be found the best red wine of the region, the Vin de Marcillac. The vineyards of Marcillac once belonged to the bourgeoisie of Rodez and were worked by labourers living in tied cottages. The vines now cover an area of 500 hectares giving 20,000 hectolitres of wine, of which 2,000 hl are of VDQS quality. The grapes employed are 70 per cent Fer Servadou and the remaining 30 per cent made up of a mixture of Cabernet, Merlot, Mouyssagues, an old local variety, and Cot. The permitted minimums of alcohol are 9.5 degrees for the red and 10 degrees for the *rosé*. No white wine is produced. The red wine has a growing reputation outside the Rouergue and is now sold as far afield as Paris. Despite this we found it astringent, like the reds of Estaing and Entraygues and it certainly did not seem worth a detour to sample; however you never can tell with wine, and one short tasting is not enough to form a reliable opinion. Most of the production is handled by an excellent modern co-operative the 'Caves des Vignerons du Vallon' at Valady. Nearby is the famous romanesque abbey of Conques, which contains one of the finest collections of medieval church treasures in the France, not to be missed if you are in the area.

The only other wine made in the Rouergue worthy of note is the Gorges du Tarn. This is a very drinkable *vin de pays* with a alcoholic permitted minimum of 9.5 degrees. It is made on the banks of the Tarn in the vicinity of St. Affrique and Millau.

Life in the Rouergue has always been very hard and the local cooking reflects the rigours of the climate and the ruggedness of the country. This is not the place to look for the kind of refined cuisine found in more favoured regions such as the Bordelais or Périgord; the food of the Rouergue is hearty and substantial, designed to fill the stomach cheaply and at the same time provide plenty of internal warmth to help combat the bitter cold of winter in the mountains. This is not to say you cannot get a good meal in the Rouergue. Hotels and restaurants here are just as well run as anywhere else in France, but their menus will usually be typically French and you will not find the range of local specialities that you might in other parts of the South-West.

The Rouergue's most famous dish is the *aligot*, a delicious mixture of puréed potatoes, fresh cream, butter and cheese. The *aligot* must not be confused with *alicot* or *alicuit*, which is a giblet stew and whose name is a corruption of *ailles cuites*. *Aligot* derives from the Latin *aliquid*, *aliquot*, or in French *quelque chose*.

Aligot

Aligot is a traditional wedding dish in the Rouergue and according to custom should be made by the man of the house: this is because it is very hard work stirring the mixture so that the cheese spins into long fine threads.

The local cheese, Tomme de Rouergue, seems to be unobtainable in England but try a mixture of Mozzarella and grated strong Cheddar. Melt the butter in a thick-bottomed saucepan with the cream. Add the mashed potato and the cheese. Now comes the chore: you have to stir the mixture, always in the same direction, so that the cheese is spun into threads. You really need two people, one to keep stirring while the other adds the crushed garlic and salt. As soon as the cheese starts to break up, serve. You can eat *aligot* on its own as a supper dish or as an accompaniment to a roast, but be warned – it is very filling and it is advisable not to drink too much liquid with it or you will feel very bloated afterwards.

500g (1lb) mashed potato
500g (1lb) Mozzarella and grated cheddar
150g (6oz) butter
150ml ($\frac{1}{4}$ pint–5fl.oz) fresh cream
2 cloves garlic, crushed
Salt

Potatoes were introduced into France in the sixteenth century as ornamental plants – there was great resistance to it as a vegetable because it was believed to cause leprosy. In the seventeenth century cultivation was forbidden and although it was permitted in the eighteenth century the potato was now suspected of weakening those who ate it and this ignorant prejudice prevented the planting of this useful vegetable. The potato's rehabilitation was accomplished by Antoine-Augustin Parmentier, who also introduced the Jerusalem artichoke to the French. Parmentier's name on the menu indicates that potatoes feature somewhere in the dish, thus shepherd's pie is known in France as *hachis parmentier*. In the years leading up to the French Revolution, when food was short and harvests failed, Parmentier managed by clever publicity to overcome the repugnance with which the potato was regarded. He presented Louis XVI with a bouquet of flowers, after which potato flowers even appeared as decoration on fine dinner services. When Parisians still refused to accept the potato as food he set an armed guard on his potato fields all day, leaving them unguarded at night, with the result that the citizens thought they must be missing something, took advantage of the lack of guards at night to steal the crop – and then demanded more!

Gradually the the potato spread throughout France and in the Rouergue the once sterile Ségala became, thanks to the use of lime and other fertilizers, one of the major potato-farming areas in the South-West. Today the Ségala produces some 200,000 tonnes a year and sells them throughout southern France. To our ears the names of the different varities sound very strange. Ackersegen, Arranbareran Urgenta, Bintje, Bea and Sirtema are all waxy potatoes, good for boiling because they keep their shape, but not so good for mashing. The Kerpondy is a more floury potato and this is the one used in the *aligot*.

Two more potato-based dishes, both very filling, from the Rouergue are *gargouillou rustique* and *étouffe-chrétien*. A *gargouillement* is a tummy rumble, something you are unlikely to suffer from after eating either of these concoctions.

Gargouillou rustique

You can prepare most of this dish the day before, boiling the waxy kind of potatoes and slicing them, chopping the bacon and onions and cooking them gently in lard or oil.

When you are ready to start the final preparations, put the cooked onions and bacon in the bottom of a fireproof dish. Crush the garlic and mix with the onions and bacon, then cover with a layer of sliced potatoes. Beat the egg and pour over the dish. Sprinkle with the parsley and cover with the grated cheese. Put into a hot oven for about half an hour, until piping hot and brown. There is unlikely to be any left over, but if there is it makes a good cold snack on its own.

For each person allow:
250g ($\frac{1}{2}$lb) cooked potatoes
2 streaky bacon rashers,
  chopped and fried
1 small onion or 2 shallots,
  chopped and sweated in lard
75 grammes (3oz) grated
  cheese (strong Cheddar or
  Cheshire)
1 beaten egg
$\frac{1}{2}$ clove garlic, crushed
Little chopped parsley

Étouffe-chrétien

As its name implies this is another very filling dish and definitely not for those watching their waistlines.

Roll the pastry into two rounds the size of a good deep pie dish. Put one round into the pie dish and cover with finely sliced potato rounds. Add one clove of crushed garlic and some chopped parsley. Mix the belly of pork and the pie veal with another clove of crushed garlic, some more chopped parsley, salt and pepper. Cover the potato slices with the mixture. Moisten the edges of the pastry and put the second pastry round on top, sealing the edges. Brush the top with a little beaten egg or milk and bake in a medium oven for about 40 minutes. You can finish the pie in true fashion, if you have a second pie dish the same size. Turn the pie out upside down onto the second dish and leave in a warm oven for 15 minutes so that the fat from the stuffing soaks into what was the top of the pie.

500g (1lb) rough short crust pastry, with 1 egg added
250g (½lb) cooked sliced potatoes
2 cloves garlic, crushed
Chopped parsley
500g (1lb) coarsely minced belly of pork
500g (1lb) minced pie veal (boned neck)
Salt and pepper

Much of the country ham sold in the South-West comes from the Rouergue Most farmers' wives have a ham, wrapped in a piece of cotton, ready for any emergency: like the occasion when we were visiting a local farm and were unexpectedly pressed to stay for supper. After a good vegetable soup and some beetroot salad, out came the ham and was handed with some ceremony to the farmer for carving. We remarked on its colour, a *bon rouge*, as the thick, chewy slices were set on our plates, and enjoyed its fine flavour. This was followed by a dish of haricot beans, a ripe charentais melon each and cheese an excellent impromptu meal.

The method of processing Rouergue ham is similar to that used for *jambon de Bayonne*, but here more saltpetre is used, which can make the meat tougher. The hams of the Rouergue, like those of Bayonne, are dry-cured: salt is rubbed into the rind and the hams are laid on a bed of rock salt, rather than being placed in a bath of saline solution or melted salt. The climate is crucial for this type of process: exactly the right amount of humidity is necessary for the rock salt to give its own moisture but not melt too much.

Another speciality found all over the South-West, but particularly associated with the Quercy and the Rouergue, is *confit de porc* (preserved pork). The following is simple and inexpensive to make – a delicious summer dish served with a green salad or boiled potatoes. It can also be eaten hot.

500g (1lb) lean pork from the loin or fillet without bones or rind
800g (¼lb) goose fat or lard
2 cloves garlic
1 tablespoon rock salt
1 large pinch black pepper
1 tablespoon armagnac
1 large glass dry white wine

Confit de porc

Mix the salt with the black pepper, peel the garlic and crush it before adding it to the salt and pepper. Rub the pork with the mixture, giving the meat a good battering so that the salt can penetrate the outer layer. Pour the white wine and the armagnac into a large cooking bowl and lay the salt-encrusted pork in the marinade, turning it over from time to time. After twelve hours of marinading, drain the meat. Melt the fat gently in a large, thick-bottomed saucepan. Add the pork, which should be completely covered with the fat. Simmer gently for at least 2 hours on a low but regular heat. When the meat is done (you can check this with the point of a sharp knife) take it out and put it in an earthenware jar. Pour the fat from the cooking round the meat and leave to cool. When the fat has set firmly, cover with a layer of freshly melted lard and keep in a cool dry place for at least a month before eating. To remove the pork from the jar, melt the fat a little so that you can take the meat out without breaking it. If you are serving the *confit de porc* you can fry some boiled potatoes in the fat to give additional flavour.

Although fresh cod is sold in the markets of the South-West, the housewives seem to prefer *morue verte*, which is cod that has been salted soon after it has been caught. *Morue sèche* has been both salted and dried and stockfish has been dried for much longer. The English word 'stockfish' comes from the Norwegian *stokkfisk*, which reappears in Italy as *stoccafisso*, in Provence as *estocaficada* and in the Rouergue as *l'estofi* or *estofinado*.

The deep-sea fishermen of France have fished for centuries in the waters off Newfoundland for cod, and their dogs earned their keep by allowing themselves to be thrown overboard to swim after and catch the fish that escaped from the hooks. Each dog retrieved twenty-five or thirty cod a day. The fish was put into salt in the ships' holds and sold on the quayside in Bordeaux.

In the days when river transport was the key to communication it was the riverside towns and villages that were the chief recipients of the Newfoundland catches. The inhabitants of the upper reaches of the Lot, in particular, seem to have always valued *morue* and stockfish highly. High up in the Rouergue, at Decazeville on the Lot, the *morue* arrived in a novel fashion – towed behind barges. Decazeville is an important coal-mining town and the coal was shipped downriver to Bordeaux in barges which made the return trip laden with iron ore. The bargees soon discovered that the week's voyage from Bordeaux to Decazeville was exactly the right amount of time needed to desalt the cod if the *morue* were streamed astern of the barge. By the time Decazeville was reached, the fish were ready for cooking! A certain Monsieur Ramadier, who was deputy for Decazeville, had no barges at his disposal, however, but he was a wealthy man and his home contained a number of luxuries, including a flushing WC. His solution to the desalting problem was to put the *morue* in the cistern (not the pan) of the WC. Every time the pan was flushed the water in the cistern was changed and some salt in the *morue* washed out.

Nowadays, stockfish is becoming rare and you are more likely to see the *morue verte* in the markets of the South-West. If you are going to try cooking an *estofinado*, you will have to soak the salt cod in cold water, skinside uppermost, resting on a sieve or a pressure cooker trivet for about twenty-four hours, changing the water at intervals. The salt used to preserve the cod is not a good salt for cooking and you should try to soak the fish until the water barely tastes of anything (you will be putting good cooking and eating salt back when you cook the fish). Most *morue* recipes are for poaching, including the *estofinado*.

Estofinado

Put the fish in a pan of cold water and bring slowly to the boil, lowering the heat so that the water just simmers. The water should not boil if you want the fish to stay white and fresh-looking. Poach for 10 minutes, skimming frequently. The *estofinado* of the Rouergue uses this basic poached cod, together with an equal amount by weight of boiled floury potatoes.

Salt cod
Boiled, floury potatoes
1 tbsp butter
1 clove garlic, crushed
Chopped parsley
Freshly ground black pepper
1–2 eggs, beaten

Skin the fish and take out any bones. Mash the fish and the potatoes together with the butter and some of the water the fish has been poached in. When the mixture is well mixed add a clove of crushed garlic, chopped parsley and some freshly ground pepper. Stir well. Make a depression in the centre of the mixture and stir in one or two beaten eggs. Check the seasoning and add more salt if necessary. Serve immediately.

Morue aux haricots

This is a similar recipe to the *estofinado*, except that the potatoes are replaced by dried haricot beans soaked overnight and cooked with plenty of water, chopped onion, garlic and a bay leaf. Keep moistening the beans while they are cooking as you will need some extra juice to make a sauce. When cooked, drain the beans and keep the remaining liquid. Fry a crushed clove of garlic and a couple of chopped shallots in a fryingpan with a little olive oil. Moisten with some of the bean liquid and add a few of the beans themselves, crushed so that the sauce becomes thick and creamy. If you like, you can do all this in the blender. Add salt, pepper, powdered thyme and chopped parsley. Stir well and set aside while you poach the *morue*. Cut a slice of bread for each guest, fry and rub well with a piece of garlic. When the *morue* is poached, remove the bones and skin. Put the haricots in an ovenproof dish. Arrange the pieces of fish on top and cover with the sauce. Finish with a topping of chopped parsley.

Salt cod
Dried, haricot beans
1 onion, chopped
2 cloves garlic
1 bay leaf
2 shallots, chopped
Salt, pepper, powdered thyme, chopped parsley
1 slice bread per person
Olive oil

GASCONY

Landes

'. . . a desolate landscape where a man can find no comforts whatsoever, no wine, no meat, no fish, no water. There is only honey, millet and pigs.'

So WROTE the twelfth century author of the *Liber Sancti Jacobi*, a guide written for pilgrims on their way to the great shrine of Santiago de Compostela in northern Spain. And indeed the medieval traveller had every reason to fear the Landes, for in those days it was one of the poorest and most inhospitable parts in all France, a desolate region little better than a desert. Few outsiders would brave the fevers and hardships of a journey across the Landes and those who did regarded the inhabitants as little better than savages.

Yet it would be a mistake to think that the Landes has nothing of interest in the way of food to offer today's traveller. On the contrary some of the finest *foie gras* to be found in the whole of the South-West is produced here; in fact the Landes has a greater output of *foie gras* than Périgord. What is more it has a reputation second to none for the excellence of its cuisine and at Eugénie-les-Bains you will find the restaurant of one of the most celebrated of today's French chefs, Michel Guérard, the inventor of *Cuisine Minceur* (slimmers' cookery).

The explanation for this seeming paradox lies in the great programme of reclamation that was undertaken in the Landes at the end of the eighteenth century and was finally completed eighty years later. The Landes has the form of an enormous triangle with its base formed by the Atlantic coast stretching south from the Arcachon basin to the mouth of the river Adour and with its point 100 kilometres inland in the vicinity of Nérac. The coast consists of a strip of sand dunes about 11 kilometres wide. Some of these dunes are the size of small hills and the most famous of them, the Dune du Pilat, near Arcachon, is 100 metres high and the highest in Europe.

Behind the dunes is a series of lagoons which originally formed because the few small streams flowing through the Landes were blocked by the shifting dunes and prevented from reaching the sea. The water spread to become swamps which have now been drained and turned into lakes where there are attractive holiday resorts offering swimming and boating. Small streams called *courants* flow out of the lakes and eventually find a circuitous way to the sea. Some of the *courants* flow through beautiful scenery reminiscent of the Everglades of Florida. They are navigable by canoes and punts and the traveller will be rewarded by the sight of all kinds of interesting flowers and birds.

Until the nineteenth century however there was nothing behind the dunes but a mournful landscape composed of barren heathland and fever-ridden marshes, inhabited for the most part by a few wretched shepherds, who journeyed through the fens on stilts, guarding large flocks of sheep. In those days the Landes had more head of sheep than any other part of France. In 1857 there were 300,000 of them. Apart from sheep farming the only other source of income came from bee-keeping. The flowers of the heathlands give the honey a delicious flavour and it can still be bought from farms in the Landes today.

Most of the inhabitants of this sad country lived in small oases of grassland called 'airials'. These were to be found in isolated spots where for some reason, usually because the land was slightly higher than the surrounding very flat country, conditions were a little more favourable. The airials would contain one or two half-timbered houses, some pigs and poultry. Occasionally there were one or two small fields where millet and rye was grown, but this was for subsistence only.

For hundreds of years nothing was done to improve the Landes or to alleviate the miserable existence of the people who lived there. It was not until 1788 that Brémontier, a famous French construction engineer, started on the immense task of holding back the dunes, which were advancing inland at a rate of between 10 and 25 metres a year, burying whole villages that lay in their path in the process. Until this was done there was little point in trying to do something about the interior. Brémontier began by constructing a palisade, well above the highest tide line, against which the sand accumulated. As the sand built up, the height of the palisade was increased until eventually there was an embankment 12 metres high, forming a permanent coastal barrier. The next step was to stop the tops of the dunes from being whipped off and blown inland by the gales. This was done by planting a species of grass called *gourbet* whose roots spread very quickly forming a dense network that held the sand in check. Behind this first line of defence, Brémontier planted a mixture of gorse and pine seeds. The gorse and broom grew quickly and helped to protect the slower-growing pine trees. By 1867 the dunes had been fixed and 80,000 hectares had been planted with pines.

The problem of how to improve the fertility and drainage of the interior had still to be solved however, but this task was undertaken by another engineer called Chambrelent at the beginning of the nineteenth century. The bleak conditions in the interior were due to a thin layer of sandy topsoil covering a layer of hard impermeable rock at a depth of 50 centimetres that stopped the growth of plant roots and created marshes in low-lying areas. Chambrelent put forward a scheme which included breaking up the hard

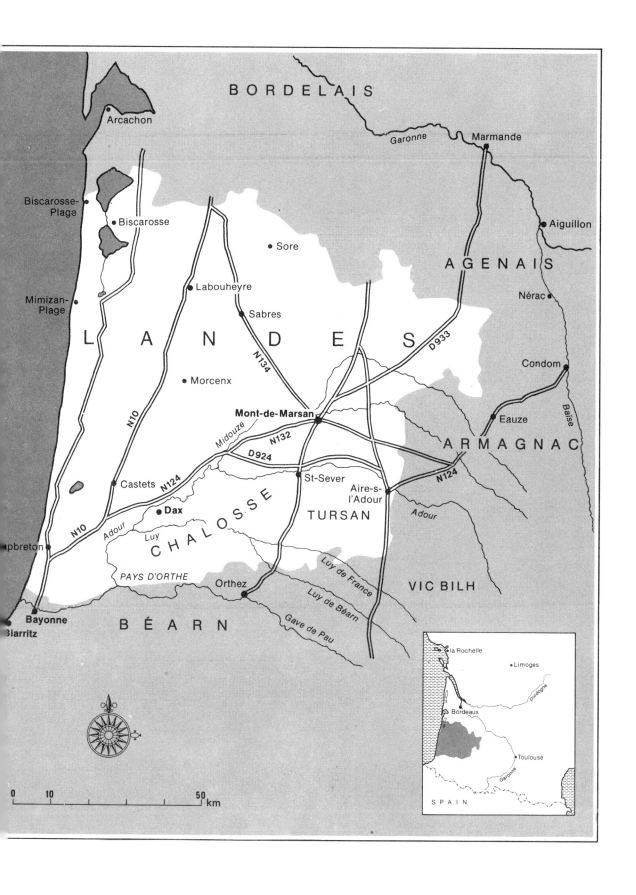

BORDELAIS

Arcachon

Biscarosse-
Plage

Biscarosse

Sore

AGENAIS

Marmande

Garonne

Aiguillon

Mimizan-
Plage

L A N D E S

Labouheyre

Sabres

Nérac

N134

D933

Condom

Morcenx

N10

Mont-de-Marsan

Eauze

Baïse

Midouze

N132

A R M A G N A C

D924

Castets

N124

St-Sever

Aire-s-
l'Adour

N124

Dax

C H A L O S S E

TURSAN

Adour

N10

Adour

Luy

VIC BILH

pbreton

PAYS D'ORTHE

Orthez

Luy de France

Bayonne

Biarritz

B É A R N

Luy de Béarn

Gave de Pau

0   10   50
km

la Rochelle

Limoges

Dordogne

Bordeaux

Toulouse

Garonne

S P A I N

rock, draining marshes, introducing fertilizers and planting pine trees. For a long time progress was painfully slow because of lack of money, until Napoleon III took a hand. A law was passed obliging the local communes to drain their land and plant trees. The Emperor himself set an example by buying and planting an enormous tract of land near Sabres, called Solferino after his famous victory. By the last quarter of the century the Landes had become an enormous forest covering nearly 60,000 hectares.

This dramatic alteration in the physiognomy of the Landes brought about far-reaching changes in the ecology of the region. The hundreds of miles of forest were soon populated by all kinds of birds, including many that the French love to hunt and to eat: pheasant, snipe, woodcock, ortolan and above all the *palombe*. Great flocks of these wild pigeons fly across southwest France every autumn on their way from Scandinavia and northern Europe to the warmer climates of southern Spain and north Africa. This annual migration arouses the same degree of fervour and excitement in the Landes that the FA Cup does in England. From the beginning of October the arrival of the *palombe* is eagerly awaited, not only in the Landes but in the Pays Basque and Armagnac as well. Workers take time off from their factories, shopkeepers shut their shops and professional men close their offices, all of them intent on bagging as many *palombes* as they can.

With such a reception committee it is a wonder that any of the birds survive at all, but the *palombes* are easily frightened and it is very hard to get near them. To overcome this difficulty, elaborately camouflaged hides are set up, both on the ground and in the trees. Some of these hidden hides are big enough to hold several sportsmen, who may have to stay there all day for several days. Naturally they take a good supply of food and wine with them and a great camaraderie grows up between members of the group, who may well meet each other in the same hides year after year. From the hides the huntsmen manipulate a complicated system of decoy birds set high in the trees to attract the *palombes* and persuade them to settle long enough for the *chasseurs* to get in a shot. The decoys are controlled by an intricate network of lines leading back to the hide, which when they are pulled make the decoy flap its artificial wings, thus catching the attention of the *palombe*. It is a highly skilled operation requiring great patience.

The *palombe* is considered to be a great delicacy and is quite often found on restaurant menus. It can be roasted but the best-known recipe is a rich casserole dish called *salmis de palombe*. It is a great deal easier to discover the secrets of the *palombes chasseurs* than to find out how to make a good *salmis de palombe*. The Landais cooks are willing enough to describe the process of trussing and roasting the birds, cutting them into pieces and adding them to the sauce, but the secrets of the sauce remain with each cook; one will add a pinch of nutmeg, another prefers to use cloves or ground ginger; sometimes a truffle or truffle peelings may be included; still others claim that the wild mushrooms and other fungi of the pine forests provide the authentic flavour, while there are those who insist that you must have a basis of rich veal stock, and so on.

In Britain you will be unlikely to find *palombes*, but here is a recipe that will transform the humble pigeon. In the Landes the *palombes* are roasted until they are almost, but not quite, done; they should still be slightly red inside. Allow one pigeon between two people and start by roasting them whole in a little butter, allowing about 30 minutes in a moderate oven. Take off the leg pieces and the breast and wings, leaving as much of the carcasses as you can for the stock. Put the pieces of pigeon in a covered casserole, pour over a little warm Armagnac and flame them until the alcohol is burnt out. Cover the casserole and set aside while you make the sauce.

Salmis de Palombe Serves 4

Heat the olive oil in a thick saucepan and add the chopped onion, diced carrots, bacon cut into strips and crushed garlic clove. Cover and allow to cook gently for 15 minutes. Add the chopped mushrooms and cook for another 5 minutes. Moisten with the veal stock and the red wine, then put in the pigeon carcasses and the bouquet garni, bring to the boil and allow to reduce by about half, adding the allspice, salt and freshly ground pepper to taste, together with a pinch of cayenne. Remove the carcasses and the bouquet garni, stir in the tomato purée and thicken with a little roux; allow to simmer gently for 15 to 20 minutes.

Reheat the pieces of pigeon gently in the casserole and cover with the sauce. Some cooks insist that the sauce should be strained and sieved before it is served, because all the goodness and flavour will have passed from the vegetables into the liquid. Certainly the texture should be smooth and velvety as you pour it over the pigeon and stir in 2 or 3 tablespoons of armagnac.

2 pigeons
150g streaky bacon (about 5oz), cut into strips
150g mushrooms (5oz), chopped
2 carrots, diced
1 clove garlic, crushed
1 onion, chopped
1 bouquet garni
1 pinch allspice
Salt, pepper and a pinch of cayenne pepper
Butter and flour for thickening
1 bottle red wine
500ml veal stock (1 pint/20fl.oz.)
2 tablespoons olive oil
1 tablespoon tomato purée

The Landes is famous for the abundance of its game, most of which is served in the local restaurants, but be warned, game is likely to be expensive and the soft-hearted may recoil from the idea of eating some of the smaller birds like the *bec-fin*, a tiny pippet, or the ortolan. A French tourist guide to the area sums up the matter admirably: 'Ortolan – a miniscule bird with red plumage which is trapped and then kept in darkness; bored by the gloom, it stuffs itself with millet and grows inordinately fat. Despite its relatively obesity, it only makes a single mouthful, and you should ask for three if you wish to enjoy its flavour: always assuming you have enough money'.

For those not partial to game, there is plenty of delicious freshwater fish, as well as eels, lampreys and crayfish, which have flourished in the newly drained lagoons and *courants*. A fish rarely seen in Britain is the shad (*alose*), which is despised by some because it has so many tiny bones. Not long ago, however, we were delighted to find *alose à l'oseille* on the menu in a Landais restaurant. Some less adventurous members of the party took the easy way out and settled for asparagus, but we chose the shad with its sorrel stuffing and, despite the bones, enjoyed it very much.

Two kinds of shad are found in the South-West: the more common is the great shad (*Alosa alosa*); the lesser shad (*Alosa fallax*) does not travel so far up the rivers to spawn. The lesser shad is distinguished from the great shad by the row of black spots on its skin. After they have spawned the shad die, as do lampreys. The first-year fry of the lesser shad, which are found in the south of the Landes, are called *astons*. They are only about 4 to 5 centimetres long, but by the second year they have grown to a length of 15 to 18 centimetres.

If you are cooking shad, it is probably best to fillet it first, as many people seem to find the bones difficult to cope with. The technique is exactly the same as for herrings, mackerel and similar fish. You will need to keep an eye out for stray bones during the rest of the cooking, but you can remove these as they appear.

Grilled (broiled) shad

Fillet the shad and make a marinade by blending three tablespoons of olive oil, a pinch of thyme, powdered bay leaves, black pepper, salt and chopped chives. Allow the marinade to stand for 5 minutes and blend again, then pour over the fish and leave for 2 hours. Meanwhile boil the dorsal bone with a couple of tablespoons of dry white wine and a pinch of basil, adding a tablespoon of water from time to time, as necessary, to keep the juices liquid. Strain and set aside to keep warm. Put the shad fillets under the grill, basting frequently with the marinade. Grill, skin-side first, for 8 to 10 minutes, according to size. When they are cooked, inspect them carefully for signs of stray bones which you can remove if you think it necessary. Arrange the pieces on a warm serving dish and cover with the wine sauce mixed with any liquid which has come from the fish during grilling.

Alternatively you can grill the whole shad slowly, sprinkling with melted butter and lemon juice from time to time, and serve it on a bed of sorrel, or you can stuff the fish with a sorrel/breadcrumb mixture and bake it in the oven.

Alose à l'oseille

1 shad
1 cup breadcrumbs
2 cups cooked sorrel
50g melted butter (2oz)
1 beaten egg
1 teaspoon sugar
Handful chopped parsley
Salt and pepper to taste
2 tablespoons olive oil
2 tablespoons dry white wine

Scale and clean the shad and stuff it with the mixture.

Mix the melted butter with the beaten egg, chopped parsley and cooked sorrel. Stir in the breadcrumbs with the salt, pepper and sugar. Stuff the fish with the mixture and tie firmly with string so that it keeps its shape.

Put the shad in foil with the olive oil and the dry white wine, salt and pepper. If there is any stuffing left over, roll it into little balls and add to the fish parcel. Fold the foil carefully and bake in a hot oven for an hour. Unwrap the parcel and turn the fish over carefully. Finish off the cooking with the fish uncovered, testing to see that the shad is not overcooked. Serve with plain boiled potatoes and salad as a main course or as an *entrée* to roast meat, braised rabbit or a chicken casserole.

In a short time, the way of life in the Landes changed out of all recognition. A number of industries dependent on the forest came into being. The pine trees were tapped for their resin, which was distilled to produce turpentine, the wood was also used for railway sleepers, pit-props and telegraph poles. More recently a number of paper mills have been built in the area. The introduction of these industries, together with the building of the first railway line through the Landes in the 1870s, brought sudden prosperity to the region and from having been one of the poorest parts of France it became for a time the richest. Most of this new-found wealth went into the pockets of a few wealthy landowners, however; the condition of the resin tappers was very little better than that of the shepherds who had preceded them, for as the forest spread the flocks of sheep diminished.

Before the planting of the forest and the draining of the marshes, the Landes was too poor to have any tradition of local cooking, yet now its gastronomic reputation stands very high and you will find excellent restaurants everywhere. The change seems to have taken place quite quickly because already by the 1880s the intrepid Edward Harrison Barker, who was making a journey on foot from Arcachon to Dax, was able to find a number of comfortable inns where he enjoyed simple well-cooked food. He certainly struck lucky at Taller, a small, village about 20 kilometres north of Dax:

My next stopping-place was Taller, a pretty village, where the people seemed to spend their lives basking like lizards. I arrived here in the full blaze of noon, and the shade of Host Lassalle's back room was so refreshing that I soon began to shiver, and was obliged to go outside again and sun myself against the southern wall.

While I am standing here the *aubergiste's* young wife is engaged on the problem of preparing an acceptable meal from such ingredients as the house affords. I have no misgivings on this subject, for there is scarcely a Frenchwomen from Dunkerque to the Pic du Midi who cannot produce in half an hour a savoury and attractive repast with next to nothing, if her heart is in it. And I can see that Madame Lassalle's heart is in her work. It is a pleasure to her to cook for a genuine stranger, from whom she may hear some news of the outer world. In almost no time she appears on the threshold, and says with a smile, '*Monsieur est servi*'. In the cool back room a white cloth has been spread over a little table, and a napkin has been laid beside a plate. In the centre is a tureen full of steaming *soupe aux choux*. Cabbage soup has a barbarous sound in English ears, but more than one hungry Englishman has, I expect, felt his heart glow with gratitude towards the clever Frenchwoman who has set it before him. Do not turn up your fastidious noses, English housewives, but humble yourselves before the French *menagère* until you have learnt her secret for making cabbage-soup. I can tell you that the ingredients are a cabbage, a piece of ham or bacon, and a dry sausage with garlic in it; but this knowledge is only half the battle. If no woman not bred in England can boil a potato or grill a chop, so no woman not bred in France can make a *soupe aux choux* or an *omelette au cerfeuil*. After the soup I have the ham that was boiled with it, and a little dish of green capsicums with oil and vinegar. The next course is a fowl, cut up, and served with a sauce which is another secret of the Frenchwoman. Then for dessert, I have a plate of figs just picked from beneath the cool broad leaves that droop from the wall of the little inn, and beautiful in their purple bloom. Hitherto in the Landes I have found the wine bad, for the *aubergistes* have brought it of the Bordeaux dealers, who have knavishly counterfeited nature; but Host Lassalle's wine is a sound and generous liquor – real blood of the grape. It comes from the Chalosse, an excellent wine-growing country, where he has a vineyard. It has the strong, sweet, and full flavour of all the red wines of the South. If it is less pleasant than the light wines of the Gironde, it is vastly superior to the compounded liquour that is so often called Bordeaux.

The rapid improvement in standards is not difficult to explain, for however bad conditions may once have been in the Landes, one did not have to go far beyond its confines to find a good table.

To the east lay Armagnac, with its reputation for good hearty food, and to the south the green foothills of the Pyrénées. Here in mediaeval times there were three small semi-independent fiefs (*petit-pays* as they are called in France): the Chalosse, Pays d'Orthe and Tursan, all of which now form part of the modern *département* of the Landes. The frontiers of the three *petit-pays* are difficult to define exactly, but they all lie south of the river Adour in an area stretching south-westwards from Aire-sur-l'Adour to Peyrehorade on the Gave de Pau.

Tursan, the most easterly of these three former fiefs is also the smallest, yet it is nevertheless important on two counts: it produces a well-known VDQS wine called Tursan, and at Eugénie-les-Bains is to be found one of the most famous restaurant in the South-West, Michel Guérard's Les Prés et les Sources d'Eugénie. It has three rosettes and its prices reflect its prestige. But if you wish to eat impeccably prepared food in the most elegant surroundings this is the place.

The vineyards of Tursan cover an area of 2,000 hectares in the neighbourhood of Geaune, 15 kilometres south-west of Aire-sur-l'Adour. There are about 1,200 *vignerons* altogether, some of them very, very small scale producers indeed, but all the wine that is sold commercially is made at the Cave Coopérative de Geaune. The Co-operative produces 25,000 hectolitres of which 15,000 is VDQS quality. The vineyards are for the most part planted with the Baroque grape, which gives a dry white wine which is light and fruity. Small amounts of red and *rosé* wine are also made. The Tannat grape predominates in the red but, following the example of the vineyards of Madiran (see page 208) Cabernet Franc and Cabernet Sauvignon are being introduced to give the wine more finesse. The *rosé* is made entirely from Cabernet grapes. The minimum alcoholic strength is 10.5 degrees for all three. Tursan is not an important wine today but in the seventeenth century it was better known and was exported through Bayonne to both Holland and England.

Apart from Tursan, the Landes produces no other wine worth mentioning but there used to be one made on the coast that was unique: it was called *Vin des Sables* and was to be found in the vicinity of Capbreton. The vines, whose roots sometimes reached a depth of five metres, were trained so low that sometimes the grapes actually rested on the sand itself. This had the effect of making the grapes ripen quickly and concentrated their sugar content. The resulting red wine was rich and heavy with a heady bouquet. It also had a distinct tang of the sea, said to be derived from the seaweed that was used as a fertilizer for the vines. Always rare, this wine is now no more than a memory.

No sight could have been more welcome to the weary medieval pilgrim than that of the Cap de Gascogne rising abruptly 102 metres above the flat plain, and surmounted by the small town of St-Sever with its magnificent Romanesque abbey. At St-Sever he knew that for the time being the worst was over. The next stage of his pilgrimage would be through the pleasant, well-wooded, gently rolling landscape of the Chalosse. Here he knew that he would find comfortable inns where he could dine well and prepare himself for the difficult passage across the mountains into Spain.

The reputation of the Chalosse for good food continues to this day. St-Sever itself, although it has a population of only 4,800, has two excellent restaurants, one with a Michelin rosette. This is because the town is a flourishing market centre for an area that specializes in poultry. Just to the south there are farms that raise hundreds of geese and ducks for their livers (the *foie gras*, for which the Landes is renowned, comes in fact from here in the Chalosse). Here, too, you will find the plump, yellow, maize-fed chickens, whose flesh is particularly succulent, which are famous throughout France for their quality. In fact, St-Sever is the headquarters of the oddly named *Syndicat de Défense du Poulet Jaune des Landes*, which exists to make sure that standards are maintained. Incidentally a subsidiary industry has grown up in St-Sever using the feathers from the geese and ducks to stuff pillows and duvets!

But the Chalosse has another claim to fame besides its poultry. Further to the west, beef cattle take pride of place and their meat is also highly prized for the flavour. No wonder, with such riches on their doorstep, that the inhabitants of the Chalosse are famed for their love of a good table.

The Pays d'Orthe lies south of Dax in a triangle formed by the convergence of the rivers Adour and the Gaves Réunis. The latter is a short stretch where the combined waters of the Gave de Pau and the Gave d'Oloron flow smoothly through a placid landscape to their final junction with the Adour 10 kilometres downstream.

In the north-east of the Pays d'Orthe the country is wooded and hilly like the Chalosse but as you go further south-west the hills peter out, the landscape becomes a flat sandy heathland and more and more pines start to appear, heralding the great forest of the Landes to the north. In the hills there is mixed farming but in the plain there are great fields of maize.

Peyrehorade, the chief town of the area, is sited at a strategic crossing place on the Gaves Réunis. It is an important market town, but its chief claim to fame is the quality of its fish, especially salmon which swim upstream between February and June each year to spawn. Unfortunately excessive fishing and poaching have seriously reduced their numbers. But if salmon are now rare, there are still plenty of other fish – roach, pike, eels and many more. The firm of La Pêcherie, which is based in Peyrehorade, is well known all over France for the high quality of its smoked salmon, but the sad fact is that demand is so great that much is now imported from Norway, Canada and Scotland. La Pêcherie also smokes eels and sells caviar and *jambon de Bayonne*.

Should you go to Peyrehorade, do not fail to visit Sorde l'Abbaye which has a fine position overlooking the Gave d'Oloron with an excellent view of the Pyrénées. This ruined abbey, whose earliest parts date from the tenth century, offered hospitality to pilgrims on their way to Santiago de Compostela. Who knows, perhaps the pilgrims feasted on salmon? Recent excavations there have revealed traces of prehistoric dwellings as well as Gallo–Roman remains.

In the Landes, as in Armagnac, they like to finish a good meal with a succulent dessert, and what better than a *tourtière*, an irresistible confection made from the thinnest of flaky pastry, stuffed with fat prunes and soaked in armagnac. Similar pastries are to be found in the Agenais, Armagnac, Périgord and Quercy under a variety of names, including the *croustade* and the *pastis*. There is much controversy about the exact nature of each and as outsiders we hesitate to be dogmatic, but it would appear that the *tourtière* has prunes as a filling whereas the other two have sliced, sweet, eating apples. There is however general agreement about the pastry part; the finest flaky pastry is rolled very thin, brushed with melted lard, goose fat or walnut oil and folded. The process is repeated again and the pastry rolled out until it is as thin as finest linen, indeed the traditional name for the pastry is *voile de mariage*.

Fiddling about with wedding veils is almost impossible for those of us who have not learnt the knack of rolling gently and firmly always in the same direction. Try using instead a small packet of frozen flaky pastry, well thawed.

Tourtière

Remove the stones from the prunes and allow to drain well. Cut the thawed out pastry into four equal parts. Take the first piece and shape it into a ball. Sprinkle the icing sugar and cornflour mix onto your rolling surface and with your rolling pin roll the pastry gently and firmly until it is very thin and about 35cm (14 inches) across. Take your largest cake tin (metal is best, do not be tempted to use glass or china) and with your pastry brush spread the oil or melted fat generously on the inside. Put the first layer of pastry gently in the tin. Arrange eight of the prunes at intervals round the inside of the tin and sprinkle with a little orange flower water and some of the icing sugar and cornflour mix. Roll out the second piece of pastry and repeat the process. Continue until you are rolling out the fourth piece of pastry, making sure that you finish off with a light brushing of milk.

Bake the *tourtière* in a hot oven, watching to see that the pastry does not brown unduly. When ready, use an apple corer to make a small hole in the centre and pour in the armagnac, rolling the tin from side to side, so that all parts receive some. Powder the top with icing sugar and serve lukewarm with extra armagnac if you like, or thin cream.

For *croustade* or *pastis* you need the same amount of frozen pastry, but the prunes are replaced with peeled, cored and sliced eating apples.

1 small packet frozen pastry (250g or 8oz)
24 large prunes soaked in tea and stewed with sugar
Orange flower water
a little milk
Walnut oil, melted goose fat or lard
2 generous tablespoons armagnac
Icing sugar mixed with cornflour in equal proportions
Extra icing sugar to powder the top when cooked

Dacquoise

The *dacquoise*, which as its name indicates is associated with the town of Dax (a rugby stronghold) follows much the same pattern except that the inside layers are filled with a mixture of ground almonds, orange flower water and egg. It can be made with either flaky pastry or a rich short crust.

Mix together the ground almonds and the same caster sugar with two teaspoons of orange flower water and a beaten egg, using a little milk for extra moistening if necessary. Instead of the sugar, you can use honey and water mixed to a thick syrup, in which case you probably won't need to add milk to the mixture. Spread this on each layer of pastry, sealing the edges well and brushing the top with milk to brown it. You can pour some warm armagnac into the centre if you like.

1 small packet flaky or rich short crust pastry
125g (5oz) ground almonds
125g (5oz) caster sugar
2 teaspoons orange flower water
1 egg, beaten

Armagnac

ARMAGNAC lies in the very heart of Gascony, bounded to the south by the foothills of the Pyrénées, to the west and north-west by the pine forests of the Landes to the north by the river Garonne and eastwards by the right bank of the Gers, a sluggish tributary of the Garonne that can turn into a raging torrent during periods of prolonged rain, as happened in the early summer of 1977 when much of the region was seriously flooded. The modern department of Gers takes its name from the river and is almost identical with the old county of Armagnac.

The land is rural in character with no large towns to speak of. Auch, the capital of the Gers, is the biggest with a population of 25,000, whilst Condom and Eauze, both well-known centres of the armagnac brandy industry, have 8,000 and 6,000 inhabitants respectively. There are few villages and the farms are widely dispersed. This sparsely populated region is famous for one product above all others, its aromatic brandy which ranks with cognac as one of the finest in the world. Some say that armagnac lacks cognac's finesse but this is an opinion that it would be unwise to voice in the hearing of the Gascons' themselves who are traditionally hot-blooded. These dark-skinned volatile people are descended in part from the Vascons, an Iberian tribe who settled this area in the sixth century AD at a time when the Roman administration was rapidly breaking down. Gascons enjoy a reputation for being proud, touchy, boastful, quick-witted and eloquent. They are also spontaneous and friendly, and nowhere in the South-West will the traveller find a warmer welcome, so long as he sings the praises of armagnac!

Perhaps the Gascon temperament is something to do with the climate of Armagnac, which can be extreme. The summers are sometimes so hot that the rivers and streams dry up completely and the heavy clay soil that covers much of the area becomes cracked and dusty. In the winter it can be bitterly cold, especially when the *bise*, a dry cold wind from the north, is blowing. Heavy rain from the Atlantic occasionally lasts long enough to swell the many small rivers and streams to the point where they burst their banks and turn the surrounding land into a quagmire, or cause serious flooding. On the whole, however, the climate is moderate with average winter temperatures of between 4 and 5° C. Frosts are rare and snow even rarer, but it does tend to be rather humid during the winter months. Spring comes late in

Armagnac and is short lived but spectacular, to be succeeded by a long, very hot, and often dry summer. Given the nature of the soil and the climatic conditions, it is perhaps not surprising that the land supports such a small population.

The county of Armagnac first came into existence in the tenth century, following the invasions of the Norsemen. In AD 853 the Vikings penetrated deep inland from Bordeaux, looting and laying waste everything in their path including the towns of Lectoure, Condom and Eauze, the latter being the Gallo-Roman capital of the area. As a result the authority of the Duke of Gascony was completely undermined and the first counts of Armagnac were able to carve out a territory for themselves. Technically the counts were vassals of the duke, but in practice they were independent. They quickly consolidated their position and rapidly extended their boundaries. By the fourteenth century they had become a force to reckon with in France and they played a major political rôle during the period of the Hundred Years' War. At this period Armagnac was a disputed territory right on the frontier between Gascony and the domains of the French king, a fact that is testified by a line of castles, *bastides* and heavily fortified churches stretching southwards from Fleurance to Masseube.

In the seventeenth century Armagnac was chiefly remarkable as a recruiting ground for the French army. It became a tradition that the younger sons ('cadets') of noble families should leave home to seek their fortunes. They really had no choice since most of the noble families of Armagnac lived in genteel poverty and could not support an extra son who contributed nothing to the household. That is why Charles de Batz, better known as d'Artagnan, left his home near Lupiac and went to Paris to join the army. D'Artagnan subsequently became lieutenant-captain of the king's musketeers, the king's own bodyguard. It was on his career that Dumas based his famous series of novels.

The economic pressures that forced Charles de Batz to leave home still apply today. The Gers is the least populated department of France: only 32 per cent of the population live in towns and 51 per cent of the working population are engaged in agriculture, figures that underline the rural character of the land. The countryside of Armagnac is delightful to drive through. The rolling wooded hills are relaxing on the eyes and the roads often follow the valley routes alongside one of the many small rivers that wind half-hidden by trees and bushes through the landscape. There are few towns or villages to interrupt a leisurely journey, and the farms are often concealed from view by trees or a fold in the landscape. It is easy enough to turn off the road and find an empty meadow by a stream where, mosquitoes permitting, you can enjoy an uninterrupted picnic. We once spent a languorous hot afternoon in the shade of a ruined mill on the banks of the Gers. The slow-moving brown river flowed over a weir at this point, creating a convenient back-eddy where we could put our bottle of

Monbazillac to cool; the birds were silent in the intense heat but enormous brightly coloured dragonflies flitted back and forth over the water as we ate our delicious *charentais* melons from nearby Lectoure and sipped our wine.

There are many such idyllic spots to be found in Armagnac, for the countryside is threaded by numerous rivers and streams which rise on the plateau de Lannemezan to the south and spread fanwise as they flow northwards. For reasons connected with the thawing of the glaciers in the last ice age, many of the river valleys, especially in the south of Armagnac, have an unusual asymetric section; the right-hand or eastern banks slope steeply and abruptly from the river, while the opposite, western banks have a longer, more gradual incline. This makes a car journey from east to west a roller-coaster ride – you climb laboriously up the long western slope to rush joyously down the eastern one, only to begin the slow ascent once more – and this pattern is endlessly repeated.

The Gascon farmers make good use of the long western slopes, planting them with a variety of crops. In the valley bottoms are the meadows; a little higher up cereals and tobacco are grown; higher still, where the slopes receive the most sun, are the vineyards. This gives an interest to the landscape not found in some other areas of the South-West, notably the neighbouring Lomagne to the north-west, where there are enormous fields of sunflowers – a marvellous sight when they are in flower but monotonous at other times.

Much of Armagnac has heavy clay soil that is very difficult to work. In the past sturdy oxen were used to drag the plough but now tractors have largely taken over and today a much greater area of land is given over to the cultivation of cereals, especially maize. In the west of Armagnac the soil is lighter and sandier and it is here, in the neighbourhood of Eauze, that the best armagnac brandy is made.

The region where armagnac is distilled, and which is legally entitled to the *appellation*, covers three-quarters of the modern department of the Gers, the extreme south-west of the Agenais (Lot-et-Garonne) and a small part of the Landes, near Villeneuve-de-Marsan. Within these boundaries Armagnac is further subdivided into Haut-Armagnac, a large area embracing the whole of the eastern half and a good portion of the south of the region; Ténarèze, a smaller stretch in the north and centre, and to the west Bas-Armagnac, with Eauze, the 'capital' of Armagnac as its main town. (Auch is the departmental capital of the Gers.)

Although armagnac rivals cognac in excellence, it is much less well known. This is in part due to the fact that the Charente, where cognac is made, is much nearer to Bordeaux and has therefore always had an outlet for its product, while armagnac had a much longer journey, either down the Adour to Bayonne or along the Garonne to Bordeaux, through what was often hostile country. The building of the railways and later better roads at the end of the nineteenth century eased the communication problem, but because the Gascons were cut off from the outside world for so long they were also less energetic in exploiting their brandy than the producers of cognac. It is only very recently that serious efforts have been made to reach export markets, so that names such as Janneau, Clés des Ducs and Marquis de Caussade are becoming better known.

Armagnac is made in an alembic, a kind of double boiler in which the

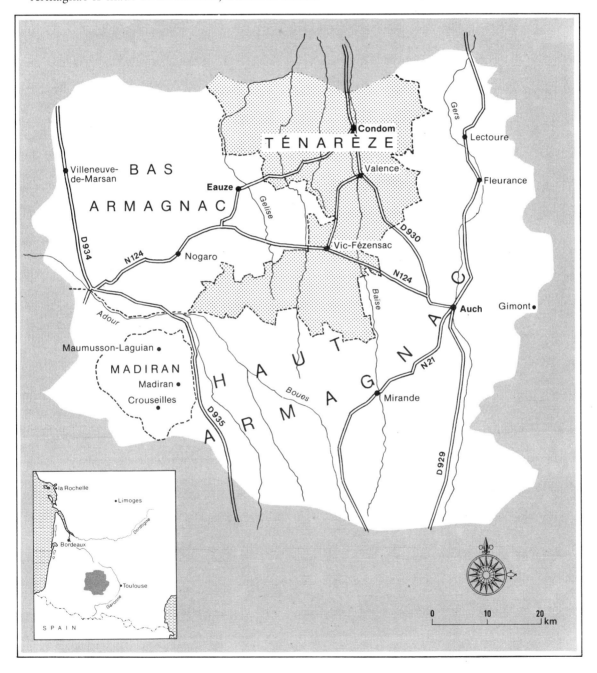

wine is distilled only once, unlike cognac which passes through the still twice. The strength of armagnac is also lower. At the end of the distillation the spirit leaves the alembic with a minimum of 52 degrees of pure alcohol compared with cognac which starts with a minimum strength of 70 degrees. During its years in the barrel it will lose by evaporation between one and one and a half per cent per year. By law armagnac must be sold with an alcoholic content of between 40 degrees and 48 degrees. But in practice bottles above 42 degrees are rarely found.

The Gascons learned the art of distillation from the Arabs whose influence was strong in this part of France until the Moors were expelled from Spain in the fifteenth century. The word *alembic* comes from the Arabic *'el embic'*. In the archives of the Musée de l'Armagnac at Condom there is a document dated 1411 which mentions an 'Ayga Ardenterius', in other words a distiller of *eau-de-vie*, but it appears that this spirit was used for medicinal purposes only. So far as we know it was not until the seventeenth century that armagnac was distilled to be drunk. Until then, Armagnac was still a wine-growing region although, during the troubled period of the Hundred Years' War and subsequently the Wars of Religion in the sixteenth century, the growers found great difficulty in exporting their product because of the difficulty of reaching a port.

In the seventeenth century, however, the Gascons were encouraged by Dutch merchants to distil their wine. The advantage of this to the Dutch was that the volume of the *eau-de-vie* was much less than that of the wine and so their transport costs over a long distance were much reduced. When the spirit reached Holland it was mixed with wine purchased from more accessible parts of France such as Périgord. The idea was to help preserve the wine as well as to fortify it. This fortified wine was shipped in the following year to ports in Germany and the Baltic.

It was the Dutch seamen who first started drinking the spirit. They were given a barrel of *eau-de-vie* on each voyage as part of their contract and seem to have acquired a taste for it that led to more and more of the imported spirit, rather than French wine finding its way into Dutch taverns. The sailors called the spirit 'Brandewijn', which is Dutch for *'vin brulé'*, or 'burnt wine'. 'Brandewijn' was anglicized into 'brandy'.

The original alembic used in Armagnac was the *'double chauffe'* which meant that the liquid was distilled at least twice to purify it. In 1801 however a chemist from Montpellier, Edouard Adam, invented a single distillation method which was further refined by a Gascon peasant named Verdier, and this *alambic armagnacais* is still in use today.

To understand how the *alambic armagnacais* works one needs to understand the basic principle of the ordinary pot still. This is simple enough; the wine, contained in a large kettle or pot, is heated so that it starts to vaporize. The first highly volatile elements, known as headings, escape into a copper coil called the serpentine, which is immersed in water. As the vapour passes through the serpentine it condenses and by the time it has reached the end it has changed into spirit. The 'headings' are full of impurities that contribute nothing to the final spirit, so they are drawn off into a barrel. Meanwhile the process is continuing and as the heat increases the alcohol in the wine is also vaporized and is collected in a second barrel. The liquid alcohol contained in this second barrel is called the '*brouillis*'. A residue of wine is left behind in the pot and this goes into the third barrel under the name of 'tailings'. The *brouillis* is returned to the pot and is distilled a second time, in exactly the same way, and this time the second barrel contains the *eau-de-vie* that, after a period of maturing in the barrel, is sold as brandy. The headings and tailings are added to the next pot of wine to be distilled.

In the case of the *alambic armagnacais*, the wine does not go straight into the pot but into a copper cauldron called the *chauffe-vin*, inside which is the serpentine. From the *chauffe-vin* the wine flows into a second receptacle which is divided into two parts: at the top is the *colonne à plateaux* and beneath it the *chaudière-en-cuivre*, which is heated by the furnace immediately below. The *colonne à plateaux*, as its name suggests, contains a

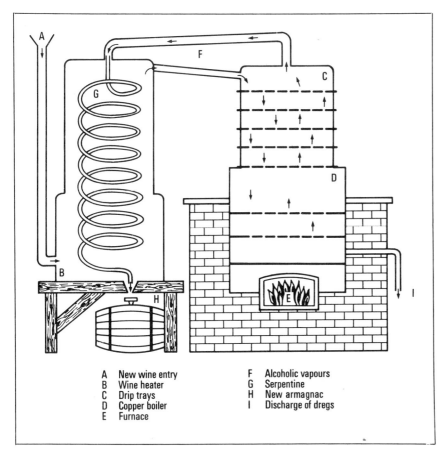

A	New wine entry	F	Alcoholic vapours
B	Wine heater	G	Serpentine
C	Drip trays	H	New armagnac
D	Copper boiler	I	Discharge of dregs
E	Furnace		

series of perforated trays and the wine drips slowly down from tray to tray becoming hotter and hotter as it gets nearer the furnace until the water, alcohol and other volatile elements all evaporate. The vapour now rises, finding its way back through the trays and becoming impregnated as it does so with the subtle aromas of the incoming wine in the process of vaporizing as it drips downwards. These aromas are preserved throughout the rest of the distillation and account for much of armagnac's individual character. The alcoholic vapour (for most of the water content disappears) continues on its way into and through the serpentine. In the case of the *alambic armagnacais*, it will be remembered, this is immersed not in water but in the wine itself, which enters at the base of the *chauffe-vin*. Thus, as the vapour descends, the serpentine is slowly condensed by the cooler wine outside, so that by the time the bottom is reached it is *eau-de-vie* and is drawn off into a barrel. Conversely, the rising wine is warmed by the serpentine and by the time it reaches the top of the *chauffe-vin* it has already attained a temperature of 80°C. Inside the *colonne à plateaux*, the temperature averages 100°C but at the base of the *chaudière* it rises to between 105°C and 110°C. Here the last traces of alcohol evaporate leaving a liquid residue full of impurities called the *vinesse*, which is regularly drained off.

Once started, the distillation process is continuous until the whole of the new vintage has been converted into *eau-de-vie*. Although the method is basically straightforward, a great deal of skill is needed to produce the best results. For example, it is claimed that even the kind of wood used to heat the alembic plays an important part: oak and alder are considered the best.

Armagnac is distilled from white wine made from a variety of grapes and here again the choice of grapes will significantly affect the final quality. In the past the grape most widely used in Armagnac was the Picquepoult, a local word meaning *pique-lèvres*, referring to the high acidity of the wine made from it, but today this has been largely supplanted by St-Émilion, Colombard and Bacco 22A. The latter is a hybrid made by crossing Folle Blanche with the American grape, Noah. It can only be grown in the sandy soil of Bas-Armagnac. Other authorized grape varieities are Folle Blanche, Jurançon, Meslier St-François, Plant de Graisse and Mozac.

All these grapes are low in sugar but rich in the subtle perfumes that distinguish brandy made in Armagnac from all others, although the wine made from them is thin, acidic and low in alcohol. By law the wine must not be racked or filtered and distillation starts as soon as the fermentation is over. The grape harvest is late in Armagnac so the distillation period begins in late November or early December and lasts until the end of April. The process goes on day and night and the roaring flames of the furnace seen against the blackness of the night make a dramatic sight. Most of the small producers in Armagnac have no alembic of their own but rely on an intinerant still, which in days of yore used to be transported slowly from farm to farm behind two sturdy blond oxen. Nowadays the alembic comes by lorry, which is quicker but much less picturesque. The larger concerns have their own stills and some of them are adopting the cognac method of double distillation, but this is frowned on by the purists.

After distillation the spirit is kept in new barrels for a minimum of a year. The barrels must be made of the local oak, most of which comes from the forest of Monlezun. This is unfortunately becoming rarer and consquently very expensive, but no substitute will do. Limousin oak has been tried instead but the resulting brandy is not armagnac. The local oak is dark and sappy and by some mysterious alchemy this helps to give armagnac its peculiar character as well as its beautiful colour. It follows that the cooper has an important role in Armagnac. Indeed the larger establishments employ their own. The cooper (*tonnelier*) chooses the trees and supervises their felling; he then sees that the logs are cut into manageable lengths from which the staves can be made. Because the oak is so full of sap the cooper cuts out the staves by hand with an adze. The staves are then left to dry out at the rate of a centimetre a year. The cooper himself matures slowly, serving an apprenticeship that lasts ten years before he is considered fully fledged. His chief art lies in making the finished barrel watertight but not airtight, for the contact of the air with the spirit contributes to the maturing process.

Armagnac must remain at least one year in the barrel before it can be sold, in which case it carries three stars on the label. If the label bears the letters 'VSOP'* it means that the brandy has been in cask for a minimum of four years, whilst the words 'Hors d'Age' indicate a minimum period before bottling of at least five years, although it could be much longer than that. Armagnac can mature in the cask for anything up to thirty years before it starts to decline, in rare cases even longer, and indeed it is possible to find bottles whose labels claim this length of age. Brandy doesn't mature in the bottle of course. In passing, it should be pointed out that the flask-shaped bottle in which armagnac is sold has no particular significance; the old bottles that can be seen in the Musée de l'Armagnac are all the same shape as a claret bottle.

It would be wrong to suppose that when you buy a bottle of armagnac the brandy it contains comes from a single barrel of a particular year. It may do, but in practice nearly all armagnac is blended. In the case of the smaller producers the blend is made by mixing different years to produce a quality that is individual to the house but does not vary too much from year to year. A good example is Château du Tariquet, a small domaine near Eauze. The château has an attractive façade flanked by small round towers. Close to the house there are oak trees and flower beds but otherwise the château is surrounded by vines, St-Émilion and Bacco 22A predominating. The *chai*, of which the proprietor Monsieur Pierre Grassa is rightly proud, dates back to the seventeenth century, the period when armagnac was first distilled to

* VSOP is short for Very Superior Old Pale. This classification is also used for cognac.

be drunk. Inside, the *chai* has a beautiful timbered roof made from the same local oak as the barrels it contains.

At Château du Tariquet, as we have said, the armagnac is the result of the careful blending in cask of spirit from different years, the exact combination being the secret of the *maître de chai*, in this case Monsieur Grassa himself. Monsieur Grassa believes fervently in upholding the traditional methods of making armagnac and the finesse of his brandy is the best of tributes to the care and skill that goes into its production.

In some of the larger firms, however, the grapes may come from a number of different growers, so the wine from which the distillate is made is already a blend. After the distillation the years are blended as at Château du Tariquet, but in some cases spirit from one area may be mixed with that from another, Haut-Armagnac with Ténarèze, for example. Such a blend could not carry the appellation of either Haut-Armagne or Ténarèze, but would be sold under the simple label, 'Armagnac Appellation Contrôlée'. The bigger companies often market several different qualities of armagnac, from the simple appellation up to a very expensive twenty- or thirty-year-old Hors d'Age. If you wish to buy a very fine armagnac the words to look for on the label are 'Bas-Armagnac', the best area, and 'Hors d'Age', but remember that all this means is that the brandy has been in the barrel a minimum of five years and in these days when all good businessmen are anxious to turn their money over as quickly as possible it probably won't be longer. If you would like a really old bottle you will have to look out for one that actually states the number of years in cask.

Should you be fortunate enough to enjoy a tasting before buying your armagnac – and there is no shortage of opportunities for a *dégustation* – you should look first of all at the colour. A young armagnac should be a pale amber, whilst an older one will be a deeper, richer shade. Unfortunately some young armagnacs have sugar and other elements added to them so that they take on a darker hue which, for some obscure reason, is how most people think a good armagnac should look. This artificial colouring makes the brandy look slightly more opaque than it should do if it has gone through the proper ageing process. A good armagnac will also have a strongly perfumed aroma and a high viscosity. The latter can be tested by swirling the spirit in the glass; this will leave a film on the inside of the glass from which long tears will slowly drip down like rain on a window pane. To the palate armagnac should be smooth and dry with an aftertaste that gives a comfortable warm glow. A poor armagnac will be fiery and will make your eyes blink.

Armagnac should alway be warmed by cupping the hands round the glass before tasting. This will help to release the fine aromas. The locals, however, claim not to need a glass to assess the quality of an Armagnac, they merely pour a little into the palms of their hands, rub them together and sniff!

Armagnac is an *eau-de-vie de vin*; in other words, like cognac, it is distilled from wine, which largely accounts for the superior quality and comparative rarity of these brandies. Most *eau-de-vie* is distilled from *marc*, the residue of the grapes that is left behind after the wine has fermented and been transferred to another container. *Eau-de-vie* can also be made from the mash of fermented fruit, hence Poire Williams, which is a pear liqueur and Eau-de-vie de Prune, a plum liqueur popular all over the South-West but especially associated with the Agenais.

Many farmers in France have the hereditary right to distill twenty litres of *eau-de-vie*, duty free, for their own use each year. At one time it was possible to transfer the privilege to a new owner when the farm was sold but the French government, worried by alcoholism in France, has clamped down and stopped the practice. This has reduced the number of people entitled to distill their own *eau-de-vie* from four million in 1956 to under two million today. Even so, every farming family seems to have its supply of *eau-de-vie* and it is common when you are invited in to be given a small dish containing two large prunes swimming in a dark alcoholic liquid or a similar dish of cherries. This is not a true brandy for the fruit has been bottled in the *eau-de-vie*. To begin with the spirit is quite clear but after a year or so it takes on the colour of the fruit while the plums or cherries swell as they absorb the alcohol. The result is quite delicious and extremely potent, as we have found to our cost!

In Périgord they make a special *eau-de-vie* called *gnole* or *gniole* from a mixture of honeysuckle, plum and mint. A bottle of *gnole* is traditionally given to an infant at birth and should last his or her whole life through, only being brought out on very special occasions like marriage.

Another drink, with quite a kick to it, that is made in Armagnac is the liqueur aperitif Pousse Rapière or 'rapier thrust'. It consists of a measure of liqueur armagnac topped up with a sparkling white wine and garnished with orange peel. The name is supposed to derive from the fanciful idea that the effect of the aperitif is like the thrust of a rapier received in a duel – this is after all the land of d'Artagnan. Pousse Rapière is now being marketed by the Domaine de Monluc in special packs containing one bottle of armagnac mixed with orange liqueur and a bottle of sparkling white wine. A less potent drink is Floc de Gascogne (Bouquet de Gascogne), a Gascon version of Pineau de Charente. It is made from grape juice drawn off before fermentation and mixed in a proportion of 3:1 with Armagnac. Floc de Gascogne has an alcoholic content of 17 degrees. Served chilled it is delicious.

The cuisine of Armagnac is overshadowed by the famous brandy, even so you can still eat very well here. The Gascons have hearty appetites and, outside the main towns, restaurant meals tend be copious and on the heavy side, so if you do stop for lunch at some small wayside restaurant it is advisable not to have any exacting plans for the afternoon!

One of the dishes that really sorts the men from the boys is *cassoulet*, a rich bean and meat stew that is so filling it is really a meal in itself. Strictly speaking *cassoulet* originated in Languedoc, east of the region covered in this book, but the eastern border of Armagnac is so close to Toulouse, the capital of Languedoc, that there are bound to be similarities in the cooking. After all, good food knows no political boundaries and the *cassoulet* is such a magnificent dish that its fame has spread far beyond the confines of Languedoc itself and is likely to be encountered on restaurant menus throughout the South-West.

The method of preparing the cassoulet and its ingredients varies from village to village but there are three main kinds: the *cassoulets* of Toulouse, of Castelnaudary, a dull little town 55 kilometres south-east of Toulouse, and of Carcassonne, the marvellous medieval walled city, 36 kilometres further on, which is one of the great tourist attractions of the area. *Cassoulet* is served in the restaurants in Carcassonne so this is a good place to try it, but if you do make sure you get your sightseeing over in the morning!

Carcassonne boasts that the *cassoulet* originated there. It is believed to have been introduced into the area by the Arabs who occupied much of the South-West in the eighth century and who are said to have shown the people of Carcassonne how to cultivate the haricot bean and combine it with other kinds of white bean and various cuts of mutton. Naturally the pre-eminence of the *cassoulet* of Carcassonne is hotly disputed and many experts claim that the Castelnaudary variety is the only true one because the earthenware pot in which it is cooked and presented is a *cassou* or *cassole*, made from the clay of Issel, a nearby village. Castelnaudary also claims to be the progenitor of *cassoulet* for another reason: according to local legend the first *estofat* (a dish of stew cooked very slowly) of haricot beans and whatever meat they could find was concocted by the townspeople to give the defenders heart during a siege by the English, at the time of the Hundred Years' War. The results proved highly beneficial and so effective that the besieging army was pushed back not just from Castelnaudary but from the whole of southern France!

The Castelnaudary *cassoulet* is made from fresh pork, ham, knuckle of pork, the *saucisses* of Castelnaudary and a type of haricot bean called the *lingot*, larger than the usual English baked bean but smaller than a butter bean. No tomato or mutton or lamb should go into the Castelnaudary variety. The *cassoulet* of Carcassonne is very similar to that of Castelnaudary, except that pieces of leg of lamb or mutton should be added, together with a quartered partridge in season. The *cassoulet toulousain*, however, is probably the variety most likely to be served in restaurants in Armagnac. It should contain Toulouse sausage, preserved duck or goose and a good helping of tomato or tomato purée. Another ingredient that you are likely to find in all these *cassoulets* is fresh pork or bacon rind; this is much prized in the South West for the way it enriches a stew or ragôut and is an essential ingredient in many recipes. The English tend to push it to the side of the plate, much to the amazement of the French – but then many things that the English do to food amaze the French!

The preparation of a *cassoulet* also varies. The Castelnaudary *cassoulet* should be taken out of the oven seven times during the cooking and stirred well so that the crust which forms on the top is broken and mixed in. It should also be cooked in a baker's oven fired by gorse from the slopes of the Montagne Noire to the north of the town; alternatively some gorse branches should be put in the bottom of the oven to give the required perfume. The *cassoulets* of Toulouse and Carcassonne need only one session in the oven and no stirring. Clearly *cassoulet*-making demands a certain amount of time and trouble: this is borne out by a story told by Prosper Montagné, the editor of *Larousse Gastronomique* and a famous Paris restaurateur, who went to his local shoemaker in Castelnaudary one day to find the shop shuttered and locked and a notice pinned to the door. Prosper Montagné thought something must be very wrong, perhaps sickness or death in the family, but when he read the notice he found the real reason: '*Fermé pour cause de cassoulet*'.

Cassoulet Serves 6–8

You can add or substitute whatever takes your fancy in the way of, say, pie veal (neck) pieces, rabbit portions, more chicken bits or sausages. Beware of beef; it does not mix well. The recipe gives a very generous amount of meat per person. If cutting down, halve the quantity but get the variety of meat.

Soak the dried beans overnight. Drain them and put them into a pan with the oddments of bones, onion, carrot, bouquet garni and garlic. Bring to the boil and cook slowly for about $1\frac{1}{2}$ hours until the beans are tender but not split. You can also add the rind of the piece of bacon and the skin of the salt belly pork to the mixture – it all helps to add flavour.

When the beans are cooked, drain off and keep the liquid. Discard the onion, garlic, carrot and bouquet garni and bones. Cut the other meats in pieces about 4cm ($1\frac{1}{2}$in) square. Fry with 3 chopped onions, olive oil and the 3 crushed cloves of garlic, 1 diced carrot. Add a little water at the end of frying to moisten the mixture.

In a very large casserole with a lid, put first a layer of beans then a layer of meat and so on until the casserole is full (or all the ingredients are used up). Finish with a layer of beans. Mix the bean liquid with tomato purée, a glass of strong red wine (more if you like), a good milling of black pepper (do not add salt because of the bacon and salt pork already in the recipe) and stock (a stock cube would do but they are a bit salty; a packet soup or instant soup might be preferable). Pour the liquid over the casserole until it comes to about 2.5cm (1in) below the top of the beans. Keep the rest of the liquid for later. Sprinkle with fresh breadcrumbs about 1cm ($\frac{1}{2}$in) thick. Cover tightly with foil and the casserole lid and cook very, very slowly for as long as you like (4–6 hours on the lowest heat or in the lowest oven temperature). Keep

$\frac{1}{2}$–$1kg$ (1–$1\frac{1}{2}lb$) *dried haricot beans*

$500g$ ($1lb$) *salt belly pork (boned if necessary)*

$500g$ ($1lb$) *breast of lamb*

Stock bones (lamb and pork bones, a pig's trotter, veal bones, etc)

1 *large onion, stuck with 2 cloves*

1 *carrot*

1 *bouquet garni*

4 *cloves garlic, whole*

3 *onions, chopped*

2 *tablespoons tomato purée*

1 *glass strong red wine*

Freshly ground black pepper

125–$250ml$ ($\frac{1}{4}$–$\frac{1}{2}$ *pint*/5–$10fl.$ *oz*) *good stock*

Fresh breadcrumbs

$250g$ ($\frac{1}{2}lb$) *pork fillet*

$\frac{1}{2}$ *chicken cut into four pieces*

$250g$ ($\frac{1}{2}lb$) *garlic sausage in cubes*

$250g$ ($\frac{1}{2}lb$) *piece streaky bacon (not too salt and cut in pieces)*

Olive oil

an eye on the level of the liquid and add more as necessary. You can also stir in the breadcrumbs every 2 hours and recover with a fresh lot. The last lot of crumbs should be allowed to settle on top and absorb surplus fat. Remove the cover and lid for the last hour to let the crumbs brown. Don't let the *cassoulet* dry out but add more liquid/wine/stock as available.

A great deal of preparation can be done in advance but it is advisable not to pre-cook the whole dish because the beans will go mushy and the *cassoulet* will become dry, but you could cook the beans the day before and do the main cooking on the day.

This may sound a great deal of trouble, but be assured, it is worth taking the time and choosing the ingredients for a good home-made *cassoulet*. If you don't much mind about flavour and are short of time there is a quick version taking about an hour:

Quick cassoulet

2 tins white haricot or navy beans (750g or 1lb 10oz)
1 can peeled tomatoes (400g or 14oz), chopped
5 shallots
2 cloves garlic
6 small pork chops
Salt, pepper, thyme and parsley
6 pork chipolata sausages
6 slices neck of lamb
Pork fat or olive oil for frying
Red wine

Chop the shallots and fry gently in pork fat or olive oil. Take the shallots out and in the same pan, fry the pork chops, then the neck of lamb and finally the sausages. In a large deep earthenware casserole put a layer of haricot beans. Mix the rest of the beans with the chopped tomatoes and add the thyme, parsley, garlic, the tomato juice and the shallots. On top of the white beans put a layer of the fried meat and sausages. Cover with the tomato and bean mixture. Put another layer of meat in the casserole and finish off with a layer of the tomato and beans. Cook in a hot oven for about half an hour. Take it out, break the top crust and pour in any juice left over or a little red wine to keep the *cassoulet* moist. Give it another half-hour in the oven and serve piping hot.

Cassoulet is a very substantial dish, so serve it with salad, green vegetables or on its own with good bread to mop up whatever juices have escaped the beans. A light dessert to follow is the only other course needed and what could be better than prune ice cream with armagnac.

Prune ice cream with armagnac

16 prunes
250ml double cream (½ pint/ 10fl.oz)
2 tablespoons sugar
250g fromage blanc or 125g cottage cheese and 125g natural yoghurt
Juice of half a lemon
Vanilla essence to taste (optional)
Prunes in armagnac for decoration (one per portion)

Many people have freezers these days but making ice cream can be a tedious business without a *sorbetière* – half freezing the mush and then beating in egg white or making the mixture so rich in cream that it becomes a most expensive dessert. There are alternative recipes that use a creamy custard mixture and these are delicious for plain or delicately flavoured ice cream. This recipe does not need a *sorbetière* and by using a mixture of double cream, natural yoghurt and cottage cheese it is economical and not too fattening. If you can buy *fromage blanc* use with the double cream instead of the yoghurt-cottage cheese mixture.

Soak the 16 prunes overnight in tea. Transfer them to a saucepan with a minimum of tea. Sweeten with the sugar. Simmer gently until cooked, then remove the prunes and continue cooking the juice until about three tablespoons of very syrupy liquid remain. Remove the stones from the prunes.

If you are not using *fromage blanc* – double cream, blend the yoghurt and cottage cheese with the lemon juice, then add the prunes, the syrup and the vanilla essence; lastly pour in the double cream and blend thoroughly, scraping the mixture back on the blades if necessary. Taste for sweetness and add more sugar or sweetener if required. You can also add a little armagnac at this stage if you like, but it would be better to pour it over the individual portions as you serve the ice cream.

If you do not have a blender, you can make a satisfactory version of this ice cream by mincing, mashing and chopping the stoned prunes and substituting a commercial vanilla ice cream for the *fromage blanc*-double cream mixture. Let the ice cream melt in a bowl and then incorporate the prune purée. Pour the ice cream into a freezer-proof mould and freeze for at least 4 hours. Serve in individual dishes with a prune on top and a dash of armagnac.

This habit of dressing the prune ice cream with armagnac is a feature of the restaurant La Phare at Moncrabeau, just north of Condom. Moncrabeau boasts an Association of Liars and if you happen to be in the area on the last Sunday in August you could be enrolled in their number, if you can tell the tallest story you know, in French of course! At other times you can sit in the Liar's throne after lunch at La Phare and read the history of this interesting custom.

Glace au Pousse Rapière

Pousse Rapière forms the basis of this ice cream, which is better if you have a *sorbetière*, but which can be made without, if you are prepared to half-freeze to a mush and then beat well before completing the freezing process.

Boil the water and melt the sugar to make a syrup and allow to cool. Mix in the cream with the syrup and turn it into the *sorbetière*. As soon as the mixture starts to thicken, pour in the Pousse Rapière and allow the mixture to freeze solid. Serve in tall champagne glasses with a little more Pousse Rapière poured over the top. You can make half the quantity of this recipe and you can also substitute *fromage blanc* for some of the cream as in the previous recipe.

500ml (1 pint/20fl.oz) water
300g sugar (just over 8oz)
100ml Pousse Rapière (just under ⅓ pint/6fl.oz)
500ml double cream (1 pint/ 20fl.oz)

If you have no Pousse Rapière, try mixing your own. You will need a bottle of dry white wine, the juice of half an orange 60g (2oz) sugar and about 10 centilitres (⅓ pint/6fl.oz) armagnac. Mix together and add the correct amount to the ice cream mixture before freezing. To serve, add a little fizzy lemonade to the rest of Pousse Rapière and pour over the ice cream. This is a pleasant drink to accompany the dessert.

Gâteau à la broche

Another Gascon speciality is *gâteau à la broche*, which is featured on coloured postcards all over the South-West, each area claiming it for its own. The recipe is included for interest more than anything else, but on *fête* days you may well see a pancake stall with its bath of fat for deep-fried waffle cakes, huge flat pans for thin pancakes, liberally laced with armagnac or fruit syrups, and the open fire with the spits for sausages or *gâteaux à la broche*.

The batter is a thick pancake batter made from flour, sugar, eggs, white wine, orange flower water or vanilla essence and oil. It is spooned onto the spit a little at a time and the spit turned so that the batter cooks. A plate underneath will catch the drips and these can be spooned on to the *gâteau* as the batter cooks and turns. There is a secret to making a *gâteau à la broche* – you need to spear a large stoned olive on the spit and cover it with a small square of linen spread with butter. The linen is tied firmly round the olive and provides a good non-slip base for the batter. As the batter drips off the olive, and cooks in the heat it forms the characteristic needle-shaped points all round the spit. When the cake is large enough, cut it in half to remove it from the spit, take out the olive centre and serve sprinkled with sugar and armagnac.

Madame Grassa's Gâteau à l'armagnac

One day, while visiting Monsieur Grassa and his family to buy some armagnac, we were invited to sample Madame Grassa's sponge savarin cake – like an enormous baba soaked in orange and armagnac syrup. We ate pieces of the cake with teaspoons and drank glasses of home-made chilled Floc de Gascogne. Monsieur Grassa was concerned that the *gâteau* would have been even better the following day, when the armagnac would have had time to soak throughout the sponge – but then he is a perfectionist!

For the cake
2 eggs
4 heaped tablespoons plain flour
4 heaped tablespoons caster sugar
1 teaspoon baking powder
Pinch of salt

Beat the sugar with the eggs until thick and creamy. Fold in the flour, baking powder and a pinch of salt. Pour the mixture into a buttered savarin mould and bake immediately in a moderate oven for 25 minutes.

While the cake is baking, prepare the syrup by warming the grated orange rind, water and sugar. Allow to boil for a moment or two and then set aside to cool slightly before straining and adding the armagnac. Keep the syrup warm while the cake is cooking.

For the syrup
Rind of 1 orange, grated
8 tablespoons water
3 tablespoons sugar
4 tablespoons armagnac

When the cake is ready, take it from the oven and allow to stand for a moment or two before turning it out onto a warm plate. While the cake and the syrup are still warm, pour the syrup round and over the sponge and set aside until the next day. You can fill the inside of the cake with crème Chantilly, but Madame Grassa feels this is over-rich.

But to go back to the cassoulet for a moment, it will be remembered that the Toulouse variety should contain some *confit d'oie*. This is not surprising for the goose plays an important role in the local economy. Geese are a frequent sight in Armagnac, being the special responsibility of the farmer's wife who nurtures them carefully in the farmyard while her husband tends the vines and cultivates the fields. More geese and ducks are reared in Armagnac than anywhere else in the South-West and the enlarged livers (*foie gras*) are just as much a delicacy here as in Périgord. They figure prominently on restaurant menus, either plain or served with quails' eggs or grapes, and in many other ways. The flesh of the goose is usually preserved in its own fat to tenderize it and served as *confit d'oie* either hot or cold, and of course it also turns up in *cassoulet*. Breasts of duck (*lou magret*) is another favourite often found on menus in Armagnac (the recipe for this is given in the Périgord section). Armagnac also specializes in the production of turkeys for the markets of Paris and Toulouse. The Gascons themselves are very fond of these birds and have a splendid way of cooking them: it is called *ballotine de dinde gasconne*, and consists of a boned turkey, stuffed with breadcrumbs, garlic and minced pork and country ham in season (the breadcrumbs can be replaced by mashed chestnuts).

The local *charcuterie* shops in Armagnac sell excellent *pâté de foie gras*, often flavoured with armagnac and of course *confit d'oie*. Most of them also stock tins of *foie gras* and other local specialities, including *cassoulet de Toulouse*. The quality of these tinned delicacies is very high and they are well worth buying. One of the best firms specializing in the field is the Comtesse du Barry whose factory is on the outskirts of the bustling little market town of Gimont, 51 kilometres west of Toulouse. A visit to a canning factory may not sound everyone's ideal way of passing a morning, but the Comtesse du Barry establishment provides a fascinating glimpse of a small factory, which takes a pride in the quality of the produce and the processes. You will see great vats of sauces simmering alongside stocks of various kinds, chickens and ducks being filleted, dried ducks' breasts, rows of *foies gras*, sausages, fine fresh vegetables and fish of all shapes and colours waiting in the trays. Of course, the exact range of activities depends on the season but there is sure to be something of interest to see. You can visit the factory any morning or afternoon Monday to Friday and then walk a little way up the road to collect your free tin of *pâté de foie de porc*, to which each visitor is entitled.

Of all the small towns we have visited, Gimont is the one that seems to evoke best the authentic spirit of the South-West. Set on a small hill overlooking miles of flat, rather boring country where enormous fields of *tournesols* (sunflowers) and maize stretch as far as the eye can see, Gimont is quite unremarkable except for its market hall. This dates from the Middle Ages and covers most of the main square and here on market days the town comes to life. Stalls are piled high with fruit and vegetables and little knots of local farmers, wearing the traditional floppy Gascon beret and with the inevitable Gaullois trailing from the corners of their lips, are engaged in animated conversation. The market straggles down the hill to another more recent hall full of ducks, geese, chickens, rabbits, guinea fowl and turkeys. Frustrated-looking dogs are tied outside while their owners drive hard bargains inside. Eventually the owners emerge, the plumes of the still live birds suspended from their shoulders, and the dogs go wild with excitement! Apart from the big car park next door to the hall you can't help feeling that the scene has hardly changed in two hundred years or more.

After a visit to the market you can adjourn for lunch to the Hôtel de France in the main square. This is one of the vanishing breed of French hotels which provides one rough and ready dining room for the local tradespeople, where the noise becomes louder and louder as the meal progresses and where suddenly, on the stroke of two o'clock, everyone disappears; other guests lunch in a pleasant old-fashioned room with white tablecloths. Even those with egalitarian principles are advised to take advantage of the posh dining room where the atmosphere is tranquil without being dull and which has the advantage of being next door to a WC that is quite luxurious compared with the one used by the locals. The food at the Hôtel de France is typically Gascon; it is plain but well cooked and the helpings are more than generous.

It was at Gimont that we bought a string of the finest garlic imaginable. This part of France is in fact top of the league when it comes to the production of garlic: the department of Tarn-et-Garonne produces 6,000 tonnes annually, amounting to 18 per cent of the total for the whole of France. The garlic capital of the area is Beaumont-de-Lomagne, 32 kilometres to the north of Gimont, where every September a garlic fair is held. It takes place in the magnificent wooden market hall which, covering an area of 3,000 square metres, is even bigger than the one at Gimont. It is a splendid example of the medieval carpenters' skills, the wooden piers and complicated structure of roof beams being remarkably well preserved, no doubt due to the annual fumigation (the aroma inside the hall can be overwhelming).

Cooking with garlic is a feature of the South-West. It is said to have been rubbed on the lips of Henri IV when he was born, and certainly no concessions are made to those squeamish noses that can detect the smell at fifty metres. Strangely enough very few local people actually smell at all offensive; we noticed this with our local farmer and his family. Garlic soup, rabbit or chicken cooked with copious amounts of chopped garlic, a boiled egg with garlic sliced into it – yet no-one ever smelled of it. Perhaps, we thought, we were not noticing the garlic because we were eating it ourselves, but the more likely solution is that the more you eat the less you smell! Ford Madox Ford describes the experience of a mannequin, or model as we should call her today, who so enjoyed the flavour of garlic that, despite her work, she was unable to give it up and carefully rationed the amount she ate, hoping to disguise the aroma. The results were disastrous and she resolved to resign her job and indulge her love of garlic for the rest of her life. She went home and cooked a *poulet béarnais*, which consists of garlic and chicken in almost equal proportions, and for the next few days she almost lived on garlic. When she went back to work, for the last time as she thought, no one complained of the smell; on the contrary they all said how well she looked – the problem was solved!

In case you are still not convinced, here are some alternative solutions offered by French friends: never cut the clove with a knife, always cut it with a knife; use a garlic crusher, do not use a garlic crusher; never use the central greenish bit of the clove, use all the clove – take your pick, but if you are in the South-West you will surely have to come to terms with garlic sooner or later.

The garlic bulbs are known in France as *têtes* and the individual segments as *gousses*; in Britain we know the first as 'heads' and the second as 'cloves'. Garlic growing in Britain seldom seems to be successful; our summers don't seem to be hot or sunny enough. Even in France there were complaints in 1978 that the garlic was very small; nevertheless we brought strings back with us and found that it kept well and was sweeter than garlic available in shops in Britain.

Early in the summer, in June or July, the market stalls offer bunches of new garlic which look more like overgrown spring onions than the garlic we are used to seeing. These can be chopped and added, discreetly, to salads or used in stews and soups. Later, in September and October, the more familiar strings and bunches appear on sale. There are three main kinds of garlic: pink, violet and white. The pink is generally smaller and is highly prized for its flavour. In the Tarn-et-Garonne it is the white variety that is mostly grown, with the violet concentrated round Lautrec in the Tarn.

You can buy small strings of garlic, weighing about half a kilo, or even one or two heads at a time. If you find a favourite supplier, it is worth buying more and hanging it in a cool airy place; it will remain juicy the whole winter and still taste sweet.

Monsieur Ramos, a friend of ours who grows sweet pink garlic in his garden on the outskirts of Villeneuve-sur-Lot, has some advice for would-be garlic growers in Britain: first you must choose only the largest segments surrounding the core, discarding the central clove because it will not grow true. Do not peel the cloves but stick them in good fine earth in November, if you are planting *l'ail rose*, or in March/April if you are putting in the white variety. Use the first three fingers to make a hole in the earth and then put the clove of garlic in the hole and firm the earth round it. Allow about 12–15cm between each clove and keep the garlic bed in a square: about fifty cloves planted in a square metre will be about right. Do not expect to grow garlic in heavy clay or loam; it will grow better in the sort of soil that produces good root vegetables. In June when the stalks and leaves are getting long, tie them in a single knot. This will help the already strong bulbs to develop and grow fat. Dig up the bulbs in July or August when the leaves are almost dried out. Hang them in bunches in a dry cool place and they should keep throughout the winter. Monsieur Ramos says you can grow garlic in the kitchen during the winter, so that you can use the leaves to flavour salads and stews. Put the head in the top of a glass pot, rather like a hyacinth, keeping the bottom just touching the water below. Stand the pot on a window ledge where there is plenty of light.

A favourite starter on menus in the South-West is the *tourin*, a light clear soup flavoured either with garlic or tomato. We had encountered the tomato variety at several restaurants, but the garlic *tourin* we regarded with some suspicion until we were unexpectedly invited to stay for lunch with a neighbouring farming family and found it served up as the first course. We were impressed: the flavour was lightly creamy and we instantly asked for the recipe. Madame Artisié was pleased: her English friends who came from London, centre of sophistication, appreciated her *tourin*! This was the starting point for a long discussion on food and cooking and we owe to her many of the recipes in this book.

Madame Artisié's tourin à l'ail

3 whole heads garlic
Goose fat, pork fat or olive oil
2 tablespoons flour
4–5 tablespoons cold water
2l (4 pints) hot water
2 handfuls vermicelli
Salt and pepper
2 egg yolks
Few drops vinegar

Peel the garlic and slice lengthwise in thin slices. Heat the garlic gently in goose fat, pork fat or olive oil in a thick saucepan for 10–15 minutes. Add flour and mix quickly for a few minutes off the heat. Then add the cold water and mix well to remove any lumps. Still off the heat, add the hot water and give a good stir, making sure you get all the bits off the sides of the pan and incorporated into the *tourin*. Put the saucepan back on the heat and bring to the boil. Let the *tourin* cook for about 15–20 minutes, then add a couple of handfuls of fine vermicelli. Remove from the heat, add salt and pepper as necessary and set on one side.

Just before you are ready to serve, reheat the *tourin* but do not allow it to boil. Then beat the egg yolks with a few drops of vinegar in a large soup tureen and pour the garlic soup over the yolks, mixing well all the time. Stir well and serve immediately with toasted bread or croûtons.

The Gascons are fond of game and *faisan* (pheasant), *perdreau* (young partridge), *bécasse* (woodcock), *bécassine* (snipe) and *ortolan* (see page 165) are all liable to appear on the menu, either roasted or in casserole and always with an added dash of armagnac. Here, as elsewhere in the South-West, one of the most popular dishes is *salmis de palombe*, a savoury stew of wild wood pigeon. The recipe is given in the section on the Landes (page 165). Another favourite is *caille* (quail). These small birds are usually served in pairs, but sometimes a single quail turns up as part of an extensive menu, stuffed with a spoonful of *foie gras* or liver *pâté* and served on a croûton of fried bread. Here is a less exotic recipe:

Cailles aux fruits

2 quail per person
1 cooked prune ⎫
1 slice apple   ⎬ *per bird*
1 slice fried bread ⎭
Butter or lard to fry
125ml (¼ pint/5fl.oz) armagnac
125ml (¼ pint/5fl.oz) chicken stock

Fry the bread, which you should have first trimmed to a size and shape to fit neatly under each quail. Peel and core an eating apple and fry the rounds gently in butter or lard and set on the fried bread in a warm place while you deal with the quail. Brown the birds lightly in the frying pan with a little butter or lard. Stuff a cooked prune inside each quail and arrange the birds in a deep baking dish or ovenproof casserole. Flame with a generous amount of warm armagnac and moisten with an equal amount of chicken stock. Cover the dish with foil and cook in a moderate oven for about half an hour. Remove the foil, transfer the quail to a serving dish, setting them on the apple rings on the fried bread. Put the birds back in the oven to keep warm and serve the juices in a small sauceboat.

Should you fail to find quail in your local shop in Britain, write to Nigel Mizen of Sprunks Farm, Dunsfold, Surrey, who provides a postal service to most parts of the country. You will have to buy at least a dozen but any you have over can go into the freezer and be none the worse for it.

Quail is also eaten in Armagnac wrapped in oiled vine leaves and cooked on a spit over a fire of vine twigs.

Tourin à l'ail, salmis de palombe, glace aux pruneaux à l'armagnac, cailles aux fruits, cassoulet: there is certainly no shortage of good things to eat in this part of Gascony, and what better to round off a satisfying meal than a glass of fine old armagnac.

PYRENEES

Pays Basque

W HAT MOST PEOPLE remember about the Pays Basque is sitting in seemingly endless traffic jams on the RN 10 as thousands of French holidaymakers flock towards Hendaye and the Spanish frontier. Even those tourists who choose to halt a while on their journey south usually see only a narrow coastal strip that extends from Bayonne to the border and is known as the Côte Basque. This is a shame, for the Pays Basque has a unique character, and inland there is not only some magnificent mountain scenery but many delightful Basque villages with their own very individual and attractive style of architecture.

The Pays Basque lies in the extreme south-west of France. To the north stretches the forest of the Landes, to the west is the Atlantic Ocean and eastwards the mountains of Béarn. The southern border coincides with the Spanish frontier, but the Basques themselves are to be found on both sides of the Pyrénées: in fact there are more of them in the Basque provinces of Spain than those of France.

The origins of the Basques are obscure but it is currently believed that their immediate ancestors were the Vascons, an Iberian people who crossed the Pyrénées in the sixth century AD and ravaged the South-West. Subsequently the Vascons settled down in the lowland region just north of the Pyrénées and in the area that later became the county of Béarn, becoming assimilated with the local population, who by then had lived under Roman rule for six centuries and whose language was based on Latin. The Vascons thus lost their individual identity, although their name survives transformed into Gascons, the 'people of Gascony' (Gascogne). In the impenetrable mountains and forests of what is now the Pays Basque, however, the Basque race and its language have survived intact until the present day.

The Pays Basque is noticeably different from the rest of the South-West: the Basques are bilingual, jealously preserving their own strange and difficult tongue, so difficult that the devil himself could not master it! In the westernmost Basque province, Labourd, there is a distinct style of architecture, small flat-roofed, half-timbered houses with whitewashed mud walls strengthened by exposed wooden cross-beams and uprights painted blood-red or bottle-green with matching wooden shutters and sometimes shady recessed wooden balconies as well. There are a number of villages – Espelette is one – with Basque houses dating back to the sixteenth and seventeenth centuries, but the style has been much copied, and everywhere, including the coast, you will find modern concrete villas whose red and green 'timbers' are no more than painted decoration.

But some of the most significant differences are due to the presence of the ocean. The Atlantic is responsible for the mild weather; in the winter it is warm and damp with heavy rainfall but little snow, while the summers are hot but tempered by cool sea breezes and punctuated by some spectacular thunderstorms. The temperate climate means that where the soil is good the land produces abundant crops, although diseases like mildew are obviously a problem.

The sea is also a great tourist attraction and, unlike most sandy beaches of the Landes to the north, swimming and surfing are both possible on the Côte Basque, so that although the coastline is a mere 30 kilometres in length it has two famous seaside resorts, Biarritz and St-Jean-de-Luz, as well as a few smaller ones. Even more important from a gastronomic point of view is that in St-Jean-de-Luz the Côte Basque has the only fishing harbour of any size south of the Gironde.

The Atlantic coast between Biarritz and Hendaye is rocky with low cliffs in places. Until quite recently fish were abundant in these waters and the Basques have long been famous as skilled fishermen. At some time during the early Middle Ages (there is documentary evidence dating back to the eleventh century) they turned to whaling. Every September at the time of the equinox schools of whales swam into the Bay of Biscay and as soon as the first sighting was made signal fires were lit along the coast and a flotilla of small boats set out to harpoon as many of the sea giants as they could. The prizes taken were divided between the fishermen and the owners of the tackle; first however the Crown took its tenth and the chapter of Bayonne Cathedral claimed the tongue.

The last of these shore-based culls took place in the 1680s, but by then the Basques had long been hunting the whale in the waters of Greenland. Early in the seventeenth century however they came into conflict with the English and Dutch whaling fleets who combined to stop the Basques landing on the coast of Labrador to carve up their catches. Undeterred the Basques found a way of rendering down the fat to make oil on board ship, a development that meant they could more than double their catch before the holds were full. The Basques also fished off Newfoundland for cod, but these waters were denied them in 1713 by the terms of the treaty of Utrecht and so the fishermen converted their ships into privateers (corsairs) and harassed British merchantmen, with great success. The expulsion from Arctic waters was only temporary however and the Basques were soon back, despite the hostility of the British, fishing for cod on the fertile Grand Banks off Nova Scotia. In 1749 the sardine appeared in the Bay of Biscay and the Basques had an alternative to deep-water fishing.

Today, St-Jean-de-Luz is the chief tunny fishing port of France, although sardines and anchovies are both important catches. The arrival of the first tuna in the Bay of Biscay each June is eagerly awaited and there is great excitement when the first of the enormous fish with its rich red flesh appears in the fish markets. In the winter a fleet of 600 vessels fishes for tunny off the coast of Senegal. An enormous freezing plant with a capacity of 1,000 tonnes has been built at St-Jean-de-Luz to store the fish prior to canning. Unfortunately overfishing has seriously reduced the stocks of all the fish on which the Basque fishermen depend for their livelihood and unless serious efforts are made to regulate fishing on a world scale the industry faces a serious decline.

Thon à l'oignon

This is a simple tunny recipe for which you need almost equal proportions of onions and tunny.

Fry the chopped onion in the oil in a thick frying pan. Add salt, pepper and sugar and cook covered on a low heat for 10 minutes, without letting them brown. Insert slices of the cloves of garlic into the flesh of the tunny, and cook gently in a little more oil and sprinkled with the vinegar in a covered pan for 30–45 minutes, turning the fish over after the first half-hour. Add the onions to the tunny for the last few minutes before serving.

1 large slice of tunny weighing about 1kg (2lb)
800g chopped onions (1½lb) chopped
Pinch of sugar
2 tablespoons olive oil
2 or 3 cloves garlic
Salt and pepper
Sprinkling of vinegar

Grilled tunny à la basquaise

Peel the peppers by putting them under the grill and browning them on all sides; put them to cool in a plastic bag so that the skin comes off easily. Remove the seeds and chop into rough pieces. Peel the tomatoes, remove the seeds and chop roughly. In a thick frying pan put the oil, the herbs, the chopped onion and the crushed garlic and the chopped peppers and the bacon pieces. Fry gently until the vegetables start to soften. Then add the tomatoes and cook for a little longer. Remove the skin from the outside of the slice of tunny, brush lightly with oil and put under a hot grill for 15–20 minutes each side, sprinkling with more oil as necessary. Put the tunny on to a hot serving dish and cover with the *sauce basquaise.*

1 large slice of tunny weighing about 1kg (2lb)
6 large fleshy tomatoes
4 green peppers
1 large onion
2 or 3 cloves of garlic, crushed
3 tablespoons olive oil
Pinch each of thyme and powdered bay
Salt and pepper
2 rashers streaky bacon, chopped

Baked stuffed tunny

This version of a tunny recipe will stretch one thin slice of the fish per person to make a whole very filling course.

Mix all the ingredients, except the tunny, for the stuffing. Moisten with a little milk if necessary. Spread this mixture on each slice of tunny (boned and skinned as far as possible) and then roll the slice into a tube and fix the end with a wooden cocktail stick. Put the rolls of tunny into an ovenproof dish, sprinkle with dry white wine and some chopped parsley. Cover with foil and cook in a moderate oven for about 1 hour. Remove the foil for the last 15 minutes of cooking. Serve with plain boiled potatoes, or creamed mashed potatoes, and a green salad.

1 thin slice tunny per person
250g (8oz) minced veal
250g (8oz) minced belly pork
1 cup fresh breadcrumbs
1 small shallot, chopped
1 clove garlic, crushed
Pinch each powdered thyme and bay leaf
1 tablespoon dry white wine
Parsley to garnish

St-Jean-de-Luz may be the chief fishing port of the Pays Basque but the capital is Bayonne, situated six kilometres from the sea at the junction of the rivers Adour and Nive. Bayonne has had two periods of exceptional prosperity, the first during the Middle Ages when Gascony was under English rule, and, like Bordeaux, the city benefited from the trade generated by the English connection, the second came in the eighteenth century and was based on the booty brought to Bayonne by corsairs, whose ships were fitted out by the city's wealthy merchants. But in most people's minds Bayonne is famous first of all for a special kind of ham. It comes as a surprise to discover therefore that *jambon de Bayonne* has never been cured at Bayonne itself but comes instead from the vicinity of Orthez in Béarn (see page 211). The connection with Bayonne grew up because the cured hams were shipped down river to be sold in the city's great market.

Bayonne is also celebrated for its chocolate, which has been made there since the seventeenth century. Drinking chocolate was one of the civilized habits of the Aztecs of Mexico. They made an infusion of chocolate, peppers, honey and maize which they believed was an elixir. The Conquistador Fernando Cortez and his soldiers copied the Aztecs and introduced chocolate to Spain where it quickly became so popular that chocolate-making soon became a lucrative business. The skill was brought to Bayonne by the Jews who fled to south-west France to escape persecution by the Spanish Inquisition.

The method of making the chocolate was simple enough: the chocolate-maker squatted in front of a small marble mortar which was warmed for the purpose. The cacao seeds were crushed in the mortar to remove the husk and the beans were then finely ground to produce a paste to which sugar and spices were added. The citizens of Bayonne soon became so addicted to chocolate that the city fathers thought fit to issue an edict in 1691 forbidding its manufacture. This piece of legislation clearly had little effect because by the beginning of the nineteenth century there were more than twenty-five firms registered as chocolate-makers in the city. Today it is still a speciality and you can sit at your ease at a café table under the arches of the Pont Neuf and enjoy a delicious cup of thick cinnamon-scented chocolate topped with whipped cream.

To the south and east of Bayonne is a region of barren heathland that stretches in a great crescent from St-Pée, near St-Jean-de-Luz, round the northern-facing slopes of Mount Urzumu, with its bald dome-like summit, and on eastwards to the lower reaches of the river Bidouze in the vicinity of Bidache. These are the Landes de Hasparren and Mixe and they give a clear idea of what the *touyas* of Béarn must once have looked like (see page 208).

The more fertile areas of the Pays Basque are all to be found south of this area. In the extreme south-west there is the valley of the river Nivelle, which flows into the Atlantic at St-Jean-de-Luz, where mixed farming predominates; further east, in the neighbourhood of St-Palais, cereals are the main crop. Higher up in the mountains to the south there is mixed farming once more, but mostly on a very small scale; so small indeed that looking at the pocket-handkerchief-sized fields of maize and hay one wonders how the farmers can possibly earn a living. Scattered amongst these fields are some small vineyards, for this is where the Basque wine, Irouléguy, comes from.

The nearest town of any size is St-Jean-Pied-de-Port, situated at the foot of one of the most famous passes into Spain, the Col de Roncevaux that leads to the pass where Roland, Charlemagne's heroic paladin, met his end, killed not by the Saracens as legend has it, but by a guerilla band of Basques. St-Jean-Pied-de-Port is a beautiful old town full of interesting buildings and with a fine citadel built in 1688 by Louis XIV's famous engineer Vauban.

We went to St-Jean-Pied-de-Port to find out what we could about Irouléguy and that is how we came to meet Monsieur and Madame Brana who own a distillery in the town. Monsieur Brana explained that there are about 120 producers spread over eight communes on either side of the road from St-Jean-Pied-de-Port west towards St-Étienne-de-Baïgorry. Between them they own roughly 100 hectares producing 3,500 hectolitres of wine in the proportion of 2,000 hectolitres of red and 1,000 *rosé*. The grapes used are the Tannat and the Cabernet Sauvignon, in equal proportions, and the vines are trained to grow high like those of Jurançon (see page 205). All the grapes are taken to the local co-operative to be made into wine so there is no single vineyard Irouléguy for sale. The wine is kept in cask for no more than six months before bottling, and like Beaujolais it should be drunk young. Indeed, because so little is produced, you are unlikely to find a bottle that is more than a year old anyway. And it is even more unlikely that you will see it for sale outside the Pays Basque and its immediately adjacent areas, such as Béarn and the south of the Landes. The minimum strength of Irouléguy is 10 degrees, but this can increase to as much as 12 degrees in a very good year like 1976.

The books say that there is a white Irouléguy, but if so we could not find it and Monsieur Brana had not heard of it. If white Irouléguy does exist you are unlikely ever to see a bottle. Still, the red and *rosé* that we tried are both fragrant, fruity and refreshing – an excellent quaffing wine but one that is stronger than it seems!

Monsieur Brana makes both the red and the *rosé* but his chief interest is in the liqueurs that he distils. He has his own pear and plum orchards from which he makes Poire William and a plum brandy marketed under the name Prune Vieille Réserve. The fruit ferments for fifteen days before being double distilled in the same way as cognac (see page 168). It is then aged in oak casks, for three years in the case of the Prune Vieille Réserve and four years for the Poire William. A Marc du Pays Basque is also made from wine unsuitable for drinking. All three are excellent but the Poire William has earned the accolade of being chosen by Michel Guérard for sale in his restaurant at Eugénie-les-Bains (see page 168) and in his shop in Paris.

While on the subject of liqueurs, it should be mentioned that the Pays Basque has one all its own called Izarra (Basque for 'Star'), which was invented in 1835 by Monsieur Joseph Grattau, founder of the Distillerie de la Côte Basque. The exact formula for Izarra is a closely guarded secret but it is known to be made from a mixture of Pyrenean herbs and flowers macerated in armagnac and distilled. The resulting *eau-de-vie* is then blended with a syrup made of sugar, honey and more armagnac. Izarra comes in two colours, bright green and bright yellow; it is, perhaps, a little sweet for some tastes, although it is delicious if drunk *frappé* (poured over crushed ice) on a hot day. The colour and sweetness give the misleading impression that Izarra is an innocuous drink, but on the contrary it is very potent. The green is 50 per cent by volume and the yellow 40 per cent.

Another drink that is very popular, not only in the Pays Basque but all over the South-West, is Sangria, which actually originates in Spain.

Sangria

1l (2 pints/40fl.oz) strong rough red wine
4 oranges, sliced
4 cloves
At least 4 peaches, but as many more as you can manage, peeled and sliced
2 tablespoons sugar
eau-de-vie to taste

Leave the wine, sugar, cloves and fruit to macerate overnight. The next day give the mixture a good stir and add the *eau-de-vie*. Two glasses of *eau-de-vie* are the maximum to a litre of wine. Remove the cloves before serving ice cold and make sure that each glass has a mixture of fruit.

This is a heady mixture and on long hot summer days you may prefer a more gentle drink. Try adding fizzy lemonade or sparkling mineral water.

or:
1l (2 pints/40fl.oz) rough red wine
4 oranges
1 lemon
½l (1 pint/20fl.oz) fizzy lemonade
12–14 ice cubes
150g (4–5oz) sugar
Quarter bottle of eau-de-vie

Slice the oranges and the lemon and put in a large jug. Add the spirit, wine and sugar and allow to macerate for 3 or 4 hours, stirring frequently and bruising the slices of fruit to release the flavour. About 10 minutes before serving, add the lemonade and ice cubes. Give another good stir before serving.

Few British readers will have *eau-de-vie* to hand and rum (which is traditionally used in Spain) makes a highly flavoured drink. Try instead vodka, or cognac, which makes a good substitute for *eau-de-vie* and allows the fruitiness of sangria to be appreciated.

Not far north of St-Jean-Pied-de-Port is the Col des Palombières. This is one of the passes through which the *palombes* (wild pigeons) fly every autumn on their way south. In some of the passes of the Pays Basque the *palombes* are driven into cunningly positioned nets. The most famous of the passes where this takes place is near the typical Basque village of Sare, about 13 kilometres south-east of St-Jean-de-Luz. The *palombe* is highly regarded as a delicacy not only in the Pays Basque, but all over the South-West (see page 165 for recipe). Many other kinds of game are to be found in the mountains. Ortolan, quail, snipe and woodcock are all hunted and occasionally appear on restaurant menus. For those who are not partial to game, the rivers are full of fish – salmon, trout, pike, lamprey and many more. Most trout now comes from trout farms, but as these are usually located alongside a river or stream they are just as good to eat as the wild ones.

The high rainfall in the Pays Basque means that the climate is so humid in the mountains that although they are not very high the upper slopes are suitable only for grazing. So, for over a thousand years, once the winter snows have gone, the shepherds have driven their sheep up from the lowlands to the mountain pastures and taken them down again in September. During the four months or so that they are looking after the sheep in the mountains the shepherds live in small rugged stone huts called *burans* where they make cheese from the ewes' milk. The best known of them is Arnéguy which is made in the mountains south of St-Jean-Jean-de-Port. It has a light yellow rind, is about 30 centimetres in diameter and about 6 centimetres thick. Arnéguy is made throughout the summer pasturing season and is cured in cold cellars for about three months. It has a delicious nutty flavour with a slight edge to it and goes well with Irouléguy. But most of the cheese made from ewes' milk finds its way to the Caves de Combalou, in the Rouergue, where it is transformed into the much more famous Roquefort (see page 147). Altogether about one-eighth of Roquefort's total production originates in Béarn and the Pays Basque.

A similar cheese to Arnéguy, but made from a mixture of ewes' and cows' milk, is Iraty. This is also cured for three months but has a much stronger flavour.

It cannot honestly be said that Basque cooking is very remarkable. On the coast there is plenty of seafood to add some variety, but inland the three famous Basque dishes, *pipérade*, *poulet basquais* and *gâteau basque* tend to turn up on menus with monotonous regularity, often all three on the same menu. Of these, *pipérade* is by far the most interesting and, if you have the right ingredients to hand, it has the great advantage that you can prepare an impromptu but delicious meal very quickly. *Pipérade* appears in various guises, sometimes as scrambled egg with a rich sauce made from tomatoes and green peppers, something like a *ratatouille*; on other occasions with the same sauce mixed into beaten egg to make a heavenly omelette, and yet again served as a vegetable sauce to accompany grilled or roasted meats. So it seems that it is the tomato/green pepper mixture that is the constant factor. This can be bought in tins and is well worth buying against an emergency.

Pipérade – omelette basquaise Serves 6

Prepare the peppers and the tomatoes. Peel and chop the shallots and crush the garlic. Cook the chopped peppers, shallots and garlic in half the oil in a thick pan. When they are starting to soften, add the chopped tomatoes and the thyme, salt and pepper. Cover and cook for about 15–20 minutes.

Break the eggs into a large bowl and beat lightly. Do not be tempted to add either milk or water. Melt the butter and add half of it to the beaten eggs. Heat the rest of the butter with the remaining oil in a large thick frying

6 large tomatoes, peeled with the seeds removed
3 green peppers, depipped and chopped
4 shallots or 2 medium onions
3 cloves garlic, crushed
Chopped parsley
2 thin slices Bayonne ham (or smoked back bacon) per person
12 eggs
50g (2oz) butter
4 tablespoons olive oil
Salt and pepper
Pinch of powdered thyme

pan. Fry the slices of bacon or ham in the pan and then remove to a warm plate. Pour the beaten egg into the pan and stir well. Add the *pipérade* mixture and stir and turn the omelette round and over so that the mixture is spread through the beaten egg. At that critical minute when the omelette is still runny in the middle, serve onto hot plates with the slices of cooked ham or bacon as a garnish and French bread for mopping up the juices. Serve with a green salad and cheese and fruit to follow.

Poulet basquais Serves 6

1 chicken cut into six pieces
4 medium onions chopped
4 green peppers, seeded and chopped
1 kilo of tomatoes, peeled, seeded and chopped
4 cloves of garlic, crushed
2 tablespoons of tomato purée
250g (4oz) of lean green bacon
2 teaspoons of sugar
1 generous pinch of thyme and also of bay
A handful of chopped parsley
Olive oil, salt, paprika, and freshly ground black pepper

Poulet basquais has two main forms: one is chicken pieces fried gently and served with the *pipérade* sauce of tomatoes, onions, peppers and garlic; the other is a chicken casserole, moistened with chicken stock and dry white wine. Some cooks like to include mushrooms although the strong flavour of the *pipérade* mixture tends to overshadow even cèpes. Others like to add the spicy Basque sausages.

This recipe is for braised chicken pieces with the *basquaise* sauce – if you prefer the casserole version, you can add equal amounts of chicken stock and dry white wine once the chicken and vegetables have been browned.

Dredge the chicken pieces in a little flour and brown gently in the olive oil. Cover and leave to cook for 10 or 15 minutes on a low heat. Take the pieces out and set aside to keep warm. In the same pan and using the same oil, fry the onions gently for two or three minutes. Add the chopped peppers, the garlic, the bacon cut into small chunks, the herbs and the sugar and continue cooking gently. After a few minutes add the chopped tomatoes, and salt and pepper to taste. Stir in the tomato purée and check the seasoning again. Cover the pan and allow the sauce to cook gently for about 15 minutes. Add the chicken pieces and continue cooking for another 30 minutes. Serve the chicken and the sauce accompanied with plain boiled rice and a green salad.

Gâteau basque

Gâteau basque will be found in every *pâtisserie* in the Pays Basque and is often served as a dessert in restaurants. It comes in for a great deal of criticism for it is too often found stale, leathery, dry and hard. This is a shame because the real thing should be light and fluffy, fragrant with rum or armagnac and sprinkled with ground almonds and icing sugar. Inspect the *gâteau* closely before committing yourself to a slice and if you suspect its age and composition choose something else. If however you are lucky and find a specimen worthy of the name you will certainly enjoy this deliciously filling dessert.

For the pastry
300g flour (8oz)
150g chilled butter (4oz)
150g sugar (3oz)
3 egg yolks
1½ teaspoons dried yeast
1 tablespoon rum or armagnac

Mix the sugar, flour and yeast together in a bowl with the three egg yolks, the armagnac and the butter in small pieces. Work the paste well with your hands, lightly but firmly. Roll it into a ball and leave to rise in a warm place for about an hour. During this time prepare the custard cream filling.

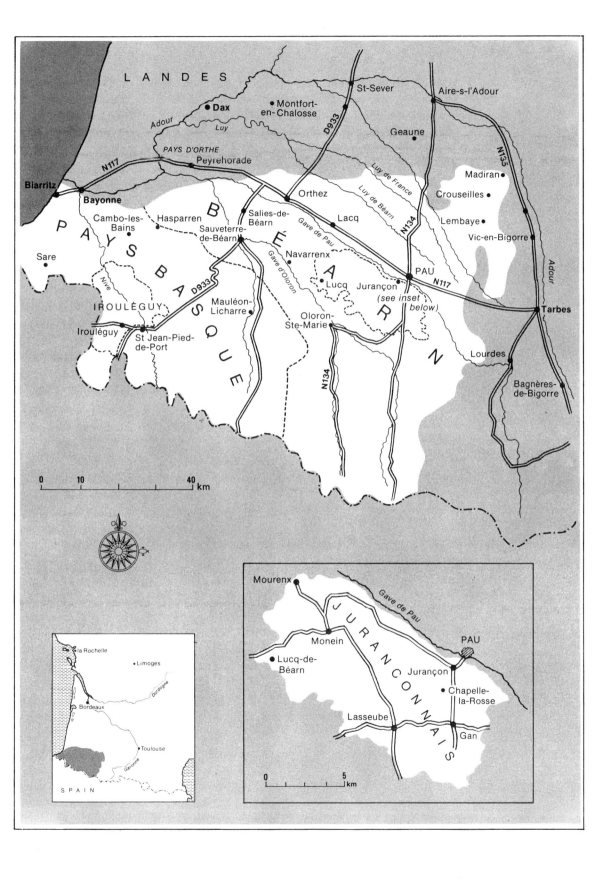

LANDES

Adour
Luy
Dax
Montfort-
en-Chalosse
St-Sever
Aire-s-l'Adour

Geaune

PAYS D'ORTHE
Peyrehorade

N117
Biarritz
Bayonne

Madiran •
Crouseilles •

N133

Cambo-les-
Bains
Hasparren
Salies-de-
Béarn
Orthez
Lacq
Luy de France
Luy de Béarn
Lembaye •
Vic-en-Bigorre •

P A Y S
B A S Q U E
Sauveterre-
de-Béarn
Gave de Pau

N134

Sare •

Navarrenx
B É A R N

D933
Gave d'Oloron
Lucq •
PAU
N117
Tarbes

IROULÉGUY
Nive
Jurançon
(see inset below)

Mauléon-
Licharre •

Irouléguy •
St Jean-Pied-
de-Port
Oloron-
Ste-Marie

N134

Lourdes •

Bagnères-
de-Bigorre •

Adour

0   10   40 km

Mourenx •

Gave de Pau

J U R A N Ç O N N A I S

Monein •
PAU

Lucq-de-
Béarn •

Jurançon •
Chapelle-
la-Rosse •

Lasseube •
Gan •

la Rochelle
Limoges •

Bordeaux •
Dordogne

Toulouse •
Garonne

S P A I N

0   5 km

For the custard filling
250ml milk (about ½ pint/
*   10fl.oz)*
3 eggs
60g sugar (about 2oz)
40g flour (a little under 2oz)
1 tablespoon rum or armagnac
100g (4oz) ground almonds
*   (optional)*
1 egg yolk to brush top of
*   cake.*

Boil the milk with the sugar and set on one side. Mix the eggs in a bowl with the flour and incorporate the hot milk, little by little, beating all the time. Put the bowl over a saucepan of hot water and continue beating until the mixture thickens. Add the armagnac and leave to cool. At this stage most recipes for *gâteau basque* add ground almonds to the custard.

When the pastry has risen use two-thirds for the base and sides of a greased and floured tart mould. Use a deep mould, at least 5cm (2in) deep. Roll the pastry to a thickness of about 1cm (about ⅜in) and line the flan case carefully. Pour the custard cream into the mould and cover with the rest of the pastry rolled into a round. Close the edges securely, pinching them with your fingers, and use the remaining egg yolk to brush over the top of the cake. You can make patterns with a fork and the egg will run into the channels and brown. Bake in a moderate oven for about 35 minutes.

You can make the custard cream filling the day before if you want it to be thick enough to hold the top layer of pastry in place.

In the village of Sare the *gâteau* has a layer of black cherry jam on the bottom layer of pastry under the custard. The *gâteau gascon* uses the same pastry mixture but the inside is filled with peeled and sliced pears which have been soaked in armagnac while the pastry is rising.

Béarn

A WARM SUNNY morning in late October. We are standing on a hilltop
looking south over a fertile valley. Immediately in front of us are rows
of tall vines that run in parallel lines down the steep southern-facing slope.
The grapes are ripening nicely but the *vendange* will not be for a few weeks
yet. The opposite side of the valley is dotted with black and white cows and
grey stone houses with enormously heavy-looking grey slate roofs. The
details show up sharply in the clear light for it has been raining earlier and
looks like doing so again. Further south we can see a range of mountain
peaks pushing up through the bloated purple rainclouds. Dominating them
all is the snow-capped peak of the Pic du Midi d'Ossau which rises to a
height of 2,884 metres. We are in Béarn in the western Pyrénées.

The vineyard we have come to see is Clos Lamouroux at Chapelle de
Rousse, just south of Pau. It is owned by Monsieur Chigé who, we have
been told, makes some of the finest Jurançon to be found in the area.
Jurançon is a wine that all Frenchmen have heard of but few have actually
drunk. It is famous because of the role it played in the baptism of France's
most popular king, Henri IV. As mentioned, the story is that when he was
born his grandfather Henri d'Albret, King of Navarre, had his lips rubbed
with garlic and moistened with the best Jurançon wine. No better publicist
could be imagined than Henri whose many amorous exploits, which were
carried on unimpeded by kingship or age, earned him the admiring
nickname, the '*vert-galant*'. Henri enjoyed all the good things of life and he
endeared himself to his people by his wish that every Frenchman should
have a chicken in his pot on Sunday.

There are many good stories about this amiable king. One of the best tells
how Henri made an unexpected call on his mistress Gabrielle d'Estrées who,
as it happened, was not alone. Her new lover barely had time to leap for
safety under the bed before Henri entered the room. The King sat down and
asked the petrified Gabrielle to have a sumptuous dinner sent up. When it
arrived he took a whole partridge for himself, handed another to Gabrielle
and tossed a third under the bed saying, 'Can't let the poor devil starve!'

Jurançon also has the rapturous endorsement of Colette who wrote: '*Je
fis, adolescente, la recontre d'un prince enflammé, impérieux, traître comme tous
les grands séducteurs: le Jurançon.*' But despite its role in French history and
Colette's enthusiasm, Jurançon is not well known outside Béarn itself. The

annual production is small and consists almost entirely of white wine. The true Jurançon is a sweet wine which, like the Sauternes or the wine of Monbazillac, is made by waiting until the grapes have been attacked by the *pourriture noble*, the 'noble rot', so that the sugar content of the grapes is concentrated and the resulting wine is rich and alcoholic (the method is described in more detail in the Périgord chapter, page 116). This means it is sometimes December before the grapes are ready to be picked and the vineyards are by then often under snow. Today, however, the *vignerons* cannot take the risks involved by waiting so long and the grapes are harvested in November. In addition, in response to changing taste, they are turning away from the production of sweet white wine to dry. This is a pity for the dry Jurançon is at best an ordinary wine and is sometimes mediocre, but one can hardly blame the producers who naturally prefer a wine that is less exacting to make, can be bottled earlier and sold more quickly.

Nevertheless, the glory of Jurançon is its sweet wine and it was because we wished to sample a bottle made by the traditional method that we had sought out Monsieur Chigé at Clos Lamouroux. Monsieur Chigé explained that he makes a semi-dry (*demi-sec*) as well as his sweet (*moelleux*) wine. The *demi-sec* is made from a grape called the Gros Manseng and the wine has an alcoholic content of 12 degrees in an average year and 14 degrees in a good one. This is higher than the permitted minimum of 11 degrees specified under the *appellation contrôlée* legislation. The sweet wine is made from two grapes, the Petit Manseng and the Courbu, in the proportion 90 per cent and 10 per cent respectively. Two-thirds of Clos Lamouroux is stocked with Gros Manseng. These grape varieties are very old and are not found outside Jurançon.

Like most other parts of France, Béarn was affected by phylloxera in the 1870s but when the vineyards were replanted original stock was used and some of the vines are reputed to be 150 to 200 years old. The method of cultivation is also unusual because the vines are trained to climb up long chestnut stakes to a height of one and a half metres before the side shoots are allowed to grow laterally against iron cross-pieces. The idea is to protect the shoots from frost by raising them well above the frozen ground (in Béarn the winters are long and can be very hard).

At Clos Lamouroux the newly made wine is kept in oak casks for eighteen months and is then decanted into stainless steel tanks leaving behind a deposit in the casks in the process. Under the *appellation contrôlée* regulations, filtering the wine to remove the sediment is not permitted. The wine is left in the tanks for a month to settle and is then bottled.

Monsieur Chigé's wine proved to be excellent. The Gros Manseng grape has a certain amount of acidity, which gives the *moelleux* in particular a refreshing tang that is not found in the more luscious Sauternes and Monbazillacs. It is also a lighter wine, paler in colour but nevertheless deceptively alcoholic. Monsieur Chigé's *moelleux* has at least 14 degrees of alcohol in an ordinary year (three more than the permitted minimum), rising to 18 degrees in exceptional ones. He also told us that the slight acidity in Jurançon makes it very long-lasting and that fifty-year-old bottles 'are not unknown. The *moëlleux* should be served chilled. The *demi-sec* was also very good, having far more character than the ordinary Jurançon *sec* commonly on sale in Béarn.

For those travellers who do not have time to search out Clos Lamouroux, the Cave Coopérative de Jurançon at Gan, 7 kilometres south of Pau on the left of the Route Nationale 134, has a good range of wine including both the *sec* and the *moëlleux*, as well as the very drinkable Rose de Béarn, a VDQS wine which, despite its name, is a red not a rosé. Although Béarn is the largest of the Pyrenean states and occupies two-thirds of the modern Pyrénées-Atlantiques *département*, it is still a very small territory, only 98 kilometres from north to south at its widest point. South of Pau, the capital, the landscape is a beautiful one full of tumbling mountain torrents (useful for cooling a picnic bottle of Jurançon!) and fast-moving rivers flowing swiftly through lush green valleys. High above tower the bare cloud-clapped peaks of the mountain range that marks the frontier with Spain. The greenness of the countryside is due not only to the many watercourses that owe their origin to the melting snows in the mountains but also to the heavy annual rainfall, for here we are not far from the Atlantic coast.

The beauty of the scenery is however deceptive, for much of the land is too mountainous or the soil too poor to cultivate. Most of the population is centred in two river valleys that stretch diagonally across the middle of Béarn, the valley of the Gave de Pau (*gave* is the local word for a torrent), which rises in the mountains of Bigorre to the east and has already reached the foothills by the time it enters Béarn, and further south, running roughly parallel to the Gave de Pau, the Gave d'Oloron which is fed by three tributaries that rise high in the mountains of Béarn itself or just across the frontier in Spain. The soil of these two valleys is very fertile and the river banks are lines with prosperous farms producing market vegetables, soft fruits and cereals.

Between the two *gaves* lies the highland region where the vineyards of Jurançon are to be found. Vines flourish in poor soil, of course, and the ountry is much less fertile, most of it being given over to vines and to grazing. Dairy cattle are a common sight in this part of Béarn, where the land is below 400 metres in height, but they are also to be found much higher up in the mountains. Indeed it can be an astonishing experience in a landscape of rocks and trees to stumble suddenly on a small green valley on whose steep green slopes a herd of cows is placidly grazing From their rich milk are made the creamy cheeses for which Béarn is famous. They are large disk-shaped cheeses with thick black or yellow rinds. The texture is smooth and the flavour very mild.

Cheese is also made from ewes' milk. At one time the Pyrenean sheep were famous all over the South-West. The shepherds drove their flocks on long journeys (transhumances) seeking winter pastures as far north as the Agenais, returning to the high slopes of Béarn for the short Pyrenean summer. Sadly the transhumances are a thing of the past, but occasional flocks of sheep are still to be found high up in the mountains. The best-known of the sheep's cheeses is Oloron, which is also called Fromage de la vallée d'Osseau. It is made in the mountain farms of the valley of Osseau from May to October. Like the cheeses made from cows' milk it is disk-shaped, about 30cm across and 9cm thick, and has a pale yellow rind. It has a stronger, nuttier flavour than the cows' cheeses but after about six months develops a rather sharp taste.

North of Pau the land is almost exclusively devoted to the cultivation of maize. This crop was originally introduced into the South-West in the sixteenth century but it was not until the eighteenth century that it began to be grown on any large scale after three disastrous harvests and hard winters had reduced the peasants to a state of famine. The growing of maize saved many lives and for the next 150 years more and more maize was grown until by the middle of the nineteenth century the crop covered 150,000 hectares in Béarn and the neighbouring Pays Basque and Landes. Thereafter a steady decline took place as the region became depopulated and the peasants who did stay turned to other crops that were less troublesome to grow. The tide turned with the introduction of a new American strain in 1948, which was more resistant to disease, could survive long periods of drought and gave harvests two or three times more abundant than the old variety. Now over 181,000 hectares are under cultivation in the same area once more. This success story has particular significance for the north-eastern part of the Béarn – the *touya*, which until recently was barren land covered with gorse and bracken. Now, thanks to the introduction of the American hybrid, together with modern chemical fertilizers and the use of bulldozers and tractors, the land has been reclaimed and what was once sterile heathland is today covered with enormous fields of maize.

Beyond the flat, rather boring landscape of the *touya* rise the low hills of Vic Bilh (Vic Bilh means Vic Vieux and is derived from the latin 'Vicus Vetulus'), one of the many tiny feudal divisions of the South-West whose identity is still jealousy conserved by the local inhabitants, even though it has had no independent existance for hundreds of years. What has probably saved the name of Vic Bilh from complete obscurity is that its southern-facing slopes produce two of the most interesting wines of the South-West, Madiran and Pacherenc du Vic Bilh. There have been vineyards in Vic Bilh since Roman times at least, but their preservation is due to the Benedictine monks who founded an abbey on the site where the village of Madiran now stands and who planted vines there sometime in the twelfth century. Not only did the monks keep viniculture alive in Vic Bilh but they improved the quality of the wine as well.

Of the two wines, Madiran is by far the more important. It is a full-bodied red having a minimum of alcoholic strength of 11 degrees and a high tannin content that means it will go on improving in bottle. The locals recommend keeping it in the cellar for at least five years. The grapes used are the Tannat and the Cabernet mixed in the proportion of not more than 60 per cent and not less than 40 per cent of either. The Cabernet contributes finesse, suppleness and a heady bouquet to the wine, whilst the Tannat gives it body.

The climate of Vic Bilh is ideal for wine-making because it comes under the influence of both the Mediterranean and the Atlantic. The weather is therefore not extreme and although there is plenty of sunshine there is not so much that the grapes become dehydrated as can happen further east. The autumn in these parts usually brings a long period of settled fine weather which ripens the grapes gradually and means that they can be picked later than in Bordeaux. The grape harvest does not begin until after 21 September and sometimes as much as three weeks after this date. This late harvest helps to give Madiran its high alcoholic content.

There are about two hundred growers in Vic Bilh. Most of them send their grapes to the Cave Coopérative de Crouseilles which was founded in 1950 and is responsible for 50 per cent of the area's production of Madiran. There are however about twenty independent producers who make their own wine. The local *vignerons* are proud of the fact that they were amongst the first wine growers in France to introduce strict quality control soon after the end of the Second World War. No Madiran was allowed to be sold unless certain stringent conditions had been met: the production was limited to 25 hectolitres per hectare and the wine had to be kept in wooden casks for a minimum of thirty-three months before bottling. In addition, the name of Madiran was restricted to wine made from grapes grown on south-facing slopes. Having met all these requirements the wine was still not allowed to be sold without a certificate awarded after it had been analysed and tasted by a panel of experts appointed by the Institut National des Appellations d'Origine.

As a result of these strict regulations the quality improved and Madiran was awarded *appellation contrôlée* status in 1948; what is more, as the wines of Burgundy and Bordeaux became steadily dearer, the quality of Madiran became better appreciated in Paris and London. The *vignerons* of Vic Bilh responded by planting more vineyards and the production increased from 10,000 hectolitres in 1950 to 30,000 today. During the same period the restrictions were eased and now 40 hectolitres per hectare are allowed and the wine need only be kept for eighteen months in cask. Even so the reputation of Madiran remains high and more and more is finding its way to other parts of France and to England.

Undoubtedly the most successful and highly respected producer of Madiran is Monsieur Denis de Robillard who at Château de Peyros makes one of the outstanding red wines to be found in the South-West. Monsieur de Robillard harvests the grapes very late, sorting them as they are picked. Unripe grapes are left and picked later and there may be as many as three separate pickings before the grape harvest is finished. The grapes are mixed in the proportion 60 per cent Tannat and 40 per cent Cabernet to make the wine that at Château de Peyros is still kept for thirty-three months before bottling. It is little wonder then that the resulting wine is very fine and that Monsieur de Robillard has no difficulty in selling all that he produces. An outstanding vintage of recent years is 1975, which he believes will go on improving for twenty-five years.

Pacherenc du Vic Bilh is a very different wine. It is white and sweet, although in bad years a dry white is produced instead. The vintage we tasted was 1977, a year of atrocious weather with months of rain in the early summer that caused serious flooding in some places. We were agreeably surprised therefore to find that the dry wine we tasted was very palatable; it had a fragrant distinctive bouquet and a flavour all its own with a hint of gunflint about it. Sadly this excellent wine is made in very small quantities by a handful of producers on the same slopes as Madiran. The grapes used are curious. The wine owes its name to the chief grape employed, the Pacherenc, which is a local word meaning '*raisin d'échalas*' ('grape of the vinestake'). Besides the Pacherenc grape (also called *Ruffiat*), Manseng, Sémillon, Sauvignon and Courbu, which here is known as Petit Sarrat, are also used to make this wine.

Pacherenc du Vic Bilh is not to be found outside Vic Bilh itself, but if you are ever in the vicinity a detour to the Coopérative de Crouseilles, near Lembeye, is well worth while. The countryside is very pleasant with occasional splendid views of the mountains to the south from the ridge that runs along the crest of the hills. When you reach the Cooperative you will be able to sample not only Pacherenc du Vic Bilh but Madiran and a very pleasant *vin de pays* called Vin des Fleurs which is a light fruity red that makes an excellent quaffing wine. The cooperative also sells Rouge de Béarn and Rose de Béarn.

In his *A Book of French Wines*, Morton Shand mentions a wine called Portet, which he says is made in Vic Bilh. We could find no trace of this wine and as Portet is a local village and Mortan Shand says that the wine was made from the Pacherenc grape, we concluded that either Portet was an old name for Pacherenc du Vic Bilh, or he had somehow got the name wrong.

If, instead of crossing the *touya* to Vic Bilh, you turn north-west from Pau and follow the course of the Gave de Pau, you will soon come to the small market town of Orthez with its famous fortified bridge, dating from the thirteenth and fourteenth centuries, spanning the river. In contrast to the once-sterile touyas, the countryside round Orthez has always been farmed and maize has been grown here since the sixteenth century and used to fatten pigs and geese. The pigs certainly seem to have thrived on this diet, because Orthez became one of the local centres for the production of *jambon de Bayonne*. The excellence of *jambon de Bayonne* is due both to the fine quality of the meat from the local porkers and to the method of curing. Part of the secret is that the ham is rubbed with salt from nearby Salies-de-Béarn, but the salt must be well rubbed in and much of the art of curing *jambon de Bayonne* depends on the skilful way this is done.

The unique flavour of Bayonne ham has spread its fame far beyond the confines of the Pays Basque and Béarn, and from the Middle Ages onwards it has been offered as a delicacy to distinguished visitors to the region. Baskets of Bayonne ham were amongst the presents showered on the young Louis XIV and Maria Theresa of Spain when they were married at St-Jean-de-Luz in 1660. On the same occasion four dozen hams were given to the Queen Mother, Ann of Austria.

Not far to the south-west of Orthez lies Sauveterre-de-Béarn. This beautiful old town sits on top of a sheer cliff, looking southwards over the Gave d'Oloron to the cloud-capped peaks of the Pyrénées. Sauveterre has a fine Romanesque church commanding a magnificent view of the mountains, and two very good restaurants, A Boste and Hôtel du Château, the latter having the additional advantage of a terrace where you can bask in the sun and admire the panorama before you. Both restaurants offer local specialities including *garbure*, *pipérade* and *poule-au-pot*.

We went to Sauveterre to visit the establishment of Monsieur Dominique Idiart, a specialist producer of *jambon de Bayonne*. We had learned of his hams in various food magazines and his name appeared in lists of recommended producers. Dominique Idiart is a round jovial young man who looks as though he plays a good game of rugby. Once he studied to be a doctor, but now he prefers curing hams to doctoring humans.

At first Monsieur Idiart was a little wary of the English couple who had turned up unannounced in his shop wanting to know about his hams. Soon, however, he warmed to his subject as he described the curing process.

First of all, to be entitled to the appellation '*veritable jambon de Bayonne*', the ham has to come from pigs bred in the three departments, Pyrénées-Atlantiques, Hautes-Pyrénées and Gers, roughly corresponding to the Pays Basque and Béarn, Armagnac and the ancient county of Bigorre that lies to the east of Béarn. The words '*Marque déposée*' on the label indicate that the pigs have been bred and fattened in the prescribed area. The salt too is special: it comes from Salies-de-Béarn, a few kilometres to the north of Sauveterre. The salt-producing spring has been there since time immemorial and at one time it actually belonged to Sauveterre, until the mayor decided to sell it to pay for the town's first drains. We had read that the salt of Salies was less good now than in days of yore, but Monsieur Idiart dismissed this as nonsense. As he said, the spring was the same, the method of collecting the salt in large pans had not changed and the chemical formula had not altered. The salt was analysed and unless it met the strict regulations laid down could not be sold as Sel de Salies.

There is a *syndicat* of recognized producers of *veritable jambon de Bayonne*, which is limited to no more than ten. When a producer dies his number dies with him and a new number is given to his successor. Monsieur Idiart's number is 17. Altogether, some two million Bayonne hams are sold every year in France. Monsieur Idiart produces between 5,700 and 5,800 hams a year, but the biggest producer in the area is the Recapet company, just north of Sauveterre, which produces over 50,000 a year. If we reckon that the ten members of the *syndicat* account between them for some 250,000 hams bearing the label '*Marque déposée, veritable jambon de Bayonne, etiquette syndicale*', then this leaves some 1,750,000 'bastard' hams sold under the name of *jambon de Bayonne*. As Monsieur Idiart explained, Bayonne hams can be made anywhere, after all they are named after Bayonne only because that was the chief port of export. With a slight smile he warned against the German and Belgian varieties. So, if you want to be sure that you are getting the real thing you must look carefully at the label.

Monsieur Idiart offered to take us round his premises to see the various processes the hams go through. To start with they are put in a large barrel with a handle. A quantity of salt is added, and the handle is turned for ten or fifteen minutes. This bruises the hams and helps them to absorb the salt more easil in the next stage of the process. Next the hams are taken to the salting pans (the *saloir*), which are enclosed racks or shelves made from wood with a layer of coarse grey salt about 10 to 15 cm deep. Two or three hams are put into each pan, depending on how many are to be cured, and are turned in the salt at intervals. The hams stay in the pans for between one and one and a half months, according to size, temperature and the judgement of the individual producer. Each salt pan is labelled with a date showing when the cure started.

The next stage in the process takes place in the *séchoir*, the drying room, but first the hams are rinsed, dried and covered with a very mild pepper, either espelette or *piment doux d'Espagne*. This pepper-covering is important because it prevents stray flies from spoiling the ham, yet it is so gentle that it does not impair the flavour.

The *séchoir* is like a dimly lit cave with rows and rows of hams hanging from the roof, each one carefully labelled with its date. The temperature is even, neither hot nor cold, and there is no smell at all – neither of hams nor salt. Drying the hams takes at least five or six months and the success of this part of the process depends on the humidity, temperature, ventilation and even the air pressure. The larger producers use specially heated drying rooms for this stage in the cure and speed up the drying time from six months to three.

We picked our way through the hams to the far wall where Monsieur Idiart was opening the shutters. The *séchoir* was suddenly flooded with sunlight and we looked out: immediately below was a steep drop to the swift-running Gave d'Oloron, beyond lay the undulating country of the foothills and in the distance the snow-covered peaks of the Pyrénées sharply defined against a clear blue sky. We were not allowed to linger over the view, however, for Monsieur Idiart was not risking stray flies damaging his hams and the shutters were closed once more.

Buying ham from Monsieur Idiart is hardly possible for most British visitors. A pig of about 140–150 kilos will have hams weighing about ten kilos, so that even half a ham weighs four or five kilos and he does not sell smaller portions. If you do decide to buy, remember that there are restrictions on importing uncooked meat into Britain. But if you are staying in France, ham can be kept in the refrigerator, wrapped in a linen cloth or cooking foil. It can also be kept in the deep freeze.

Monsieur Idiart also told us what to look for in a good-quality ham: when held up to the light a slice of the ham should be beige and slightly transparent. When cooked, whether in a frying pan or casserole, it should remain pink. If the ham is hard it is generally old. If the inside is soft, this means it is a young ham and not too salty.

If you don't buy any ham, at least you could try Monsieur Idiart's *pâté de campagne pur porc* (*specialité Basque*) or a tin of *confit de porc*, enough for two hearty appetites, because it is all meat with a minimum of fat and juices. Try heating the *confit de porc* in a casserole in the oven with a few lightly fried button mushrooms. Serve with boiled new potatoes and a salad.

What greater contrast could there be to the amiable porker of Béarn's lowlands than the nimble-footed, elusive *isard*, the chamois-like mountain deer of the Pyrénées. At one time *isard* used to feature on the local menus, but now the species is so rare that it is protected and any restaurant offering it as a delicacy should be treated with suspicion. *Sanglier* (wild boar), on the other hand, can be hunted within a strictly prescribed period during the winter months and at this time it can be offered for sale in the local shops and served in the restaurants. Unfortunately this means that it will not be available during the summer tourist season between the end of May and the beginning of October.

There are, however, beautiful fish in the rivers, including trout and salmon. On the tympanum of the cathedral at Oloron-Ste-Marie is a medieval sculpture of two fishermen each carrying a salmon. The salmon are so large that one of the men is almost staggering under the weight: a fisherman's story, perhaps? Salmon bones, engravings and sculptures have been found in the area dating from the Magdalanian period, some 30 to 40 thousand years ago.

Today, by contrast, the salmon is rare in the rivers of Béarn and the Pays Basque as a result of overfishing the rivers themselves in the early years of the century and also because of the continued excessive catches in the waters off Greenland and Labrador. The earliest salmon fishing regulations in the

South-West are to be found in the *Tribunals and Customs of Béarn* dating from the eleventh century. These forbade the netting of adult salmon and anyone who was caught had to pay a heavy fine. In the sixteenth century the rivers were so full of salmon that the troops garrisoned at Sauveterre-de-Béarn petitioned against having to eat the fish more than twice a week.

Salmon are still found in the Gave d'Oloron, the upper reaches of the Gave d'Ossau and the Gave d'Aspe, Saison and the Nive. They also appear occasionally in the Gave de Pau, despite the barrage of Baigts-de- Béarn and bad pollution. Much work is being done to try to increase stocks, and control pollution and there are strict rules on poaching, but a recent virus epidemic has reduced the salmon even further. Nevertheless, strenuous efforts are being made by local fishing societies to encourage the salmon back to the rivers, even to the extent of experimenting with salmon eggs and hatcheries.

Navarrenx, on the Gave d'Oloron, has long been famous for its fine salmon and the French Salmon Fishing Championships are held there every year, once at Easter and a second time in July. There is a dam at Navarrenx with a salmon ladder where the great fish can be seen making enormous leaps out of the foam on their way to the spawning grounds upstream.

Even if your salmon comes from less romantic places than the *gaves* of the South-West, you can still enjoy the regional flavour of the Béarn or the Pays d'Orthe.

Braised salmon au vin blanc

4 slices of fresh salmon (1 per person)
2 wine glasses dry white wine
4 shallots
80g butter (about 3oz)
25 millilitres double cream ($\frac{1}{2}$ pint/10fl.oz)
2 wine glasses fish stock (made from boiling fish heads, skin and bones with onions and equal parts of dry white wine and water)
Salt and pepper

Sprinkle the slices of salmon with salt and pepper. Peel and chop the shallots. Butter an ovenproof dish. Put a layer of shallots in the bottom, then the salmon slices, and finish with the rest of the shallots. Moisten with the fish stock and the dry white wine. Cover with foil and put into a hot oven for 10 minutes. Then lower the heat and cook slowly for 45 minutes. The fish is cooked when the flesh comes off the central bone easily. Drain the slices of salmon and remove the skin and as many bones as possible without spoiling the shape of the slices. Arrange the salmon on the serving dish. Reduce the liquid by rapid boiling and allow to cool a little before adding the cream and heating gently. Add a knob of butter to the sauce and whip quickly with a fork over the heat, before serving over the salmon.

Baked salmon with mayonnaise

4 slices fresh salmon
2 shallots, chopped
Chopped parsley
2–3 tablespoons dry white wine
Mayonnaise (opposite)

A slightly different baked salmon dish can be made with a rich egg mayonnaise.

Blend mayonnaise ingredients in a blender until the mixture is thick, adding more oil if necessary. Put the slices of salmon in an ovenproof dish with the chopped shallots, parsley and the dry white wine. Spoon the egg mayonnaise over the salmon slices and round the dish. Cover with foil and bake in a moderate oven for an hour. The mayonnaise will cook rather like an omelette round the fish. If there is any mayonnaise left over, spoon it over the hot salmon just before serving.

For the mayonnaise
2–3 eggs
Little white wine vinegar
Chopped parsley
1 clove garlic, crushed
Olive oil mixed with sunflower
*   or corn oil*

Sauce béarnaise

For most people, Béarn's chief contribution to the culinary art is *sauce béarnaise*, yet ironically it seems unlikely that there is any direct connection between this famous (some would say infamous!) sauce and Béarn at all. It is generally agreed that *sauce béarnaise* was invented by the chef of the Pavillon Henri IV, a famous restaurant on the outskirts of Paris, and that the name is a reference to Béarn's most illustrious son, rather than to his kingdom. It is true that Count Austin de Croze believed there was a link with Béarnais cuisine but he was unable to produce any convincing evidence to support this theory. Still, whatever the truth of the origins of the sauce, the Béarnais have taken it to their hearts and it turns up quite often on restaurant menus as an accompaniment to roast beef, lamb or grilled steaks or chops.

Recently, scientists have been experimenting with *sauce béarnaise*, especially with the 'resurrection of coagulated *sauce béarnaise*'. John and Carol Perram with Professor Claus Nicolau were faced with a revolting mess of curdled *sauce béarnaise* and their scientific solution appears to be to add a few more drops of vinegar. The description of the successful experiment was given in *Nature* magazine and the resulting publicity caused a number of cooks to come forward with their own successful solutions, the most popular being to allow the sauce to cool and then beat it drop by drop onto a teaspoonful of boiling water in a clean basin. The problem is that to be successful *sauce béarnaise* must consist of 'a stable colloidal suspension consisting of a hydrophobic phase suspended in a low pH aqueous phase'. Or as Oliver Gillie of the *Sunday Times* paraphrased it, 'a lot of tiny fat-covered spherical droplets equally attracting and repelling one another under the influence of Van de Waals forces'!

Be that as it may, *sauce béarnaise* is troublesome to make and should not be attempted if you are short of time. Make sure the equipment you are going to use is completely clean and the ingredients are at room temperature. Above all keep calm.

3 egg yolks
150g unsalted butter (5oz)
5 dessertspoons tarragon
*   vinegar*
5 dessertspoons of dry white
*   wine*
2 shallots
Handful of chervil or parsley
2 small branches fresh
*   tarragon or 1 teaspoon*
*   dried tarragon*
Salt and coarsely ground
*   black pepper*

Chop the shallots finely and put them in a small saucepan with half the chopped chervil or parsley, one sprig of tarragon, the vinegar and the dry white wine, the salt and the pepper. Bring to the boil over a gentle heat and reduce the liquid until about two tablespoons remain. Strain the liquid and press the pulp firmly to obtain all the juice. Set aside to cool.

When quite cold, beat in the egg yolks little by little. Put the mixture in a small bowl which will fit easily over a saucepan of hot, *not boiling*, water. Cut the butter into small pieces, chop the rest of the tarragon and chervil very finely. Put the small bowl over the hot water, stirring all the time with a small fork. Add the butter, a tiny piece at a time, stirring carefully until the mixture has the consistency of a thick mayonnaise. Check the seasoning and serve with the chopped tarragon and chervil sprinkled over.

If you make the sauce in advance and have to reheat it, take special care. Find a larger bowl than the one you originally used for making the sauce and pour some hot water into it. Then put your sauce back into the little bowl and stir gently for about half a minute. Even this is risky and it would probably be better to have the sauce cold rather than risk the panic of trying to resurrect a curdled one at the last minute.

Poule-au-pot

Another famous Béarnais dish is the *poule-au-pot*, sometimes called *poule-au-pot à nostre Henri* after Béarn's popular king. The secret of a good *poule-au-pot* is to use a boiling fowl, not one that is so tough that even long cooking will not make it edible but still something more mature than a flabby battery chicken. There are three parts to this recipe: the boiling fowl itself, the stuffing and the stock. Let us start with the stuffing.

Mince the chicken livers, the gizzard, the veal, bacon and pork and mix well together. Peel and chop the onions and fry gently in a little of the butter. Add them to the minced meat. Mix the breadcrumbs with the meat, adding the crushed garlic and the chopped parsley, the allspice and the armagnac and incorporate with the minced meat, using the egg beaten with the milk to moisten the stuffing. You will need half this stuffing for the inside of the chicken; the rest is used in the stock.

In the largest saucepan or cast-iron casserole (it must in any case be large enough to hold the chicken and the vegetables) put 4 litres of water (about 8 pints). Add the chicken giblets, the onion stuck with cloves, the bouquet garni and bring to the boil. Clean and peel the vegetables (except for the cabbage and potatoes) and add to the saucepan. Then add the stuffed chicken and simmer gently, covered, for about 2 hours. Meanwhile, blanch the outside leaves of the cabbage and drain them. Into each leaf, spread some of the remaining stuffing; roll up each leaf and tie with linen thread. Add the stuffed cabbage leaves to the chicken in the pot with the peeled potatoes in pieces and the chopped cabbage heart. Continue cooking for another 30–45 minutes until both chicken and vegetables are done.

Serve the stock first – as a soup if you like with a stale bread base. Then serve the chicken surrounded by the vegetables and stuffed cabbage rolls, with mustard, gherkins, pickled onions and salt. Like the *garbure* and the *pot-au-feu*, the *poule-au-pot* is a *plat complet*. Cheese and fruit would be good to finish the meal.

Garbure

This is another famous Béarnais dish. Although it is often described as a soup, *garbure* is more like a *pot-au-feu* and filling enough to make a meal on its own. The origins of the word are obscure, but it seems likely that it comes

---

The Stuffing
120g chicken livers (about 4oz)
150g streaky bacon (about 5oz)
250g lean pie veal (8oz) or neck of veal
250g fresh belly pork (8oz)
Gizzard
Large cup fresh breadcrumbs
3 onions
2 cloves garlic, crushed
Handful chopped parsley
3 tablespoons butter
1 egg
3 tablespoons armagnac
Milk for mixing
Pinch of allspice
Salt and pepper

The Stock
Chicken giblets
1 small cabbage
3 large carrots
1 stick celery
1 bouquet garni
4 leaks
3 turnips
3 large potatoes
1 onion stuck with 3 cloves
1 clove garlic

from the Spanish, *garbias*, meaning a stew. Some experts argue that *garbure* is derived from *garbe*, a 'sheaf' or 'bunch' and point out that a bunch of vegetables – cabbage, beans, peas – forms the basis of the dish.

Different versions of *garbure* are to be found throughout the South-West, all having the same basic ingredients: a piece of salt pork cooked with vegetables. It is the choice of vegetables that makes them different. Cabbage usually plays the leading role in a *garbure*, together with potatoes, but haricot beans, peas, onions, carrots, herbs and, inevitably, garlic all play a part. Some cooks prefer goose fat to fry the vegetables, others say that only pork fat or lard will do, while some prefer a mixture of the two with a tablespoonful of melted butter or oil added. But everyone agrees that the *garbure* should be cooked in an earthenware casserole and that it should be so thick that the ladle stands up on its own!

Here is a standard recipe for *garbure*, but you can vary the vegetables according to what is in season. It serves four to six people.
Soak the pork or bacon in cold water overnight. Put it in a large saucepan and cover with cold water. Bring to the boil, remove the meat and throw away the water. (This will remove the worst of the salt.)

Chop the cabbage, and peel and cut the rest of the vegetables (but not the garlic) into rough pieces. Put the whole lot into the same saucepan with two good tablespoonfuls of goose fat or lard and fry gently; this helps the vegetables to keep their shape.

Now put the meat in the saucepan with two litres of water and bring slowly to the boil. When the water is simmering, add the thyme and the parsley and all the vegetables, except the cabbage and potatoes. If you like, you can also put in a pinch of powdered cloves, a heaped teaspoon of dried basil and a good grind of black pepper. Simmer gently for an hour.

Transfer to a large earthenware casserole and finish cooking in a moderate oven. Add the potatoes and the chopped cabbage before you put the casserole in the oven and be sure to check the seasoning – more pepper may be needed.

Continue cooking for another 30–40 minutes in the oven. At the last moment you could sprinkle grated cheese on top, turning the oven to high so that the cheese will brown. Serve from the casserole. If you like, you can take out the meat and serve it after the vegetables as a separate course with a green salad. *Garbure* can be cooked the day before it is eaten and any leftovers will improve by being reheated later.

In parts of the South-West, *garbure* has *confit d'oie* or *cou d'oie farci* added. Elsewhere, garlic sausage, ham shank on the bone, Bayonne ham and pork rind are all included. Like *cassoulet*, *garbure* is not a dish for weaklings and the only thing you are likely to be able to face afterwards is a long snooze.

*1kg (2lb) salt pork or green
  collar in a piece
1 small green cabbage
1 clove garlic
1 large onion
3 leeks
1 small turnip
4–5 medium potatoes
2–3 small carrots
2 tablespoons goose fat or lard
Small tin butter beans or
  cooked white haricot beans
1 tablespoon peas or green
  sliced beans
Pinch thyme
Handful of chopped parsley*

Envoi

Driving north through the Bergeracois in Périgord, on the first stage of our long journey home, we notice that the vineyards on either side of the RN 21 are full of activity: the *vendange* is in full swing. It is a beautiful warm day at the end of October and most of the vine leaves have already changed colour to a pale translucent yellow, or in some places a rich red. The whole scene is bathed in the clear soft light from the retreating sun. All the signs are that this is going to be a very good vintage. In a month or so the first truffles will appear in the markets of Périgord and Quercy and soon after fresh *foie gras*. In the meantime, in Armagnac, they will be lighting the first fires and starting to convert the new vintage into brandy.

It seems such a shame to leave all this, but never mind, we shall be back again in the Spring and meanwhile we can pass the long winter evenings, trying out the new recipes we have discovered, drinking the wine we have brought back and savouring our many pleasant memories of this land of Cockayne.

APPENDICES

APPENDIX 1
Bordeaux Appellation Contrôlée Wines with Permitted Minimum Strengths.

Appellations		*Degrees*
Barsac	Blanc	13°
Blayais	Blanc	10°
	Rouge	10°
Bordeaux	Rouge	10°
	Blanc	10.5°
Bordeaux clairet ou rosé		11°
Bordeaux-Côtes-du-Castillon	Rouge	11°
Bordeaux-Haut-Benauge	Blanc	11.5°
Bordeaux-Mousseaux	Blanc	10°
Bordeaux-Supérieur	Blanc	11.5°
	Rouge	10.5°
Bordeaux Supérieur Côtes de Francs	Blanc	11.5°
	Rouge	10.5°
Bourg, Bourgeais,	Blanc	11°
Cérons	Blanc	12.5°
Côtes-de-Blaye	Blanc	11°
Côtes-de-Bordeaux-St-Macaire	Blanc	11.5°
Côtes-de-Bourg	Rouge	10.5°
Côtes Canon Fronsac	Rouge	11°
Côtes-de-Fronsac	Rouge	11°
Entre-Deux-Mers Haut-Benauge	Blanc	11.5°
Entre-Deux-Mers	Blanc	11.5°
Graves	Blanc	11°
	Rouge	10°
Graves-Supérieures	Blanc	12°
Graves de Vayres	Blanc	10.5°
	Rouge	
Haut-Médoc	Rouge	10°
Lalande-de-Pomerol	Rouge	10.5°
Listrac	Rouge	10.5°
Loupiac	Blanc	13°
Lussac-St-Émilion	Rouge	11°
Margaux	Rouge	10.5°
Médoc	Rouge	10°
Montagne-St-Émilion	Rouge	11°
Moulis	Rouge	10.5°

Appellations		*Degrees*
Néac (merged with Lalande)	Rouge	10.5°
Parsac-St-Émilion	Rouge	11°
Pauillac	Rouge	10.5°
Pomerol	Rouge	10.5°
Premières Côtes de Blaye	Rouge	10.5°
	Blanc	11°
Premières Côtes de Bordeaux	Rouge	10.5°
	Blanc	12°
Premières Côtes de Bordeaux followed by a commune name	Rouge	11.5°
	Blanc	12.5°
Premières Côtes de Bordeaux-Cadillac	Blanc	12°
Premières Côtes de Bordeaux-Gabarnac	Blanc	12°
Puisseguin-St-Émilion	Rouge	11°
Sables-St-Émilion	Rouge	10.5°
St-Émilion	Rouge	11°
St-Émilion grand cru	Rouge	11.5°
St-Émilion grand cru classé	Rouge	11.5°
St-Émilion Iͤ grand cru classé	Rouge	11.5°
St-Éstèphe	Rouge	10.5°
St-Georges-St-Émilion	Rouge	11°
Ste-Croix-du-Mont	Blanc	13°
Ste-Foy-Bordeaux	Blanc	12°
	Rouge	10.5°
St-Julien	Rouge	10.5°
Sauternes	Blanc	13°

APPENDIX 2
The 1855 Classification of Red Wines of the Médoc

	Commune
Premiers crus	
Lafite	Pauillac
Latour	Pauillac
Margaux	Margaux
*Mouton-Rothschild	Pauillac
Haut-Brion	Pessac (Graves)

Deuxièmes crus	
Rausan-Ségla	Margaux
Rauzan-Gassies	Margaux
Léoville-Las-Cases	St-Julien
Léoville-Poyferré	St-Julien
Léoville-Barton	St-Julien
Durfort-Vivens	Margaux
Lascombes	Margaux
Gruaud-Larose	St-Julien
Brane-Cantenac	Cantenac
Pichon-Longueville	Pauillac
Pichon-Longueville-Lalande	Pauillac
Ducru-Beaucaillou	St-Julien
Cos-d'Estournel	St-Estèphe
Montrose	St-Estèphe

Troisièmes crus	
Kirwan	Cantenac
Issan	Cantenac
Lagrange	St-Julien
Langoa	St-Julien
Giscours	Labarde
Malescot-St-Exupéry	Margaux
Cantenac-Brown	Cantenac
Palmer	Cantenac
La Lagune	Ludon (Haut-Médoc)
Desmirail	Margaux
Calon-Ségur	St-Estèphe
Ferrière	Margaux
Marquis d'Alesme-Becker	Margaux
Boyd-Cantenac	Margaux

Quatrièmes crus	
St-Pierre-Sevaistre	St-Julien
St-Pierre-Bontemps	St-Julien
Branaire-Ducru	St-Julien
Talbot	St-Julien
Duhart-Milon	Pauillac
Pouget	Cantenac
La Tour-Carnet	St-Laurent (Haut-Médoc)
Lafon-Rochet	St-Estèphe
Beychevelle	St-Julien
Le Prieuré-Lichine	Cantenac
Marquis-de-Terme	Margaux

Cinquièmes crus	
Pontet-Canet	Pauillac
Batailley	Pauillac
Haut Batailley	Pauillac
Grand-Puy-Lacoste	Pauillac
Grand-Puy-Ducasse	Pauillac
Lynch-Bages	Pauillac
Lynch-Moussas	Pauillac
Dauzac	Labarde
Mouton-Baron-Philippe	Pauillac
Du Tertre	Arsac
Haut-Bages-Libéral	Pauillac
Pédesclaux	Pauillac
Belgrave	St-Laurent

* Promoted to premier cru in 1973

Cinquièmes crus contd   *Commune*

	(Haut-Médoc)	Clerc-Milon-Mondon	Pauillac
Camensac	St-Laurent (Haut-Médoc)	Croizet-Bages Cantemerle	Pauillac Macau (Haut-Médoc)
Cos-Labory	St-Estèphe		

APPENDIX 3
The 1959 Classification of the Graves

Red Wines (classified in 1953 and confirmed in 1959)

Château Bouscaut	Cadaujac
Château Haut-Bailly	Léognan
Château Carbonnieux	Léognan
Domaine de Chevalier	Léognan
Château Fieuzal	Léognan
Château Olivier	Léognan
Château Malartic-Lagravière	Léognan
Château La Tour-Martillac	Martillac
Château Smith-Haut-Lafitte	Martillac
Château Haut-Brion	Pessac
Château La Mission-Haut-Brion	Pessac
Château Pape-Clément	Pessac
Château Latour-Haut-Brion	Talence

White Wines (classified in 1959)

Château Bouscaut	Cadaujac
Château Carbonnieux	Léognan
Domaine de Chevalier	Léognan
Château Olivier	Léognan
Château Malartic-Lagravière	Léognan
Château La Tour-Martillac	Martillac
Château Laville-Haut-Brion	Talence
Château Couhins	Villenave d'Ornon

APPENDIX 4
The 1855 Classification of the Sauternes

Grand Premier cru

Yquem	Sauternes

Premiers crus

La Tour-Blanche	Bommes
Clos Haut-Peyraguey	Bommes
Lafaurie-Peyraguey	Bommes
Rayne-Vigneau	Bommes
Suduiraut	Preignac
Coutet	Barsac
Climens	Barsac
Guiraud	Sauternes
Rieussec	Fargues
Rabaud-Promis	Bommes
Sigalas-Rabaud	Bommes

Deuxièmes crus

de Myrat	Barsac
Doisy-Daëne	Barsac
Doisy-Védrines	Barsac
d'Arche	Sauternes
Filhot	Sauternes
Broustet	Barsac
Nairac	Barsac
Caillou	Barsac
Suau	Barsac
de Malle	Preignac
Romer	Fargues
Lamothe	Sauternes

APPENDIX 5
The 1955 Classification of St-Émilion

Premiers Grands crus classés

A. Château Ausone
   Château Cheval-Blanc

B. Château Beauséjour (Duffau)
   Château Beauséjour (Fagouet)
   Château Belair

Château Canon
Clos Fourtet
Château Figeac
Château La Gaffelière-Naudes
Château Magdelaine
Château Pavie
Château Trottevieile

Grands crus classés

Château l'Angelus*
Château L'Arrosée*
Château Balestard-la-Tonnelle*
Château Bellevue
Château Bergat
Château Cadet-Bon
Château Cadet-Piola*
Château Canon-la-Gaffelière*
Château Cap-de-Mourlin*
Château Chapelle Madeleine*
Château Chauvin
Château Corbin (Giraud)
Château Corbin-Michotte
Château Coutet
Château Clos-des-Jacobins*
Château Croque-Michotte*
Château Curé Bon*
Château Dassault
Château Fonplégade*
Château Fonroque*
Château Franc Mayne
Château Grand-Barrail-Lamarzelle
   – Figeac
Château Grand-Corbin Despagne
Château Grand-Corbin Pecresse
Château Grand Mayne
Château Grand Pontet
Château Grandes Murailles
Château Guadet-St-Julien*
Château Haut-Corbin
Château Haut Sarpe
Château Jean Faure
Clos des Jacobins
Château La Carte
Château La Clotte*
Château La Clusière

Château La Couspaude
Château La Dominique*
Clos La Madeleine
Château Larcis-Ducasse*
Château Lamarzelle
Château Lamiote
Château Larmande
Château Laroze
Château Lasserre
Château La-Tour-du-Pin-Figeac*
Château La-Tour-Figeac*
Château Le Châtelet
Château Le Couvent
Château Le Prieuré
Château Matras
Château Mauvezin
Château Moulin-du-Cadet
Clos de l'Oratoire
Château Pavie-Decesse
Château Pavie-Macquin
Château Pavillon-Cadet
Château Petit-Faurie-de-Souchard
Château Petit-Faurie-de-Soutard
Château Ripeau*
Château Sansonnet
Château St-Georges-Côte-Pavie
Clos St-Martin
Château Soutard*
Château Tertre-Daugay
Château Trimoulet
Château Trois Moulins
Château Troplong-Mondot*
Château Villemaurine*
Château Yon-Figeac

APPENDIX 6
Cheeses of the South West

You will find every kind of cheese, from Brie to Gruyère, on a market stall in the South West, but the factory-made cheeses from the Pyrénées are particularly popular and widely available. When they have a hard black rind it usually indicates that the cheese is made from cows' milk; an orange rind from ewes' milk. The cheeses listed below are those to look out for when you are in a particular locality.

Name	Animal	Region/Department
Amou	Sheep	Landes/Landes
Arnéguy (also called Ardi-Gasna)	Sheep	Pays Basque/Pyrénées-Atlantiques
Aligot	Cow	Rouergue/Aveyron
Bleu des Causses	Cow	Rouergue/Aveyron
Bleu de Quercy	Cow	Quercy/Lot
Cabecou d'Entraygues[1]	Goat	Rouergue/Aveyron
Cabecou de Rocamadour	Goat	Quercy/Lot
Echourgnac	Cow	Périgord/Dordogne
Iraty	Cow/sheep	Pays Basque/Pyrénées-Atlantiques
Laguiole[2]	Cow	Rouergue/Aveyron
Laruns	Sheep	Béarn/Pyrénées-Atlantiques
Oloron (also called Esbareich)	Sheep	Béarn/Pyrénées-Atlantiques
Poustagnacq	Sheep	Landes/Landes
Roquefort	Sheep	Rouergue/Aveyron
Tardets	Sheep	Pays Basque/Pyrénées-Atlantiques

1 The name *cabecou* derives from a Langue d'Oc word meaning 'little goat'. These small cheeses, only 12mm thick and less than 4cm across, are found all over the South West and are sold in varying stages of ripeness, so you can buy according to your personal preference, always assuming you like goat's cheese.

2 This is a Cantal-type cheese. Cantal is made outside the area covered in this book but is commonly met with. Something like a farmhouse Cheddar, it is deservedly popular.

APPENDIX 7
Useful Addresses

General

GIVISO (Groupement d'Intérêt Économique des Vignerons du Sud-Ouest),
50 boulevard Carnot, Agen 47000. Tel (58) 66 75 99.

FNCRA (Fédération Nationale de Comités Regionaux d'Expansion, de
Promotion et de Propagande des Ressources Agricoles, Alimentaires et
Touristiques de leur province), Ariège, Aveyron, Gers, Haute-Garonne,
Hautes-Pyrénées, Lot: Directeur M. Prugniaud, Chambre régionale
d'agriculture, 30 rue de Languedoc, Toulouse 31068, tel (61) 52 38 29.
Dordogne, Gironde-Landes, Lot-et-Garonne, Pyrénées-Atlantiques:
Directeur M. Pousset, Chambre régionale d'agriculture, 33 rue Vauban,
Bordeaux 3300, tel (56) 44 53 19.

Bordelais (Gironde)

Food

Henri Minart, Specialités gastronomiques, artisanale d'Aquitaine, 4 quai de
Queyries, 33100 Bordeaux, tel (56) 86 27 21. *Confit d'oie, confit de canard,
palombe confite, truffes, miel,* etc.

Wine

General:

Conseil Interprofessionel des Vins de Bordeaux, 1 cours du 30 juillet, 33000
Bordeaux, tel (56) 44 37 82.

Maison du Vin, 1 cours du 30 Juillet, 33000 Bordeaux, tel (56) 44 37 82.

La Vinothèque, 8 cours du Juillet, 33000 Bordeaux. An 'arabian nights'
collection of wines to taste and buy.

Barton & Guestier, Château de Dehaz, 33290 Blanquefort, tel (56) 44 51 44.
Shipping company owned by Seagram; no introduction necessary.

Calvet, 75 cours du Médoc, 33003 Bordeaux, tel (56) 29 75 75. No
introduction necessary.

Maison Sichel, S. a.r.l., 19 quai du Bacalon, 33300 Bordeaux, tel (56) 29 52 20.
Well-known shippers and owners of two famous Bordeaux châteaux
(Château Palmer and Château Angludet). Tours of the châteaux can be
arranged. Introduction is needed. Apply to H. Sichel and Sons Ltd, 4 York
Buildings, London WC2N 6JP, tel 01-830 9292.

Local:

Blaye: Maison du Vin, Allées Marines, 33390 Blaye.

Cadillac: Maison du Vin, Château des Ducs d'Épernon, 33410 Cadillac.

Margaux: Maison du Vin, 29 rue de la Tremoille, 33460 Margaux, tel (56) 58 40 82.

Pauillac: Maison du Vin, quai Ferchaud, 33250 Pauillac.

St-Émilion: Maison du Vin, place Clocher, St-Émilion, tel (56) 51 72 17.

Sauternes, Barsac: Office Viticole de Sauternes et Barsac, place de l'Église, Barsac, 33720 Podensac, tel (56) 27 15 14.

Périgord (Dordogne)

General

Office Départemental du Tourisme, 16 rue Wilson, 24000 Périgueux.

Food

Brusle, J.-C., Halle de Coderc, 24000 Périgueux, tel (53) 08 35 94. Fresh truffles in season, *foies gras, confits d'oies, rillettes d'oies*, etc.

Champion, Maison, 21 rue Taillefer, 24000 Périgueux, Tel (53) 53 43 34. For *foies gras, confits*, etc.

Conserves de la Ferme, R. Crouzel, 24590 Salignac-en-Perigord, tel (53) 28 80 83. *Truffes, cèpes, foies gras d'oie, rillettes d'oie, cassoulet périgourdin.*

Dalis, Claude, 24290 Montignac. *Eau-de-vie* and liqueurs.

Wine

Bergerac, Cave Coopérative de, Boulevard de l'Entrepôt, 24100 Bergerac, tel (53) 57 16 27.

Cabaroque, Domaine de, Madame Yourassovski-Cabanne, Cabaroque, route de Lauzun 24, Monbazillac.

Conseil Interprofessionel des Vins de la Region de Bergerac, 2 place du Dr Cayla, 24100 Bergerac, tel (53) 57 12 57.

Fleix, Cave Coopérative du, le Fleix, 24130 La Force, tel (53) 46 20 15.

Fontindoule, Domaine de, Monsieur Cros, Fontindoule 24, Monbazillac.

Monbazillac, Cave Coopérative de, BP No. 2, Monbazillac, 24240 Sigoulès, tel (53) 57 06 38.

Monbazillac, Château de, BP No. 1, 24240 Sigoulès, tel (53) 57 34 36.

Tailières, Château de, par Mouleydier-Bergerac. *Suc de Monbazillac, liqueur de vieux cep.*

Unidor (Union des Coopératives Vinicoles de la Dordogne), 24100 St-Laurent-des-Vignes, tel (53) 57 40 44.

Agenais (Lot-et-Garonne)

Food

Auberge à la Ferme, Bossu, route de Savignac, 47150 Monflanquin. *Foies gras d'oie et de canard.*

La Boutique des Pruneaux, G. and A. Coustel, porte de Paris, 47300 Villeneuve-sur-Lot.

Caban, J'Le Barail' Brax 47310 Laplume, tel (58) 66 95 43. *Prunes d'Agen,* fruit in armagnac, stuffed prunes.

Catellin, Louis, 47140 St-Sylvestre-sur-Lot. Asparagus in season.

Corres, M., 47 Mas d'Agenais. *Conserves, pâtés gascon.*

Coulanges, Marc, 131 rue Montesquieu, 47000 Agen. *Foies gras.*

Ponthoreau J.P. rue Maréchal Joffre, 47400, Tonneins. *Jambon de Tonneins, pâté de campagne, charcuterie,* etc.

Wine

Donzac, Cave Coopérative de, 82340 Auvillar, tel (63) 39 91 92. Vin de pays de l'Agenais.

Cave Coopérative 'Les Vignerons des Coteaux de Duras', 47120 Duras, tel (58) 93 71 12.

Les Vignerons Réunis des Côtes de Buzet, Buzet-sur-Baize, 47160 Damazan.

Société Coopérative Vinicole des Côtes du Marmandais, Beaupuy, 47200 Marmande.

Quercy (Lot)

Food

Conserves Artisanales, P. Armand, Fontames, 46230 Lalbenque, tel (65) 31 62. *Pâté du Quercy au foie de canard, fois gras d'oie truffés, terrine du Quercy,* etc.

Wine

Clos la Coutale, Aymard et Berned, propriétaires-récoltants, Vire, 46700 Puy-l'Évêque.

Clos de Gamot, Jouffreau et fils, Prayssac 46220.

Les Côtes d'Olt, 46140 Parnac, tel (65) 36 11 56.

Rigal et Fils, 46140 Parnac-Luzech, tel (65) 36 11 45.

Roque, Louis, 46 Souillac. For *vieille prune liqueur, vieille noix,* and *lou quercynol aperitif.*

Syndicat Interprofessionel du Vin de Cahors, Chambre d'agriculture du Lot, avenue Jean Jaurès, 46001 Cahors.

Rouergue (Aveyron)

Food

Le Papillon, 12250 Roquefort-sur-Soulzon, tel (65) 60 90 03. Fine Roquefort cheese.

Wine

Viguier, Emile, Les Buis, 12140 Entraygues, tel (65) 44 50 45. Vin d'Entraygues et du Fel VDQS.

Landes

Food

Barthouil, Peyrehorade, Landes 40, tel (58) 73 00 78. *Conserve de luxe, jambon de Bayonne, foies gras, saumon fumé,* caviar.

Conserveries Lafitte, 49 rue des Carmes, Dax 40, tel (58) 74 19 39. *Specialités
landaises, foies gras, pâtés, confits,* etc.
Dubernet, M., 40500 St-Sever, tel (58) 76 01 20. *Cassoulet à l'oie, daube
landaise, jambonneau â la gelée, jambon de Bayonne,* etc.
Junca, R., place de la Fontaine Chaude, Dax 40, tel (58) 74 06 72.

Wine

Cave coopérative de Crouseilles, 64350 Lembeye, tel (59) 33 70 93. Wines of
Pacherenc du Vic Bilh and Madiran.
Peyros, Château de, Corbères, 64350 Lembeye, tel (59) 33 70 51.
Syndicat de Défense et de Contrôle des Vins de Madiran et du Pacheranc du
Vic Bilh, Château de Crouseilles, 64350 Lembeye.
Tursan, Cave Coopérative de, 40320 Geaune, tel (58) 76 51 25. Wines of
Tursan – red, *rosé* and white VDQS.

Armagnac (Gers)

Food

Comtesse du Barry, Gimont 32200. *Foies gras d'oie et canard, confits à la graisse
d'oie, salmis de palombe, cassoulet,* etc. Excellent tinned food.
Espiet, Roger, 32700 Lectoure. *Conserves régionales, jambon de Bayonne.*

Spirits
Armagnac
Janneau Fils S.A., BP No. 55, 32100 Condom, tel (62) 28 15 15.
Tariquet, Château du, Monsieur Grassa et Fils, 32800 Eauze, tel (62) 09 87
82.

Bearn: Pays Basques (Pyrénées-Atlantiques)

Food

Les Foies Gras de Navarre, 34 rue Louis Barthou, 64000 Pau. *Lièvre à la
royale au foie truffé, bécasse fourrée, foie gras truffé, morilles au natural, girolles
au naturel, salmis de palombes,* etc.
Fromagerie Pardou, 64440 Laruns, Valée d'Ossau 64. Cheeses: *les cinq monts,*
and *le roy des vallées.*
Idiart, Dominique, rue Léon Berard, 64390 Sauveterre-de-Béarn, tel (59) 38 5
75. *Jambon de Bayonne, confit de porc, pâté pur porc,* etc.
Recapet et Cie, 64390 Sauveterre-de-Béarn. *Jambon de Bayonne.*

Wine and spirits
Brana, Etienne, 64220 St-Jean-Pied-de-Port. *Prune vieille réserve* liqueur, *poire
William, eau-de-vie,* Irouléguy wine.
Cave Coopérative d'Irouléguy, St Jean-Pied-de-Port, 64220.
Cru Lamouroux, Jean Chigé, propriétaire, Chappelle de Rousse, 64000 Pau.
Gan-Jurançon, Coopérative Vinicole Intercommunale de, 64290 Gan, tel (59)
68 70 03.
Syndicat des Producteurs de Vins à Appellation Contrôlée Jurançon, 5 place de
la République, 64000 Pau, tel (59) 27 98 44.

Bibliography

General background

Guides

Michelin Guides Verts: Côte de l'Atlantique, Périgord (Berry, Limousin, Quercy), *Causses*, (Cévennes – Bas Languedoc), *Pyrénées*, published by Pneu Michelin, Services de Tourisme, 75 Boulevard Pereire, Paris 17.

Les Guides du Livres de Poche, Gironde – *Landes: Côte Aquitaine*, ed. Jacques-Louis Depal, *Pays Basque, Béarn*, Le livre de Poche, Paris, 1976.

Les Landes, Guide touristique, 1976.

Le Lot et Garonne, Guide officiel, Editions Larrieu-Bonnel, Toulouse, 1975.

Les Guides Bleus, Pyrénées, Gascogne, Librarie Hachette, Paris, 1972.

HARRISON BARKER, E., *Two Summers in Guyenne: A Chronicle of the Wayside and Waterside*, Richard Bentley and Son, London, 1894.

HARRISON BARKER, E., *Wandering by Southern Waters: Eastern Aquitaine*, Richard Bentley and Son, London, 1893.

HARRISON BARKER, E., *Wayfaring in France*, Richard Bentley and Son, London, 1890.

CHAVENT, Jean-Paul, *Le Périgord*, Solar, Paris, 1976.

CLARK, Eleanor, *The Oysters of Locmariaquer*, Secker and Warburg, London, 1965.

FAUCHER, Daniel, d'ESTALENX J.-F., de GORSSE, Pierre, CUZACQ René, *Visage de Gascogne, Béarn, Comte de Foix*, Horizons de France, 1968.

FÉNELON, Paul, SECRET, Jean, CRUZET, René, GOT, Armand, *Visage de Guyenne*, Horizons de France, Paris, 1966.

FÉNELON, Paul, *Périgord enchanté*, Arthaud, Paris, 1966.

HESS, John L., *Vanishing France*, Quadrangle/The New York Times Book Co., New York, 1975.

ORMSBY, H., *France: A Regional and Economic Geography*, Methuen, London, 1931.

PÈRE, André et le groupe Gersois de l'école moderne, *Armagnac, coeur de Gascogne*, Bibliothèque de travail, No. 656, Cannes, 1967.

SCARGILL, Ian, *The Dordogne Region of France*, David and Charles, Newton Abbot, 1974.

SOL, Chanoine E., *Le vieux Quercy: usage anciens*, Bibliothèque de la maison des oeuvres, Cahors, 1969.

WHITE, Freda, *Three Rivers of France (Dordogne/Lot/Tarn)*, Faber, London, 1952.

WHITE, Freda, *West of the Rhône*, Faber, London, 1964.

Periodicals

Cuisine et vins de France, dir. Odette Kahn, monthly magazine founded by
  Curnonsky, Paris.

Périgord gourmand, ed. Guy Fournier, Depeyrat, Sarlat, Dordogne.

Périgord-magazine, Quercy-magazine, ed. René Dessagne, Les magazines de
  France, Limoges.

La table et ma cuisine, ed. Bernard Charretton, Paris.

Agri-Sud, ed. Michel Poux, Fédération Nationale de la Presse Agricole et
  Rurale, Toulouse.

Food general

BERANGER, Georges et Jacqueline, *Géographie gourmande de la France*, Editions
  Robert Laffont, Paris, 1978.

BURGAUD, Françoise, ed. *La cuisine de A à Z régionale: Sud-ouest, Périgord*, Le
  Livre de Poche, Paris, 1978.

SOPEXA, *La France à votre table: the gastronomic routes of France*, Le carrousel
  publicité, Paris, 1967.

COUFFIGNAL, Huguette, *La cuisine Landes, Gironde, Périgord*, Solar, Paris, 1977.

COUFFIGNAL, Huguette, *La cuisine des pays d'Oc*, Solar, Paris, 1976.

LABARRE, Irène, *La cuisine des trois B*, Solar, Paris, 1977.

de CROZE, Austin, *Les plats régionaux de France*, Editions Montaigne, Paris,
  1928.

DAVID, Elizabeth, *A Book of Mediterranean Food*, John Lehmann, London,
  1950.

DAVID, Elizabeth, *French Country Cooking*, John Lehmann, London, 1951.

DAVID, *French Provincial Cooking*, Michael Joseph, London, 1960.

ELLIS, Aidan, *Guide de Fromage* (English edition), Henley-on-Thames, 1973.

GOT, Armand, *Sa majesté la truffe*, Editions de la truffereine, Bordeaux, 1966.

GRACIEUSE, *La Bonne Cuisine Méridionale de Tante Gracieuse*, Les Éditions
  Provencia, Toulon, 1947.

GRIGSON, Jane, *Charcuterie and French Pork Cookery*, Michael Joseph, London,
  1967.

GRIGSON, Jane, *The Mushroom Feast*, Michael Joseph, London, 1975

MONTAGNÉ, Prosper, *Larousse gastronomique*, English edition, Paul Hamlyn,
  1961.

PAMPILLE, Madame Léon Daudet, *Les bons plats de France cuisine régionale*,
  Artheme Fayard, Paris, 1934.

PRICE, Pamela Vandyke, *Eating and Drinking in France Today*, Tom Stacey,
  London, 1972.

RAMSBOTTOM, James, *Mushrooms and Toadstools*, Collins, London & Glasgow,
  1953.

ROBERTSON, Jean and Andrew, *Food and Wine of the French Provinces: A
  Traveller's Guide*, Collins, London and Glasgow, 1968.

ROOT, Waverley, *The Food of France*, Cassell, London, 1958.

Wine general

DUMAY, Raymond, *Guide du Vin*, Stock, Paris, 1967.

FAITH, Nicholas, *The Winemasters*, Hamish Hamilton, London, 1978.

JACQULIN, Louis, POULAIN, René, *Vignes et Vins de France*, Flammarion, Paris, 1960.

JOHNSON, Hugh, *The World Atlas of Wine*, Mitchell Beazley, London, 1971.

LECHINE, Alexis, *Encyclopaedia of Wines and Spirits*, Cassell, London, 1967.

MORTON SHAND, P., *A Book of French Wines*, Jonathan Cape, London, 1928, revised edition 1960.

ROWE, Vivian, *French Wines, Ordinary and Extraordinary*, Harrap, London, 1972.

TINGEY, Frederick, *Wine Roads of France*, Charles Letts, London, 1977.

Food and wine in the regions

Armagnac

SAMALENS, Jean et Georges, *Le livre de l'amateur d'Armagnac*, Solar, Paris, 1975.

Various authors *Recettes Gasconnes*, Auch, 1977.

Bordelais

BONTOU, Alcide, *Traité de cuisine bourgeoise bordelais* Féret et fils, Bordeaux, L. Mulo, Paris, 1921.

PENNING-ROWSELL, Edmund, *The Wines of Bordeaux*, Penguin, London, 1976.

PRICE, Pamel Vandyke, *A Guide to the Wines of Bordeaux*, Pitman, London, 1977.

Périgord

FANLAC, Pierre, *Gastronomie en Périgord*, Périgueux, 1971.

GOT, Armand, *Monbazillac: Hosanna de Topaze*, Sadag, Bellegarde, 1949.

La MAZILLE, *La bonne cuisine du Périgord*, Flammarion, Paris, 1929.

LASNET de LANTY, Henriette, *Cuisine Périgourdine*, Paris, Unide 1976.

PENTON, Anne, *Customs and Cookery in the Périgord and Quercy*, David and Charles, Newton Abbot, 1973.

Rouergue

COUFFIGNAL, H., *La cuisine rustique: Auvergne, Rouergue, Limousin*, Robert Murel, Forcalquier 1970.

MERLIN, A., BEAUJOUR, A. Y., *Les Mangeurs de Rouergue: cuisine paysanne contre gastronomie*, Duclot, Paris, 1978.

Indexes
General Index including wine

Index of recipes and other references

italic page nos. indicate actual recipes